MUHAMMAD
FORTY INTRODUCTIONS

ALSO BY MICHAEL MUHAMMAD KNIGHT

MUHAMMAD
FORTY INTRODUCTIONS

MICHAEL MUHAMMAD KNIGHT

SOFT SKULL  NEW YORK

MUHAMMAD: FORTY INTRODUCTIONS

Library of Congress Cataloging-in-Publication Data
Names: Knight, Michael Muhammad, author.
Title: Muhammad : forty introductions / Michael
Muhammad Knight.
Description: New York : Soft Skull, [2019] | Includes
bibliographical references.
Identifiers: LCCN 2018040347 | ISBN 9781593761479
(pbk. : alk. paper)
Subjects: LCSH: Muhammad, Prophet, -632—Hadith.
| Muhammad, Prophet, -632—Biography. | Hadith—
Texts.
Classification: LCC BP135.8.M85 K65 2019 | DDC
297.6/3—dc23
LC record available at https://lccn.loc.gov/2018040347

Cover design by salu.io
Book design by Wah-Ming Chang

Published by Soft Skull Press
1140 Broadway, Suite 704
New York, NY 10001
www.softskull.com

Soft Skull titles are distributed to the trade by
Publishers Group West
Phone: 866-400-5351

Printed in the United States of America
1 3 5 7 9 10 8 6 4 2

To Azreal with love, from Azreal Wisdom

CONTENTS

MUHAMMAD
FORTY INTRODUCTIONS

1

INTRODUCING THE INTRODUCTIONS

> 'Ali bin Hujr reported to us that Ishaq bin
> Najih reported to us on the authority of Ibn
> Jurayj, on the authority of 'Ata' bin Rabah, on
> the authority of Ibn 'Abbas, who said:
>
> The Messenger of God (God bless him
> and give him peace) said, "Whoever pre-
> serves for my community forty hadiths from
> the Sunna, I will be an intercessor for him
> on the Day of Resurrection."[1]

Who is this Messenger of God for whom the stakes of memory are so high? For more than twenty years now, I have worn
his name as my own, but still ask the question. If the above
narration serves as our first glimpse of him, what does it show
us? How much of the man could we retrieve from the promise
he makes here?

Before approaching his words, we must first walk through
names. This narration comes to us from the *Forty Hadiths* collection by Imam al-Nasawi (d. 915), who cites as his sources

a chain of teachers: al-Nasawi reports from a scholar of the preceding generation, 'Ali bin Hujr (d. 859), who cites an earlier authority, who in turn cites an older scholar than himself. At the end of the chain, we find Ibn 'Abbas, Muhammad's cousin, telling us what Muhammad had said.

After the chain of names, we encounter Muhammad's title, Messenger of God (*rasul Allah*), and immediately after this we read a prayer for peace and blessings upon him: our knowledge of Muhammad comes to us through those who loved him and believed in his prophethood. Finally, we arrive at the message: Muhammad tells us that anyone who preserves forty hadiths from the Sunna will have Muhammad himself advocating for that person on the Day of Resurrection.

The narration introduces key terms. The word used here for "narration," *hadith*, literally means "news" or "report" and signifies the sayings and actions of Muhammad, or things said and done in his presence to which he did not object; this particular hadith therefore speaks on the virtues of the body of knowledge to which it belongs. *Sunna*, meaning "custom" or "precedent," has come to represent the body of reported memories concerning Muhammad's statements, habits, and preferences, establishing both his teachings and personal behavior as a template for how to live as a human in the world.

This hadith tells us that there is a Day of Resurrection and that the Messenger of God, many centuries after the end of his prophetic mission and earthly life, continues to play a crucial role in the salvation of humankind. He can act as our lawyer, interceding on our behalf. We see that an articulation of Islam centered primarily on the hadith tradition could offer a profound departure from one centered on other sources, such as the Qur'an; the Qur'an does not clearly name Muhammad as an intercessor on the Day, and many readers interpret the Qur'an as expressing a generally pessimistic view of humans' prospects for intercessors with God. It is within the hadith tradition that Muhammad's advocacy becomes available, and the narration informs us that it becomes available specifically to the person who preserves forty hadiths from the Sunna.

The Arabic word used for "preserve" in this narration carries meanings associated with memorization. For historical settings in which oral tradition wielded greater authority than written texts—and in a world before paper technology, let alone the digital storage of information—to preserve knowledge meant becoming an embodied archive. The hadith memorizer commits to defending Muhammad's historical memory against the losses wrought by time and, by doing so, serves the broader salvation of humankind, and thus earns Muhammad's help for his or her own salvation. This hadith empowers its own narrators, promising them extraordinary privilege in the next world.

The Messenger did not leave behind a written autobiography or a copy of his daily schedule; we know him only through the memories of those who had been in his presence, who shared their recollections with those who had been born too late to know him. The names we walk through here show us the mediations by which Muhammad becomes the Muhammad whom we can access. Family members and friends who gave their reports as eyewitnesses to Muhammad, designated with the capitalized title Companions, became powerful custodians of the sacred past, and themselves continue to speak via their students, their students' students, and so on. The Muhammad we find on this page is not simply an individual person who lived at a particular moment in history, but an assemblage formed by encounters between generations. In addition to being a specific body that lies entombed in Medina, Muhammad is also an oral tradition spanning centuries.

The scholarly producers of this oral tradition, while reporting with conviction in Muhammad's supreme authority as the Messenger of God, in turn authorize him: they wield the power of their reputations as scholars and pious Muslims to vouch for these words as reflecting Muhammad's actual speech. In this roster of scholars reporting on Muhammad (and one another), we witness the prophetic assemblage as it takes form.

The collected body of oral traditions reporting Muhammad's words and actions is not the work of a single scholar, but of thousands of individuals. Nor is this marked as the domain of a united Muslim community held together by shared methods or a uniform roster of trustworthy experts. The people who knew and followed Muhammad in his own lifetime appear in the sources as having disagreed with one another on matters of correct belief and practice, and often gave conflicting accounts of what Muhammad had said. In the generations after Muhammad, networks of transmitters based in specific geographic centers came to be associated with particular theological, legal, or sectarian positions. But as scholars traveled between cities such as Basra, Kufa, and Baghdad to collect narrations of the Prophet, these local networks increasingly blended into one another, giving the appearance of a singular, monolithic body of scholarship. The collection of oral traditions into book form further masked the heterogeneity of Muhammad's reporters, presenting these thousands of scholars as collaborators in a shared project.

One communal identity—that is, Sunni Islam, popularly marked with the collective *ahl al-sunna*, or People of the Sunna—has become specially designated for its investment in the Sunna. But we should remember that "non-Sunni" does not mean "non-follower of the Sunna." Within Shi'i Muslim tradition, for example, we also witness great investment in the priority of Muhammad's words and actions. Observing historical disagreements between Sunni and Shi'i Muslims (not to mention the enormous capacity for disagreement and multiple opinions within each tradition), we recognize the Sunna as a contested territory. Not everyone agrees as to what it means, where it can be found, or how it should be lived out, but the vast majority of Muslims, including Sunnis and Shi'is alike, agree that it matters.

The full body of hadiths is immeasurably vast, and the scholars of oral tradition mentioned here have each preserved many more than forty hadiths: our original source for these words, Muhammad's cousin Ibn 'Abbas, appears in one seminal collection as the credited reporter for nearly 2,000 narrations. Imam Bukhari, recognized as the greatest Sunni authority on hadiths, was said to have learned 300,000 (with only 1 percent of these narrations—not counting repetitions—meeting Bukhari's standard of authenticity to merit inclusion in his collection). Before the modern transformation of these archives into mass-printed books and online databases, the hadith corpus would not have been navigable for average people. This knowledge remained marked as the domain of a highly specialized field of scholars who devoted their lives to learning not only the hadiths themselves, but the names of thousands upon thousands of hadith reporters (along with information concerning their biographical details and scholarly reputations) and a complex methodology for evaluating each hadith's level of reliability. Muhammad's promise of intercession grants incalculable advantage in the next life to those who dedicate themselves to learning and teaching.

While affirming the scholars' otherworldly prestige, however, the hadith also democratizes their privilege, enabling the masses to share in access to Muhammad's help. Thousands of hadiths, like the one cited here, consist of only a single sentence of Muhammad's words; one does not have to undergo full training and lifelong dedication as a scholar to memorize a mere forty. This narration simultaneously grants supreme advantage to hadith scholars—entering us into the structure by which they become privileged and authorized—and gives the rest of us a share of that advantage for our own salvation.

*

This project seeks to introduce Muhammad by employing a literary genre that takes inspiration from the above hadith: the *arba'in*, the forty-hadith collection. If the preservation of forty hadiths earns a right to Muhammad's advocacy in the next life, a forty-hadith text becomes more than scholarly discourse. It is a performance of piety itself, like a fast or pilgrimage, which seeks the pleasure of God and reward in the realm of the unseen. The forty-hadith collection reflects Muhammad's prescription put into action.

Throughout Muslim literary history, scholars have compiled arba'in works, and this format seems to lend itself naturally to the genre of "intro to Islam" literature. Before modern media technology and literacy, the hadith corpus became somewhat more accessible to a general public through the arba'in genre, in which a scholar could present a selected handful of jewels from the tradition. Arba'in books could operate as the literary equivalent of a Friday sermon, providing an easily digestible sample of narratives on a particular topic or theme. These books hold particular convenience for Islamic pedagogy: within the constraints of the forty-hadith genre, scholars could focus on a singular concern and narrow down the enormous hadith corpus to a few dozen reports, providing an opportunity to define Islam's essence in light of their own priorities.

Surveying topics in the genre throughout history, we find that each of Islam's "five pillars" (bearing witness to the oneness of God and prophethood of Muhammad, praying five times daily, paying zakat or alms, fasting in the month of Ramadan, and performing the pilgrimage to Mecca) has been the theme for numerous forty-hadith collections. Scholars have devoted arba'in works to various aspects of the Qur'an, reporting Muhammad's statements on topics such as the Qur'an's oral recitation, particular *suras* (chapters) of the Qur'an, or even the special merits of a single verse—as in a collection of forty hadiths focused entirely on 2:255, the famous *'ayat al-kursi*, or Throne Verse. Themes relating directly to Muhammad himself, such as the noble character of his wives or the virtues of praying for him, have also become the focus of forty-hadith collections.

Arba'in authors have commonly used the genre to advocate for what they regard as the central values and priorities of Islam. Ascetics compiled forty-hadith collections praising asceticism; mystics provided hadiths that were relevant to mysticism. The larger canon of hadiths representing Muhammad's sayings and actions remains so immense that one could dig up forty narrations to further almost any agenda. We find collections devoted to ethics, jurisprudence, marriage, mercy, justice, charity, martyrdom, manners, worship, medicine, signs of the end times, and the special virtues of locales such as Syria. As rulers gave patronage to favored scholars and commissioned books that furthered their interests, arba'in works addressed contemporary political issues and made calls for action: in the era of the Crusades, Sultan Nur al-Din Zangi commissioned the scholar Ibn 'Asakir (1105–1176) to compile a forty-hadith collection on the merits and obligations of military jihad.[2] Scholars could also wield the arba'in genre as a powerful propaganda tool in sectarian debates. If Sunni and Shi'i Muslims disagreed on a point such as the merits of early caliphs, an arba'in volume could provide evidence to settle the issue for one side or the other.

Due to the importance of direct teacher-to-student transmission in classical hadith scholarship, producing an arba'in work also serves to showcase the compiler's pedigree of master teachers and superior lineage, offering a succinct but potent display of scholarly credentials. Shah Wali Allah Dihlawi (1703–1762), for example, compiled an arba'in volume of hadiths that he had heard directly from his teacher, Abu Tahir al-Madani, which Abu Tahir had received through unbroken chains of transmission tracing directly to the Prophet's great-grandson Zayn al-'Abidin, who had heard them from his father, Husayn, who had heard them from his father, 'Ali.[3] Drawing forty hadiths from such a specific chain—and one with such prestigious transmitters as the descendents of the Prophet—serves to illustrate Shah Wali Allah's depth as a hadith scholar and his link to venerated figures of the sacred past. As scholars employed the medium to establish their own credentials, the forty-hadith genre even inspired a vanity subgenre, in which scholars showcased their mastery by compiling arba'in collections based on exceedingly restrictive criteria. In one of the more amazing examples, Ibn 'Asakir—who, in addition to his arba'in work on jihad, compiled forty-hadith collections on the Prophet's wives and the virtues of his Companions—produced a collection in which each of his forty hadiths came from a different teacher, hailing from a different town, transmitting the hadith from a different Companion of the Prophet, addressing a different topic. Similarly, Sadr al-Din al-Bakri compiled a forty-hadith collection in which each hadith came from a different Companion and addressed a different topic, with the added condition that each of his forty hadiths must have been found in a distinct forty-hadith collection.[4] In another momentous endeavor, the modern Palestinian scholar Yusuf an-Nabhani (1849–1932) compiled *al-Arba'in Arba'in*, a meta-arba'in project in which he organized 1,600 hadiths into forty unique forty-hadith collections on specific topics.

Far and away the most famous forty-hadith collection belongs to the Syrian scholar al-Nawawi (1233–1277). Instead of a collection that focused on a particular topic or issue, al-Nawawi endeavored to compile a more comprehensive work in which each hadith served as the foundation for a particular aspect of Islam. The assembled collection would serve as the ultimate introductory pamphlet to guide Muslim belief and practice. Al-Nawawi's *Forty Hadiths* became widely circulated as an accessible primer for general audiences, its fame growing in modernity amid translation and mass printing to such a degree that if you say "forty hadiths" today, Nawawi immediately comes to mind. For countless Muslims, al-Nawawi's collection provides a primer that boils down the immense tradition of Islam to a manageable core. If al-Nawawi intended to make each hadith stand as a foundation, his arba'in collection could conceivably provide the first step for forty journeys. Each hadith would open a portal into many more hadiths, guiding one's way through the hadith corpus at large. The forty-hadith collection can thus become a collection of introductions.

I thought about al-Nawawi and the forty-hadith genre while preparing to teach Islamic Studies courses at Kenyon College in Gambier, Ohio. My teaching schedule for that fall semester included "Classical Islam," an introductory lecture course that would start with Muhammad and the Qur'an, and "Muhammad," a senior seminar that involved a heavier reading load but nonetheless assumed no prior knowledge and was meant to provide an introduction to the Prophet. While reflecting on my priorities for these courses, especially my Muhammad seminar, I considered the theoretical problems of introducing Muhammad. Any introduction, purporting to give you the "basics" or "main idea," must first decide where the basics or main idea is located. Because an introduction by definition faces limits of space and depth, it must decide what it can afford to leave out; it must neglect some materials and privilege others. For this reason, the introduction does not only introduce, but also produces and creates the artifact that it seeks to present. In establishing a center, it invents the thing that needs a proper introduction. To some extent, every introductory syllabus, reflecting the topic as creatively imagined by its designer, inevitably becomes a work of fiction.

An introduction is especially challenging with a figure such as Muhammad, whose life and legacy undergo endless reimagination in Muslim traditions. There is more than one Muhammad to consider. Which should become the center for an introduction? Muhammad the lawgiver and statesman? Muhammad the general and battlefield hero? Muhammad the prophet of monotheism, heir to biblical figures such as Moses and Jesus in what some would call "Abrahamic" tradition? Muhammad the visionary mystic who ascended into the heavens? Muhammad as an example of the perfect body or even a cosmic principle whose light preexisted not only his physical form, but the world itself? Muhammad the husband, father, grandfather, friend? Muhammad the orphan?

As Muslims engage Muhammad's life as a resource to answer questions in their own lives, some ideas about Muhammad become more immediately relevant than others. In *The Lives of Muhammad*, Kecia Ali even anticipates Muslims writing of the Prophet as a modern business executive:

Can Muhammad be seen as a model CEO? Perhaps. After all, early Muslims wrote about him as a

shepherd, because all prophets were shepherds; and
mid-twentieth-century Egyptians wrote about him as
a socialist reformer, because that is what they needed.
Why should a businessman not write about him as
the epitome of executive skill?[5]

During my research for this project, I actually found such an
endeavor: *40 Hadith Reflections on Marketing and Business*,
in which the author promises to reveal the "hidden gems of
marketing in Islam," demonstrating the miraculous relevance
of a man who lived in seventh-century Arabia for modern
capitalism.[6]

In today's world of live-streamed sermons, the forty-hadith
genre continues to reconstruct Muhammad's legacy and value
on new platforms. In the wake of Donald Trump's ascent to
the presidency, for example, the popular shaykh Omar Suleiman presented a series of lectures titled "40 Hadiths on Social
Justice," offering resources from within the prophetic tradition for those working to enact change. One Muslim even
compiled a "40 Hadiths on Social Media" booklet, applying
Muhammad's guidance to the challenges of modern communication via relevant hadiths such as "The excellence of a person's Islam is that he leaves what does not concern him," and
"The servant who conceals the faults of others in this world,
Allah would conceal his faults on the Day of Resurrection."[7]

Non-Muslims (and Muslims responding to them) often
mold their image of Muhammad in relation to images of
Islam that they encounter in contemporary media—that
is, they define Muhammad in terms of violence, religious
intolerance, radical politics, and reactionary patriarchy.

As Kecia Ali's work points out, the modern biography of Muhammad, whether written by a critic or defender of the Prophet, consistently reports his life in such a way that gives priority to modern concerns. Whether one seeks to trace a direct line from Muhammad to the horrors of ISIS or to rescue him from Islamophobia networks, these conversations highlight the ways in which we create Muhammad with the questions we ask of him. Our questions are historically specific, informed by our own experience, and are not the same questions that would have been asked of Muhammad in a different age. When Martin Luther wrote about Muhammad, the concepts of a secular state, "Western civilization," and feminism did not exist, so Luther never asked whether these things were compatible with Muhammad's worldview; Christians in sixteenth-century Germany would not think to condemn Muhammad as patriarchal, homophobic, or antisecular. While Muhammad's opponents today highlight his participation in slavery and concubinage, and Muhammad's defenders present him as a fierce opponent of racism and reformer of slavery, these attacks and defenses would not have been intellegible as such for many in the nineteenth-century American South (though some proslavery American authors in the nineteenth century, aware of differences between Muslim and American slaving practices, cited Muslims as a positive example of slavery's historical diversity and potential to exist in a more benevolent form).[8] While American critics of Muhammad today often emphasize the age of his wife A'isha as a mark against him, others writing prior to the late twentieth century barely noticed that Muhammad married a young girl, focusing instead on his practice of plural marriage. Even if the sources do not change, our changing values and attitudes transform what we find in them.

Faced with the problem of introducing Muhammad to primarily non-Muslim students as I designed my syllabus, I wished that they could get forty introductions, each offering a distinct way of looking at Muhammad for the first time. If every introduction must leave things out, perhaps forty introductions could reduce our loss. At one point, I imagined how we might introduce Muhammad with one hadith per unit over the course of a forty-week semester. (This desire did not last too long, I assure you.) As each hadith in a forty-hadith work necessarily calls upon other hadiths, not to mention a wealth of references beyond the confines of hadith literature, an arba'in collection designed for an "intro to Muhammad" syllabus could both provide a series of snapshots of Islamic tradition and invite further investigation.

But are we looking here at "Islamic tradition" or at Muhammad himself? The hadith at the start of this chapter provokes a conversation about hadiths' authenticity and the question of whether sifting through these thousands of narrations can reliably give us the historical Muhammad. This hadith's valorization of the scholars who preserve Muhammad's Sunna finds its mirror in a widely reported hadith in which Muhammad states, "Whoever lies about me deliberately, let him take his seat in the Fire."[9] Muhammad was apparently aware that Muslims might invent hadiths in his name, and Muslim scholars quickly recognized the flood of forged hadiths that circulated throughout an expanding Islamic domain after Muhammad's death. Faced with the crisis of false hadiths, early hadith masters developed a sophisticated methodology for determining whether a reported statement of Muhammad was reliable, based primarily on evaluating the moral character and scholarship of each hadith's transmitters. If you were a scholar of hadith traditions in the early centuries of Islam, properly documenting your sources meant that you could name the scholar who taught you a specific hadith, that this scholar had named his/her teacher, and that this teacher had named his/her teacher, and so on, providing a chain of teachers and students that ideally traced back through the generations to a Companion, someone who had personally known the Prophet. Any missing or defective links in the chain, such as an unknown transmitter or someone who had been stigmatized for a poor memory, inappropriate behavior, or excessive sectarianism, weakened the reliability of the transmission.

Contemporary scholarship questions whether these methods of reporter evaluation achieved what they promised, producing a variety of conclusions. From a skeptical point of view, Muhammad's reported statement "Whoever lies about me deliberately, let him take his seat in the Fire" would itself be most likely a lie, reflecting not a genuine warning from the Prophet but rather the anxieties of later Muslims after hadith fabrication was already widespread. Harald Motzki, however, argues that by careful analysis of transmission chains and their relation to textual content, we could possibly attribute some hadiths to the earliest Muslim generation. Motzki cautions that this does not exactly prove that specific hadiths really originated from Muhammad's own mouth, but rather that it helps us identify hadiths that are old enough to be plausibly attributed to the era of people who had known him.[10]

Some scholars have sought to complicate the authenticity question. Wael Hallaq treats contemporary challenges to hadith authenticity as a "pseudo-problem," arguing that premodern hadith masters were not caught up in the zero-sum game over authenticity that compels modern skeptics and apologists alike.[11] Denise Spellberg and Asma Sayeed, suspending the authenticity question, have instead focused on the representation of women in hadith sources to ask new questions about gender in the tradition.[12]

The irony of the hadith considered here, promising Muhammad's intercession for the preserver of forty hadiths, is that Sunni scholars regarded this hadith itself as weakly evidenced, undermined by defects among its reporters (though the tradition gets a more charitable verdict in Shi'i hadith scholarship). Critics denounced Ishaq bin Najih, one of the transmitters for this particular version, as a fabricator of hadiths. However, Sunni doubts over the hadith's reliability did not stop Sunni scholars from producing an immense body of literature inspired by it. Perhaps the paradox of a call for preserving authentic history being possibly inauthentic itself provides a compelling launchpad for introducing Muhammad. At the very least, this paradox becomes a critical disclaimer. Muhammad as a historical person cannot make himself directly available to us unaffected by the dynamic and creative traditions that have grown around him. An arba'in work does not simply deliver forty facts of the Prophet's life and teachings, but instead gives us forty stories, each passing through multiple rounds of mediation—through its chain of transmission, its lineage of subjective human storytellers—and finally mediated by the arba'in author, who extracts the hadith from among countless thousands because it satisfies the needs of his/her own meticulously curated project. Every forty-hadith work, as a unique reconfiguration of materials, holds the potential to invent Muhammad anew. My own forty-hadith collection remains inescapably mine.

When choosing hadiths for my arba'in, I did not hold much stake in the judgments of premodern hadith masters (or, for that matter, contemporary secular scholarship) as to whether a particular hadith could pass a classical authenticity test. The entity that we're calling Muhammad remains much bigger than that, and there is more than one way to vet a hadith. Premodern Sunni and Shi'i scholars developed different methods for assessing a hadith's chain of transmitters; modern scholars who cast doubt on the reliability of these methods have sometimes offered alternatives; many Muslims would forgo transmitter evaluation altogether and instead measure a hadith's content against his or her personal, intuitive sense of Islam or what s/he understands as the message of the Qur'an; and some others might discover the truth of Muhammad through personal encounters with him in dreams and mystical visions. My forty-hadith project does not claim to bring forth the historical Muhammad, but rather treats Muhammad as an unstable archive of elements that combine, scatter, and reassemble in ongoing relation to his (and our) changing contexts. In any given setting, the most powerful makers of Muhammad's meaning from this archive are not necessarily the hadiths with the most rigorously vetted scholarly approval; hadiths with canonical privilege are not always the most relevant for understanding Muhammad or the communities that love him. I have attempted to recognize the significance of the canon while also recognizing it as a product of power struggle, giving us Muhammad as envisioned by the winners while marginalizing and excluding other voices. I have sought Muslim traditions that offer representations of Muhammad that speak from outside canonical privilege. I have listened to the "anti-canon," the sources specifically marked as forged and unacceptable; they, too, contribute to Muhammad's multiple legacies, and often become our only way of engaging Muslim voices that would have otherwise disappeared from history. Attempting to distinguish "pure" Islam from its various cultural expressions would resemble the study of a language in its "modern standard" form: a theoretical version of the language in its ideal state, free of pollution and change from local dialects, as imagined by professional grammarians rather than experienced in real life. For languages as well as religious traditions, this means a scholar's fantasy construction that cannot be found at any street corner or market. Mine is a hadith collection that does not privilege "modern standard Muhammad" over the Muhammad of local dialects on the ground, the Muhammad of street corners and markets.

What I ended up with was neither a detached academic textbook in which I write as a disembodied intellect offering analysis from above the fray, nor a pamphlet that claims to speak for "mainstream Islam" (as though there were such a thing). The project became my own walk with Muhammad. Can this arba'in still read as traditional? Its chosen organizing principle seems "traditional" enough; it adheres to a particular genre within Muslim literary tradition that goes back nearly to our oldest examples of Muslim writing. And though elements of my approach and final result would fail to satisfy many Muslims' notions of traditional hadith litera-ture, I did adhere to one traditional hadith scholar's practice: performing two short cycles (*rakat*) of prayer for every hadith selected, starting with this one. With mindfulness of my lim-itations, the process of compiling an arba'in became a way of reintroducing the Prophet to myself.

2

PUNK ROCK AND BEDOUIN PISS

Anas narrated:
   A Bedouin urinated in the masjid, and some of the people rushed at him. Then the Messenger of God (God bless him and give him peace) said, "Do not interrupt his urination." Then he called for a bucket of water and poured over it.[13]

Perhaps no other hadith does more to justify my own encounter with the Prophet. Reading of Muhammad's kindness and patience with hopes of successfully imitating him, I am hopeless. Instead, I read this hadith as if I were the masjid pisser.

In 2003, blessed with easy access to photocopiers, I self-published a novel, *The Taqwacores*, about a community of punk-rock Muslim kids. The story overflowed with the signatures of punk culture: crass language, offensive humor, rebellion and provocation, a proud embrace of blasphemy, and a refusal to apologize or negotiate with the dominant culture's demands and sensitivities. It was, in many ways, rude for the sake of being rude. If pressed today, I could contextualize the taqwacore scene within Islamic tradition. These punk Muslims represented a kind of lawless and ecstatic Islam that echoed the misfit piety of dervish groups found across Muslim Asia—communities such as the Abdals, who practiced public nudity, indulged in hashish and music, and abandoned the constraints of Muslim legal traditions.[14] Some scholars have in fact defended my work by forging these connections, insisting that even if my punk-rock Muslims defy popular expectations of what Muslims could be, they nonetheless find ancestors of their own in premodern Islam. When I was writing the novel, however, I had never heard of *malamatiyyas* or *qalandars*, and felt little desire for "classical tradition" to sign my permission slip. So much of punk's value came through its promise that we can live unapologetically, in our own skins and on our own terms, with or without the endorsement or forgiveness of our elders. No precedent or genealogy was required.

As the novel traveled through a succession of publishers, translations, film treatments, and media attention, I became known in American Muslim communities as the punky guy who wrote outrageous things. To this day, I am one of the most problematic writers in the American Muslim universe. At academic conferences even today, people sometimes seem surprised that I could show up in the expected uniform of a professor and give serious presentations without dropping fuck bombs or kicking tables over.

In the years after my initial release of the photocopied and spiral-bound *Taqwacores*, I have often felt uncomfortable with the novel, and have continued to pump out books, hoping that the new stuff might push my younger work farther into the distance. I won't outright disown *The Taqwacores*—Muslims still reach out to me to say that it did something for them, and the book has even attracted some accidental conversions to Islam—but facing a shelf of books with my name on them, I'm still afraid of what I might find in my million-plus words. Some of it—perhaps most of it, or all of it, depending who you ask—amounts to walking into a masjid and spilling urine in front of better people than myself. Throughout these books, I have often been selfish and heedless in my treatment of sacred things. Even if my authorial voice has grown more polite or academically measured over the years, my positions themselves fly far beyond the pale of most responsible "orthodoxies." Whether written in a provocative punk-rock voice or with a scholarly performance of theory-dropping, I am still too friendly with the wrong sectarian crowds, and in several cases these wrong crowds remain wrong even to one another: no marginalized heretic is necessarily an ally of every other marginalized heretic. In a few Muslim contexts, my name is piss.

When interviewed about my more controversial work, I am almost always asked a variant of one question: "What response have you received from Muslims?" The inquirers often seem to expect—or hope—that I'll feed them tales of outraged "fundamentalists" who express shock and horror at my words, supporting a popular narrative that presents Muslim communities as incapable of dealing with individual subjectivity and provocative art. Thinking in scripts informed by the Salman Rushdie affair, my interviewers might even hope for stories of death threats and condemnation from a bearded old patriarch in a turban whose stern glare offers an antimodern mirror against the West.

I can brush that narrative aside. In my encounters with various Muslim communities, I have received patience and generosity that my work had not earned. Yes, Muslims occasionally write to me expressing anger and hurt, but the overwhelming response—even beyond Muslims who might share my grievances and struggles—has been charitable. Muslim readers have addressed me as their brother and welcomed me into their masjids and homes. In showing compassion and patience with an uncouth voice in the community, they reflected the practice of Muhammad, who did not fly into a rage when a Bedouin urinated in the mosque. While his Companions lost their heads, the Prophet gently insisted that they let the man finish relieving himself, and then simply wash out the waste with water.

The masjid pisser becomes a teaching moment for Muhammad, a test for his Companions, and a demonstration of patience and superior manners as part of the prophetic Sunna. If some readers would see my books as repeating the Bedouin's behavior in a place of prayer, the response to my books from many Muslims would fulfill the precedent that Muhammad had established. In my own lived experience as a Muslim, I cannot find a hadith that better introduces Muhammad and the way that Muslims seek to follow his example today.

3

THE PROPHET IN HIS WORLD

Abu Hurayra narrated:
The Prophet (God bless him and give
him peace) said, "The Hour will not be established until the people of my nation copy
the deeds of the nations that came before
them and follow them span by span, cubit
by cubit." It was said, "O Messenger of God,
like the Persians and Romans?" He said,
"What people except those?"[15]

It is hard to speak with much confidence about pre-Islamic
Mecca (the city in which Muhammad was born), Medina
(the city in which he died), or their locale, the Hijaz region of the Arabian Peninsula. Our earliest source on the
origins of Islam remains the Qur'an, which presents itself as
a series of God's addresses directly to Muhammad and his
community but does not reflect his immediate surroundings
in a way that would satisfy historians. Before approaching
Muhammad as a historic individual in a particular context,

perhaps we should consider the world that made Muhammad possible.

Arabia in the generations leading up to Muhammad was a frontier land, a liminal space between major empires, and northern Arabia factored prominently in long-standing Roman-Persian rivalries. Though the Hijaz region was too uninviting to allow full conquest or attract sustained imperial interest, it was never so isolated that it could remain unaffected by these empires and their economic, military, or theological trajectories.

To the northwest of the Hijaz was the Byzantine Empire, heir to the Romans. A little more than two centuries before Muhammad's birth, the Roman emperor Constantine I (r. 306–337) legalized the Christian faith and embarked on a process of Christianizing the empire. But while Christianity became the empire's official confession and a series of councils sought to precisely define the faith's official limits, Christianity on the ground remained messy and unstable— characterized by a variety of competing churches and "heresies" and imprecise boundaries between local polytheisms of the preceding era and the new universalism. At the Near Eastern peripheries of the empire, some Arab communities were drawn to Christian conversion by multiple routes: to embrace Christ no longer meant joining a persecuted, marginalized fringe movement, but rather offered a chance for closer connections to imperial Roman culture.[16] Arabs were also moved to embrace Christ through encounters with wandering "desert holy men," Christian monks and ascetics who called people to piety, mediated between human communities and forces of the unseen, resolved disputes between

neighbors, and performed miracles of healing and exorcism.[17]
Amid instability, insecurity, the silence of oracles, and declin-
ing religious institutions, such figures filled a vacuum; for this
reason, writes Peter Brown, "The rise of the holy man is the
leitmotiv of the religious revolution in Late Antiquity."[18] In
particular, Syria was recognized in the late Roman period as
"the great province for ascetic stars."[19]

To the northeast of the Hijaz, analogous to modern Iran
and Iraq, was the Sasanian or Neo-Persian Empire, the Byzantines' rival across centuries of Roman-Persian war. Like the
Byzantines, the Sasanians anchored their power in an official
commitment of faith: they sponsored Zoroastrian teachings
and practices, and sought to establish the image of a united
empire characterized by uniformity of belief and ritual—
though, as with the Byzantines, this promotion of an official
imperial faith could not fully suppress or control the considerable diversity among its ruled peoples. We can include the
Sasanians' imperial Zoroastrianism as part of the monotheistic turn characterizing late antiquity. (For its notion of the
conflict between good Ohrmazd and evil Ahriman, many
would describe Zoroastrian tradition as "dualistic" rather than
monotheistic; however, contemporary scholarship reevaluates
this master narrative, suggesting that the contrast of dualism
versus monotheism has been uncritically projected onto Zoroastrianism from outside scholars working in biblical terms.[20])
Zoroastrian and Christian traditions seemed to parallel each
other in the ways that canonization of their scriptures took
place at roughly the same time and alongside imperial faith
projects of Sasanian and Byzantine rulers, for whom a central-
ization of theology seemed crucial for a truly united empire.[21]

To the south of the Hijaz, we find a third confessional empire, Aksum, which corresponds roughly to modern Ethiopia and Eritrea and at times claimed a range of territory including portions of modern Sudan, Djibouti, and Somalia, as well as the southern Arabian Peninsula with a colonial presence in what is now Yemen. Aksum is said to have been one of only four empires on the planet in its time to issue gold coinage, evidence of its economic and imperial prestige.[22] In the first half of the fourth century CE, Aksum's King Ezana I became Christian, and launched a centuries-long process of establishing Christian confession throughout the empire. Roughly contemporary to the Christianization of Aksum (and perhaps in response to it), ruling elites in the rival kingdom of Himyar (in present Yemen) gravitated toward Jewish conversion. By the end of the fourth century, South Arabian polytheism had been all but abandoned, with shrines and temples to astral gods deserted and crumbling.[23]

Monotheisms encountered each other as they traveled along trade routes. Himyarite Jews called God by the name Rahman or Rahmanan; their unique construction of Jewish tradition has been called Rahmanism. This South Arabian designation for God seems to have been a personal name rather than an Arabic word, though the Arabic r-h-m root letters connote mercy and compassion, and the name echoes the Syro-Aramaic and Judeo-Aramaic *rahmana*, "merciful."[24] As a name for God, Rahman made its way north into the Hijaz, as evidenced by the Qur'an's numerous references to God as Rahman, particularly those portions typically dated as its earliest revelations. All but one of the Qur'an's 114 suras begin with the phrase *bismillah ar-rahman ar-rahim*, though modern English translations tend to render this phrase as "In the name of God, the Compassionate, the Merciful," erasing Rahman as a personal name and rendering it an essentially interchangeable synonym of Rahim. For Meccans to whom Rahman remained unfamiliar and foreign, and who were unsure as to whether the names Allah and ar-Rahman referred to the same being, the Qur'an answers their confusion: "Call upon Allah, or call upon Rahman, by whatever name you call him, for to him belong the most beautiful names" (17:110).

Aksum-Himyar conflicts often became strategic threads in Roman-Persian power struggles. In the 520s, Himyar's Jewish king slaughtered Christian elites who were sympathetic to the Byzantines. Early in his reign, the Byzantine emperor Justinian I sought Aksum's help in controlling Himyar as part of his war game against the Sasanians. His plan was undermined by the rise to power of an Aksumite Christian general, Abraha, who overthrew the Christian king that Aksum had installed in Himyar and declared himself sovereign. Abraha's inscriptions make reference to "the help of Rahmanan and his Christ"[25] and attest to Abraha's military activity in central Arabia, conceivably placing him within reach of Mecca. According to pre-Islamic poetry and Muslim historical tradition, Abraha attempted to conquer Mecca in 570, the year of Muhammad's birth, only to be thwarted by miraculous intervention: the army's elephants refused to advance upon the Ka'ba, and birds bombed Abraha's troops from above with hardened clay; the Qur'an apparently refers to the event in its 105th sura, "The Elephant."[26]

The Hijaz region thus existed within a triangle of imperial forces that authorized themselves as protectors of monotheistic faith. By 570, they were all empires in decline. Aksum and Himyar had collapsed. The Byzantines were devastated by earthquakes and plagues, Justinian I's overspending, and numerous Christian communities' resistance to imperial efforts to impose a singular, united Christian orthodoxy.[27] Both the Byzantines and Sasanians became weakened by the ups and downs of their continual conflict, and the Sasanians had fallen to both diminished trade and internal strife.[28] The deterioration of these empires provided the perfect opening for Muhammad's movement to emerge.

By 670, the political landscape had been transformed in ways that Muhammad's contemporaries could not have anticipated. From the capital, Damascus, Muslims ruled as an imperial superpower over not only the Arabian Peninsula but also the entirety of the former Sasanian domain and much of what had been Byzantine territory, covering an expanse that reached from Mediterranean Africa to Afghanistan. This new superpower, like the confessional empires that it supplanted, authorized itself with claims to a divine mandate, and its rulers considered themselves heirs to a prophet.

But what's a prophet?

To designate Muhammad with the label of "prophet" is to place him in a special category of history-maker that was known and understood across Mediterranean antiquity. For many readers today, the most recognizable specimens in this category would have been prophets from Israelite tradition, but ideas of prophethood transcended any singular nation or locale. Insofar as we could think of anything in Mediterranean antiquity as global, prophethood reflected a globally recognized mode of knowledge; Egyptians, Greeks, Romans,

Babylonians, Persians, and monotheists and polytheists alike accepted that unseen beings could communicate with humankind through specially selected human messengers. The Sasanian kings represented themselves as defenders and preservers of the teachings of Zoroaster, a human who received privileged knowledge from the unseen. The Sasanian Empire also hosted the rise of the prophet Mani, who preached what he regarded as a universal message that fulfilled the teachings of previous masters such as Jesus. According to statements attributed to Muhammad in canonical sources, the prophets preceding Muhammad numbered as high as 125,000. The considerable intersection and exchange between societies in the ancient world also meant that local notions of prophethood developed in conversation with other cultures; prophetic figures in what are now Syria and Iraq, for example, were the products of flows between broader Hellenic and Persian imperial and economic domains. When Muhammad identified himself as a prophet, it seems that no one had to ask him, "What's a prophet?" The category awaited him.

Our earliest biographical sources on Muhammad repeat tropes of prophethood familiar in Mediterranean antiquity: his birth and childhood being distinguished by numerous extraordinary events and learned sages' predictions of his future greatness; the bodily signs that marked a divinely ordained status on his flesh; his mediation between humankind and the realm of the unseen; his reception of divinely revealed scripture and law; his smashing of idols and revival of monotheism; his apocalyptically tinged critiques of a decadent society, calls to renewed morality, and warnings of divine wrath and impending doom; his ascension into the heavens to encounter angels, past prophets, and even God; his linkage to a primordial way of life associated with Abraham; his initial rejection and persecution by the powerful members of his society, followed by triumph over his enemies; his compassion for orphans, slaves, and other disenfranchised members of his community; and his performance of miracles, such as the splitting of the moon or the causing of dried-up wells to overflow. His biography fulfilled a template of what people expected to see in prophetic lives and presents him as the culmination of prophetic history.

In enumerating the ways in which Muhammad's biography can plug into popular motifs of prophets and holy men, my concern isn't to establish whether such details really happened or instead to reflect embellishments by later mythmakers; rather, it is to consider ways in which the historical setting of seventh-century Arabia enabled "prophet" as a thinkable possibility. The "prophet" or "holy man," mediating between seen and unseen worlds, was a recognized vehicle of change; as Muhammad struggled to transform his society, he did so with terms and concepts that were already comprehensible to both his community and himself. And while Muhammad's movement achieved an enormous historical impact on the world, it also emerged naturally from the connections and collisions of various forces and flows around him.

*

Having zoomed out our lens to look at the world around Muhammad, what happens when we zoom in to focus on the Hijaz? Scholars on Muhammad face the opposite challenge that Jesus scholars face: whereas François de Blois describes Jesus as a "biographically intangible figure located in a very well documented historical milieu," Muhammad is in contrast a "biographically at least plausible figure located in a historical vacuum."[29] It's hard to say anything about Muhammad's setting with confidence.

As in the case of Muhammad's biography, the problem with making definitive fact-claims on pre-Islamic Mecca and Medina is that our sources are almost entirely post-Islamic. These later sources define the region in the pre-Islamic era as steeped in polytheism and "ignorance" (*jahiliyya*). The central shrine in Mecca, the Ka'ba, is reported to have been surrounded by up to 360 images of gods and goddesses. While this image of dominant polytheism would present Muhammad's mission as a dramatic break from the past, sources also mention Jewish and Christian tribes and individuals (as well as *hanifs*, unaffiliated monotheists) as part of Hijazi culture, and trade routes provided linkages between central Arabia and the ideas of neighboring lands. Moreover, Muslim sources also present monotheism as having been Mecca's original theological orientation. According to this tradition, the Ka'ba was first constructed by Abraham and his son Ishmael; long before its function as a center of polytheist pilgrimage, it was a house dedicated to their one god. In its radical overturning of a polytheistic society's norms and values, therefore, Muhammad could be seen as having restored what had been there first.

Did Muhammad's mission begin as a lone preacher's monotheistic stand against a society defined by polytheism?

Or did his prophethood ride a historical wave, in harmony
with the trends of the age? Should we understand Muhammad as an absolute break or as part of a flow? G. R. Hawting
argues that "long before the seventh century the balance of
power was decisively in favor of monotheism."[30] By the time
of Muhammad, perhaps the Hijaz's local pantheons were already vanishing; or perhaps they had vanished. Monotheism
could have already become an integral and "mainstream" element in Mecca. While the Qur'an engages in constant attacks
against polytheism, Hawting argues that its true target might
not be self-identified polytheists but rather other monotheists whom it judges as having lapsed or compromised. One
could further speculate that whatever "idols" had once been
venerated in Mecca were demolished long before Muhammad's arrival, and that later interpreters of the Qur'an, reading the revelation in an entirely different context, misread the
anti-polytheism polemics as addressing actual polytheists in
Muhammad's own time.[31]

Monotheism and polytheism represent constructed categories that different communities define in different ways.
Self-identified monotheists often accuse one another of polytheism, as seen in Protestant polemics against Catholics or
Muslim polemics against the Christian trinity, or even in
the frequent arguments among Muslims over what violates
Islamic monotheism's limits. For Hawting, the fact that Meccan polytheists regarded the characters of al-Lat, al-'Uzza,
and Manat as angels and/or God's daughters suggests that
they maintained their own sense of monotheism—even if
this meant a particular monotheism that the Qur'an rejects
as inadequate.

Whether or not Hawting's argument proves satisfying, his project of reconsidering the history of pre-Islamic Mecca points to the poverty of our sources and the degree to which claims on the jahiliyya period remain speculative. Hawting describes the problem by imagining how scholars could study early Judaism if they only had access to Christian sources.[32] Some extreme revisionists went so far as to deny that Muhammad ever existed; though they later dialed back their claims, Muhammad's biography remains frustrating for historians, and contemporary scholarly debate as to what our sources can tell us continues. The claim that there was never a Muhammad at all no longer receives serious consideration; we recognize that there was a person known as Muhammad, that there was some sort of monotheist revival/reform movement associated with him, and that the text of the Qur'an took its recognizable shape in the generation of people who would have personally known him (at the latest). But the Qur'an does not give us anything close to a substantive account of the setting in which it appeared, let alone a biography of Muhammad.

The rigorous hadith masters of the ninth century memorized many thousands of narrations about Muhammad, but were more interested in engaging the details of his life to make judgments about correct belief, worship, and law than in producing a coherent cradle-to-grave narrative of his life. And again, we face the problem of whether the hadith masters' science of distinguishing reliable from fabricated hadiths delivered on its promise. When it comes to Muhammad, we might lose hope of answering our question "Who was the person?" but still ask, "What was the event?" None of this requires that we deny Muhammad as an exceptional human being or insist that individuals cannot have the agency to change history, but only that we consider the Muhammad-event as more complex than a "founder" model of religion—or a patriarchal "great man" model of writing history—would often allow. Even if we were to surrender our claims of access to Muhammad as a historically recoverable life, we could glean something about his movement by looking at the world in which this Muhammad-event came simultaneously as a rupture and a continuity in organic harmony with its world.

My students often express amazement that Muhammad's movement emerged from "out of nowhere" to become the world's dominant civilization in a matter of a few decades. Yes, the "out of nowhere" dimension is genuinely amazing: in a minor trading town beyond the outer reaches of vast empires, a monotheist revival movement took shape that would come to rule much of the known world within an inconceivably short period. Without denying the spectacular rise of Islam, however, we can also consider the Muhammad-event as fitting naturally within its time and place—whether this amounts to a sequence of historical accidents or the fulfillment of divine plan.

4

THE HADITH OF GABRIEL

'Umar narrated:

While we were sitting with the Messenger of God (God bless him and give him peace) one day, a man came to us in extremely white clothes and with extremely black hair. No traces of travel were seen on him, and none of us knew him. He sat in front of the Prophet (God bless him and give him peace), then touched his knees to his knees and put his palms on his thighs, and he said, "O Muhammad, report to me on surrender."

The Messenger of God (God bless him and give him peace) said, "Surrender is that you testify that there is no god but God and Muhammad is his messenger, that you stand for prayer, that you pay zakat, that you fast in Ramadan, and that you perform hajj to the house, if you are able."

The man said, "You have spoken the

truth." We were astonished at his asking him and pronouncing him truthful. Then he said, "Report to me about faith."

(Muhammad) said, "That you believe in God, his angels, his books, his messengers, and in the Last Day, and in predestination, both in its good and its evil." (The man) said, "You have spoken the truth. Then report to me on beauty." (Muhammad) said, "That you should serve (or worship) God as though you can see him, for you cannot see him but he can see you."

He said, "Report to me about the Hour." (Muhammad) said, "The questioned does not know more than the questioner." He said, "Report to me about its signs." (Muhammad) said, "That the slave will give birth to her mistress, that you see the barefooted, naked, destitute shepherds competing in building." Then (the man) left. I hesitated, and then (Muhammad) said, "O 'Umar, do you know who that questioner was?" I said, "God and his messenger know better." He said, "That was Gabriel. He came to teach you your din."[33]

For many readers, the Hadith of Gabriel presents the essence of God's instructions for humankind. For precisely this reason, the hadith master al-Nawawi (1233–1277) included it in his *Forty Hadiths*, and contemporary scholars Sachiko Murata and William C. Chittick use it as a framing device for their introductory survey, *Vision of Islam*. Examining Gabriel's

questions to Muhammad regarding the definitions of surrender (*islam*), faith (*iman*), and excellence (*ihsan*), Murata
and Chittick suggest that these three dimensions help us to
understand more fully the tradition that we call Islam and
the person that we label a Muslim (that is, someone who *does*
Islam).

The hadith is not only a discourse providing a checklist
of required beliefs and actions, but also functions as a miracle
story that proves Muhammad's prophethood with the observable appearance of an angel, in fact the most prominent angel.
Murata and Chittick note the shock and confusion that this
"stranger from the desert"[34] might have caused in Muhammad's Companions: a man suddenly shows up in Medina who
is unknown to everyone, but somehow displays none of the
visible wear and tear that would have marked him as a trav-
eler. In the Medina of nearly fifteen centuries ago, this was
unthinkable. The mysterious man also seems noteworthy for
the extreme contrast of his dark hair and white garments. He
sits to face the Prophet of God, touches their knees together,
places his hands on the Prophet's thighs, addresses him in-
formally, and asks questions regarding the unseen realm but
approves of Muhammad's responses as though he had already
known the answers and is merely giving a quiz. "After the
man leaves," Murata and Chittick write, "Muhammad waits
awhile, allowing his companions to think about this strange
event," before finally revealing that the mysterious man was
Gabriel and that, in his questions, he taught them their *din*,
a term which would typically undergo translation today as
"religion."[35]

The teller of this story, 'Umar ibn al-Khattab, was a

father-in-law of the Prophet and became one of the "rightly guided caliphs" after Muhammad's death. The account draws some prestige from his special authority, but also adds to it: 'Umar was certainly not a prophet, but still he appears here as the recipient of an especially privileged access to transcendent knowledge, first as a Companion to the Prophet but also as a human who saw Gabriel with his own eyes.

The Hadith of Gabriel, when considered as a story told by 'Umar, might cause us to rethink categories. If a thirteenth-century Sufi intellectual or ascetic described an incident in which s/he personally witnessed the angel Gabriel, we would immediately place the story within a tradition of Islamic "mysticism." We're less likely to think of 'Umar—hearty war hero, caliphal statesman, and righteous legislator—as someone who belongs in a conversation about mysticism. But, according to this narration, he saw some things that people don't normally see.

'Umar's narration can also say something to the "founder" model with which we often approach religious traditions. Today, we tend to take for granted that there is a thing called Islam, and that we can locate this Islam in the category of "religions," specifically a special class that we have termed world religions. We also tend to think of religions as usually having founders, and thus name Muhammad as the founder of Islam. From a perspective that holds Muhammad as having been a genuine prophet, however, Muhammad was not Islam's founder; he only transmitted to humankind what he had received from the Creator of the universe. Moreover, Muhammad's religion was not something unique to him, but rather was the religion of all prophets, including the biblical prophets such as Jesus, Moses, Abraham, and even the first human, Adam. The founder model can meet challenge here in another sense, as we note that the Hadith of Gabriel does not technically come to us from Muhammad. 'Umar, speaking as an eyewitness, provides our window to the event. The founding of Islam, if we want to think of Islam as having been founded at a particular moment in history, did not occur as one gifted individual feeding meaning to a passive audience and singlehandedly delivering an intact system. Rather, we can conceptualize the emergence of Islam as a collaborative process, starting with members of a community who witnessed Muhammad's prophetic experience, and entered into its assemblage as active participants by telling their stories to later generations. As our source for Gabriel's examination of Muhammad, having memorized Gabriel's questions and Muhammad's answers to preserve the din, 'Umar can be considered a founder in his own right. Even beyond 'Umar, we could recognize the thousands of hadith transmitters as founders for their preservation and active production of prophetic memory.

*

Gabriel's first question to Muhammad concerns *islam*, which we typically transliterate without translating: the Arabic word for "surrender" or "submission" becomes a capitalized Islam, the name for a religion, with its adherents labeled as Muslims. Yet it is not clear that Muhammad's religion always had a name, let alone that he would have named his religion Islam; Muhammad lived in a time before our modern conception of "world religions" that existed as properly named systems. (The

Qur'an speaks of Christians and Jews as communities, for example, but has no terms for "Christianity" or "Judaism.") The Qur'an makes references to surrender; one such verse (5:3), naming surrender (*islam*) as humankind's duty (*din*), popularly appears in translation as "Islam" being named humankind's "religion." This is how we write our modern categories and concepts onto premodern revelations.

Muhammad defines islam/surrender with a list of actions that are famously described elsewhere as the "five pillars." First, one performs surrender by bearing witness to the oneness of God and the prophethood of Muhammad: one enters the community by way of expressed testimony, as opposed to privately held faith. Second, surrender requires adherence to the mandated prayers. Third, a performer of surrender (that is, a *muslim*) pays a charity tax. Fourth, fast in Ramadan, the month in which Muhammad first began to receive the revelations that would become the Qur'an. Finally, surrender means performing the pilgrimage to God's house in Mecca. These five items represent the islam quarter of the din that Gabriel had come to teach. Gabriel categorizes the rest of the din with other labels.

After inquiring about the meaning of surrender, Gabriel asks about faith (*iman*). The Qur'an seems to draw distinction between surrender and faith; in 49:14, the Qur'an states, "The Arabs say, 'We have believed.' Say, 'You have not believed, but say, "We have surrendered," for faith has not entered your hearts.'" These particular Arabs had performed the necessary acts of surrender to enter into Muhammad's new community, but they had not yet adopted his message with personal conviction.

In his answer to the question of faith, Muhammad defines the faith-centered dimension of din with six crucial items: belief in God, angels, revealed scriptures, prophets, the Day of Judgment, and *qadar* (God's decree, or predestination). To many, Muhammad's response to Gabriel would read as a complete and self-evident presentation of Islam as a faith tradition: there is only one God, who is all-powerful and will judge human beings for their actions; this singular God guides human beings toward proper belief and behavior by sending them messengers from among themselves, these messengers being endowed with divinely revealed scriptures through angelic mediation. This short statement provides, as much as we can critically claim to nutshell anything, Muhammad's narrative of existence and human destiny.

For those interested in the question of historical authenticity, the Prophet's mention of qadar might raise a red flag. Throughout the hadith corpus, we find Muhammad making reference to tribal conflicts, sectarian disputes, and theological controversies that took place in the generations after his death. From a faith conviction in Muhammad's status as the Prophet, this isn't necessarily a problem; Muhammad had access to knowledge beyond what we would normally expect for human beings. From a particular lens of historical criticism, however, hadith literature becomes suspect when it depicts Muhammad as anticipating the concerns of a post-Muhammad world. The Prophet including qadar as a critical point of belief can be interpreted as a reference to intellectual debates that began after he died.

In the early centuries following Muhammad, Muslims debated the tension between human free will and divine predestination. If humans did not possess free will, how could God—presumably perfect in his justice—reward or punish them for their actions? On the other hand, if humans indeed had the ability to freely act in the world, did this compromise God's status as the singular controller over all things that he had created? To hadith scholars who relied on transmitted prophetic knowledge as the only key to solving problems of the Qur'an's meaning, rationalist theologians who asserted free will blasphemously denied God's qadar; hadith scholars thus branded them with the slur of *Qadariya*, lumping various thinkers together as a singular sectarian heresy. And in the Hadith of Gabriel, Muhammad seems to confirm this judgment. In his exchange with Gabriel, Muhammad affirms acceptance of the Day of Judgment and then immediately affirms acceptance of God's qadar, both of which stand as critical checkpoints at the border between belief and unbelief. It seems reasonable to ask whether one party's position on the question of qadar has been projected retroactively upon this hadith, whether Muhammad is being made to referee a controversy that had not existed during his own earthly life.

The hadith's presentations of surrender and faith could push back against a common narrative about Muslim tradition, namely that Muslims throughout history have been far more concerned with questions of orthopraxy (norms of ritual and law) than orthodoxy (norms of belief). It is often imagined that, in contrast to Christians, who divided into various churches and persecuted one another because of points of theological controversy, Muslims were uninterested in theology and instead fought one another over matters of earthly authority. Historically speaking, this position is not defensible; Muslims have a long record of struggling to define and police the boundaries of correct belief. In the Hadith of Gabriel, Muhammad presents the din as anchored both in external practice and private faith.

Satisfied with Muhammad's explanations of islam and iman, Gabriel then asks about *ihsan*, which can be translated as a making/doing of the good and beautiful. According to Murata and Chittick, ihsan departs from islam's focus on action and iman's focus on belief to emphasize intention. Defined in the Hadith of Gabriel as worshiping God as though you see him, ihsan thus reflects an intersection between performative acts and the conditions of faith: calling Muslims to perfect both behavior and conscience. In another version of this hadith, Muhammad supplements this intensified consciousness of God with a renewed commitment to humanity, explaining that ihsan also means to "love for humankind what one loves for himself." This resonates with the Qur'an, which instructs us to practice ihsan with our parents, relatives, orphans, people in need, neighbors near and far, close friends, travelers, and—because slavery existed as a norm in the Qur'an's context—"those whom your right hand possesses" (4:36). In her discussion of prejudices and tensions between South Asian and African American Muslim communities, Jamillah Karim writes of ihsan as a high road in which Muslims practice forgiveness, compassion, and generosity. Pointing out that the Qur'an presents ihsan in close relation to justice (*'adl*), Karim sees an ethics of ihsan as a path for correcting wrongs and healing wounds: to practice ihsan means "creating beautiful relations between people, built on mercy and trust, so that as we confront sensitive issues of power and privilege in our communities, we are more likely to listen to one another, care about our future together, and work with one another for change."[36] Even animals are entitled to ihsan, as a number of hadiths report Muhammad telling us to comfort the animals that we slaughter and use sharp blades to spare them from undue suffering, as "God has decreed ihsan in all things."[37]

The notion of din as consisting of surrender, belief, and "making beauty" might prompt a question: Which element of the din took priority? Does the fact that Gabriel asks first about islam (at least in the most popular version) mean that islam is the most important, perhaps a prerequisite for the other two? Comparing mentions of faith and surrender in the Qur'an, Fred Donner argues for a prioritization of belief, and thus refers to the first members of Muhammad's movement as Believers rather than Submitters. Could this construct have been named Iman instead of Islam? Probing the story's structure for its inner meanings, Muslim intellectuals such as the thirteenth-century mystic 'Aziz ibn Muhammad Nasafi detect an ascending hierarchy in the order of terms. With each question, according to Nasafi, Gabriel raises the stakes. Gabriel first asks Muhammad about surrender, which means fulfilling a set of required acts that could conceivably be performed without sincerity or much thought. One can recite the testimony to God's oneness and Muhammad's prophethood, mouth the words of prayers and go through the physical motions, give the required zakat, abstain from food during the days of Ramadan, and participate in the rites of hajj as though one simply needs to cross out items on a divinely revealed to-do list. But Gabriel's inquiry then progresses from practice to faith, privileging one's internal condition and sincerity of belief above his or her rote performance of required actions. According to Nasafi, islam represents the domain of the *'ulama*, the clerical scholars who concern themselves with questions such as the proper way to wash before prayer, whereas the higher second stage, iman, represents the domain of philosophers. The third and highest stage, ihsan, represents the path of Sufism. All of these stages are "true" and exist in harmony with the divine revelation, but as one moves along the upward trajectory from islam to ihsan, one departs from the scholars' *madrasa* to the gnostics' *khanaqah*, the Sufi lodge. For Nasafi, this marks a graduation from lower to higher states.[38] In their minings of the Hadith of Gabriel for its secret jewels, Sufis privilege their own pursuits as the highest level of the din that Gabriel taught, while preserving the practice-centered knowledges and institutions that keep the rest of Muslim society running.

After Muhammad's explanation of ihsan, Gabriel asks him about the Hour. Especially when one reads what are regarded as the earliest revealed portions of the Qur'an, the urgency of the Hour is a dominant theme: *You are doing wrong,* the early suras tell us in no uncertain terms, *and you need to fix yourselves because God can bring this whole world down at literally any moment.* The Qur'an's apocalyptic motifs help to situate its revelation within the broader religious landscape of Mediterranean antiquity, in which numerous communities appear to have been interested in a conclusion to worldly time. Narratives of imminent disaster, the arrival of an awaited redeemer, upheavals of the present world order, and an ultimate Last Judgment had grown particularly significant among marginalized groups in the Byzantine Near East, such as "heretical" churches that fell under imperial persecution. Apocalyptic ideas also flourished among Zoroastrian communities. Modern scholarship sometimes paints an image of the first Muslims as an apocalyptic movement driven by an idea that the Hour was coming soon, which might explain why the community seems to have been unprepared for Muhammad to die before the end of history.[39]

While Muhammad lived in an age characterized by apocalypticism, the specific discussion of end times in this hadith did not necessarily come from Muhammad himself, and could have been a later attribution. Regarding the exact time of the Hour's arrival, Muhammad confesses to Gabriel the human limits of his knowledge, but instead offers signs that can reveal when the Hour approaches: the slave gives birth to her mistress, while the poor and the shepherds compete with each other in building. As with other apocalyptic texts, such as the Christian Bible's book of Revelation, the signs remain sufficiently vague that a reader in virtually any time or place could read them as referring to her own context. And like the book of Revelation, this textual artifact seems to refer to events in its own present—which possibly means an era after Muhammad's death. The slave giving birth to her mistress could reflect the anxieties of Arab Muslim elites as a small ruling minority in a vast (and overwhelmingly non-Arab) empire. Just as Christian faith confession had offered some pre-Islamic Arab communities new access to Byzantine imperial culture, numerous non-Arabs under Arab rule found routes to enhanced social mobility via Muslim conversion. Meanwhile, elite Arab Muslim men were fathering children with their non-Arab wives and slaves; just a century after the passing of Muhammad, Patricia Crone writes, "the Arabs were no longer the people that their grandfathers had been," and "Islam was becoming everyone's property."[40]

The shepherds' competition in building can also reflect a transformation that would have been unthinkable to the earliest Muslims; barely a century separates the nomadic tribes, small towns, and caravan raiders of Muhammad's community from the establishment of Baghdad as a virtual capital of the known world. To those who lived to see both the traces of a fading era and signs of the coming golden age, these sweeping changes could have seemed apocalyptic in scale.

Following their short exchange, Muhammad's mysterious interviewer leaves, after which Muhammad identifies him as Gabriel and reveals that he had come to teach the people their din. Again, the mention of din provokes a critical pause. In English translations of the sacred sources, *din* typically becomes "religion," as though an English word of considerable instability even within its own specific history can comfortably line up to a word found in seventh-century Arabic. It's not exactly unreasonable to translate *din* as "religion," but we should at least do so with awareness that religion as we know it isn't a universal concept that has existed in the same way in all times and places. References to islam, iman, and ihsan all become points at which we might carelessly turn the Hadith of Gabriel into a mirror that only reflects back to us our own world and its dominant regime of sense.

The three dimensions of islam, iman, and ihsan can also complicate the question of how "religious" we consider ourselves. In my life as a Muslim, I move along multiple spectrums; depending on the mode of measurement, I might think of myself as more or less religious than I would at other times. I do not always think of my personal connection to Islam in terms of "faith"; being Muslim relates to lots of things beyond the question of whether I bear witness to a number of truth claims. On the other hand, when someone asks me if I am a "practicing" Muslim, I don't always know how to answer. Yes, I do things that I regard as Muslim things; are these the practices that my inquirer had in mind? My iman, islam, and ihsan are like dials that can each be turned up and down without necessary or consistent relation to the others. There are times at which I become more involved with embodied acts of surrender and increase my participation in Muslim communities, but do not hold the same intellectual commitments that would qualify me as an "orthodox" Muslim in any given space. As a young convert drawing lines between his Christian past and Muslim future, I valued correctness of faith over everything; more than two decades later, I don't consistently maintain that investment. Can someone surrender without believing? I have known atheists who continued to attend congregational prayers at their mosques and maintain the fast in Ramadan; they drew profound benefits from their acts of islam but claimed no supernaturalist iman whatsoever. Conversely, not every believer adheres to the disciplines of surrender. I could, on occasion, approach an internal condition of belief closer to what most Muslims regard as theological "orthodoxy," but not necessarily find this change represented in my embodied actions. And sometimes, I engage traditions of Islamic ethics and etiquette for a sense of ihsan, the project of becoming human. As a third dimension of the din, ihsan means that our "religion" is not composed entirely of things that everyone could immediately and intuitively recognize as "religious." The din consists not only of faith conviction and ritual, but also a way of being in the world; if we understand kindness, generosity, and humility as no less definitively crucial to our capitalized Islam than theological questions or the correct motions of prayer, then ihsan can preserve a space as palpably "Islamic" even when no one in the room believes or prays.

5

THE END OF PROPHETHOOD

Anas narrated:
    If Ibrahim, the son of the Prophet (God
bless him and give him peace), had lived, he
would have been a righteous prophet.[41]

In 33:40, the Qur'an describes Muhammad as "Messenger of God and Seal of the Prophets." Muslims often read these offices of "messenger" (*rasul*) and "prophet" (*nabi*) as virtually interchangeable, and readers generally take Muhammad's distinction as the "Seal" to mean that prophethood concludes with him.

We should look at our terms and the Qur'an's use of them. The Qur'an mentions numerous human beings who have been chosen by God to receive divine revelations and teach their nations. Examining its usage of "messenger" and "prophet," Hartmut Bobzin demonstrates that figures from biblical tradition bear the designation of "prophet" (*nabi*) and that the Qur'an prioritizes their shared "Abrahamic"

biological heritage. Some of these figures bear both titles—
Jesus, for example, is both prophet and messenger—but a
slight distinction remains. No nonbiblical messenger apart
from Muhammad himself is called a prophet, and no biblical
messenger is not also a prophet.

Through his descent from Ishmael, Muhammad shares
Abrahamic lineage with the Israelite prophets. Bobzin argues, however, that if we rearrange the Qur'an's verses to read
them in the chronological order of their revelation (so far as
contemporary scholarship theorizes that we can actually do
this), we find that the Qur'an first begins to call Muhammad a prophet after his migration to Medina. It happened to
be in Medina, according to traditional sources, that Jewish
communities increasingly became Muhammad's conversation partners, allies, and opponents; this also finds reflection
in a chronological reading of the Qur'an, since the Medinan
verses appear to be more concerned with engaging Jewish and
Christian critiques, whereas the Meccan verses deal more directly with polytheists. It would seem that in the Qur'an's
original milieu, "messenger" and "prophet" carried different
social and political consequences; the more generic label of
"messenger" did not express the precise claims to authority,
particularly in relation to the Israelite prophetic lineage, reflected in Muhammad's role as prophet.

The only verse in the Qur'an that names Muhammad
as the Seal, 33:40, begins with the statement "Muhammad
is not the father of any of your men," and appears within a
sequence that dissolves Muhammad's relationship as adoptive
father to Zayd ibn Harith. The Qur'an connects the conclusion of prophethood to Muhammad not having a son; this

connection is reflected in the report that when Muhammad's son Ibrahim dies as an infant, Muhammad declares that his son would have grown to become a prophet. The narration intensifies the gendering of prophethood, given its silence on the fact that Muhammad did have a daughter who outlived him. Muhammad's daughter Fatima never factors into the category of prophethood, though Shi'i hadith canon does present her as receiving privileged communications from the angel Gabriel, which she in turn dictated to her husband, 'Ali, who passed it down through their family.[42]

The Qur'an seems to further masculinize prophethood in its treatment of the Virgin Mary, whom the Qur'an does not name as a prophet, despite her apparently meeting the prerequisites: biological descent from Abraham, privileged communication from Gabriel, miraculous interventions from God in her natural processes, and service as a guided teacher and sign to her community. Mary's life looks like that of a prophet or messenger, but she is not explicitly included on the roster. The Qur'an's lack of comment on Mary's possible prophethood could reflect a world in which a woman prophet wasn't fathomable; but this also means that the Qur'an never tells us that we *can't* call her a prophet. Ingrid Mattson and Barbara Stowasser note that Andalusian scholar Ibn Hazm (994–1064), leading figure in the Zahiri legal school, rejected the majority opinion that excluded women from prophethood, arguing "convincingly" that Mary belongs among the prophets.[43] Drawing from classical interpretations that regarded *rasul* as a higher class than *nabi*, however, Ibn Hazm's inclusion of Mary nonetheless preserved a gendered hierarchy: Mary could be a prophet, but not a messenger.

The gendering of prophethood could allow for compelling loopholes. In his immense encyclopedia *Nihayat al-'Arab*, an-Nuwayri (1279–1333) provides the anecdote of a woman who was charged with claiming prophethood and then brought to the caliph. When interrogated over her faith in Muhammad, she affirmed that she believed in everything that Muhammad had taught. The caliph then asked her about Muhammad's statement "There will be no prophet after me (*la nabiyya ba'di*)," to which she retorted that Muhammad had not said, "There will be no *prophetess* after me (*la nabiyyata ba'di*)"![44]

The belief that Muhammad is the last prophet is seen by many Muslims as a nonnegotiable border between Islam and not-Islam. The Ahmadiyya community, for instance, undergoes state persecution in Pakistan for its commitment to its founder, Mirza Ghulam Ahmad (1835–1908), who claimed to have received revelations and identified himself in a mystical sense with Muhammad. This could be a case of bad timing and modern-world problems: if the Ahmadiyya had originated a few centuries earlier, they might have been categorized as a Sufi order rather than a "heretical cult," and perhaps even received some government patronage. Instead, the Pakistani government has rendered it illegal for Ahmadi Muslims to self-identify as Muslims under the threat of criminal punishment. As intepretations of Pakistan's anti-Ahmadi blasphemy laws, recent efforts have been introduced to restrict Ahmadi participation in social media. The Nation of Islam (NOI) receives similar condemnation from many Muslims for its belief that Elijah Muhammad had encountered Allah in person. In another historical context, the NOI might have also located its doctrinal platform within Sufi tradition as an initiatic Muslim lodge; on occasion, Minister Farrakhan himself has articulated NOI concepts in Sufi terms.

For religions to be "modern" does not always mean that they stretch or dissolve their borders and become more inclusive; just as often, modernity concretizes and intensifies borders that were once more fluid. While one could argue for the finality of prophethood as a somewhat consistent priority throughout Muslim history, this concept—and the point at which someone violates it—undergoes new kinds of regulation in the age of global communication and self-styled Islamic Republics.

6

WHO CREATED GOD?

Anas narrated:

The Messenger of God (God bless him and give him peace) said, "God, Exalted and Majestic, said, 'Your umma will not stop talking about this and that until they say, "This God created the creation, so who created God?"'"[45]

As every hadith can open portals to a thousand other hadiths, this short prediction of future theological mischief leads me to one of the famous hadith traditions so widely discussed and analyzed that it gets its own name: the Hadith of the Slave Girl. In this story, Mu'awiyya bin al-Hakam remorsefully confesses to Muhammad that out of anger over a lost goat, he had slapped his slave girl. The Prophet tells Mu'awiyya bin al-Hakam to bring the girl to him. The Prophet then asks her, "Where is God?" She answers, "In the sky." Muhammad then asks, "Who am I?" to which she replies, "You are the Messenger of God." The Prophet declares her a believer and orders Mu'awiyya bin al-Hakam to set her free.[46]

The narration first establishes a link between the slave girl's freedom and her faith: in the same breath, the Prophet performs two speech acts that join her to the community of believers and take her out of slave status. The narration also establishes qualifications for belief that at once seem exceptionally precise and vague. The slave girl recognizes the man in front of her as the Messenger of God, and then issues a single statement on God: God is located in the sky. *Fi-l-sama'*. These two words take her across boundaries.

The slave girl's statement of faith stands in sharp contrast to the various pamphlets and websites in modern Muslim contexts that present bullet-pointed checklists for doctrinal correctness, or for that matter to the long history of Muslim theologians condemning one another over their ideas concerning God's attributes. The Prophet does not press this slave girl for a refined position on the relationship of God's attributes to his essence, the status of the Qur'an as created or eternal, or the problem of reconciling humans' free will and God's absolute power over all things. He does not ask for a systematized theology.

It's possible that in the slave girl's context, locating God in the sky might have marked a difference between her faith and that of another community. It's also possible, depending on your views of hadith authenticity, that this narration comes from a later time—perhaps amid the Muslim debates that accompanied an influx of Greek, Persian, Indian, and Chinese intellectual streams during the early 'Abbasid caliphate—and reflects the anxieties of Muslim scholars in the generations after Muhammad's death.

Historically, there's no such thing as a singular "Islamic theology" any more than there's a singular Christian theology: in both traditions, appearances of historical coherence and unity come only after sectarian conflicts, power struggles between and within institutions, the formulation of official creeds to shut down threatening heresies and stabilize thought, and even responses to theological difference with coercive force. Muslims have offered all kinds of ideas about God, while understanding their ideas as "Islamic." For his provocative theologies and cosmologies, Andalusian mystic Ibn al-'Arabi was accused of pantheism. In the South Asian context, communities named Muhammad and 'Ali as avatars of the Hindu god Vishnu. *Ghulat* ("exaggerator") movements in early Islam regarded the Prophet, 'Ali, and other members of their family as divine. Muslims in the Nation of Islam believe that God came to Detroit in 1930 as a man with a body, and defend their belief using the Qur'an and prophetic traditions. Whether or not it's recognizably Islamic to your eyes, it's Islam for them.

The sacred sources provide numerous openings. In the Qur'an, like the Bible, God describes himself in a variety of ways, enabling readers to draw multiple conclusions about him. God affirms that there is nothing like him (42:11), but also describes himself in very human terms, referring to body parts such as hands (39:67) and his act of sitting on a throne (7:54). Relatively early in Muslim intellectual history, a growing class of highly trained Muslim theologians perceived tension between God's absolute, incomparable transcendence and the ways in which he sometimes describes himself. Some argued that such verses had to be understood allegorically, lest someone imagine the creator of all the worlds as literally having a physical body and existing within definable space and time. Others insisted that it was unacceptable to question God's right to describe himself as he saw fit: if God says that he has hands, then God has hands, even if his hands exist beyond our comprehension. This does not have to mean that God's hands are like *our* hands, or anything that we might conceive as hands; but it does demand that if God does not explain the meaning of his hands, then we cannot take it upon ourselves to speculate as to what he meant. God says that he has hands and that he is like nothing in creation: both statements are true. Our religion does not need more than what God and the Prophet had given; if Muhammad himself did not explain a cryptic verse of the Qur'an to his Companions, they did not need it explained.

As with God's discussions of his hands, some Muslim intellectuals objected that we cannot take it literally when in the Qur'an God refers to himself as "he who is in the sky" or when the hadith traditions tell us that he sometimes descends to the lowest heaven for greater physical proximity to his creation. Their opponents refrained from speculating on God's intended meaning. If God says he descends to the lowest sky, that's what he does. The method of accepting God's self-descriptions *bi-la kayf,* or "without asking how," represents the position of the Hadith Folk networks, whose scholars became the vanguard of a sectarian movement that would ultimately give us Sunni Islam as we now know it. In narrations such as the Hadith of the Slave Girl, the hadith scholars give us a Muhammad who affirms their position and rebukes their intellectual rivals.

Similar to the Hadith of the Slave Girl, the Prophet's anticipation that someday people would ask, "Who created God?" possibly reflects a sectarian counter to the rationalist philosophers and cautions against overly speculative and abstracted theology. Muhammad seems to be warning that these exercises could misdirect someone from the heart of the matter. In some traditions, the question appears not as Muhammad's prediction but as an actual challenge posed to him by a group of Jews; their question provokes the revelation of the Qur'an's 112th sura, which affirms God as eternal, unbegotten, and incomparable. In response, the Jews then demand that Muhammad report the shape of God's arm to them, causing Muhammad to become angry and provoking another revelation of Qur'an verses: "They do not think of God as he ought to be thought of . . . Glorified and exalted is he above what they associate with him."[47]

The name of God, like any other artifact of language, remains a social construction that can be deconstructed, unpacked, interrogated, and exposed for its historical instability, perhaps rendering the name incapable of signifying anything at all. Of course, someone *did* make God; you "make" God when you process culturally received ideas of God and adhere to a concept of God in your mind. For practitioners of apophatic or "negative" theology, this could bring a comfort, even a route to the purest tawhid; God becomes "more God" when we cross out our names for him, recognizing the failures of our language and concepts to bring forth the Real. But deconstruction doesn't feed everyone. There are Muslims who conceive of God in straightforward terms as a king, lord, and judge who sits on a throne, feels anger and compassion, and watches over us in ways that seem kind of human; others want God as something less personal and more abstract; and some would render God virtually contentless and devoid of concepts. The Prophet's advice against overdoing speculative theology reminds me that I can suspend these projects, sign on for a confession bare and vague enough to accommodate dramatic differences of experience and interpretation, and join the other bodies in the masjid—even if my theologies are unacceptable, and even if I cannot bring myself to commit to what everyone else in the room seems to embrace as an "orthodox" set of faith convictions.

7

MUHAMMAD THE "PURE GREEK"

Yazid al-Farisi narrated:

I saw the Messenger of God (God bless him and give him peace) in a dream during the governorship of Ibn 'Abbas in Basra. I said to Ibn 'Abbas, "I saw the Messenger of God (God bless him and give him peace). Ibn 'Abbas said, "The Messenger of God (God bless him and give him peace) said, 'The Devil cannot imitate my form, so whoever saw me in a dream, saw me.' Can you describe to me the man that you saw?"

"Yes, I can describe him. A man between two men. His body and flesh were brown inclining to whiteness. Smiling, eyes with kohl, beautiful features of his face. His beard was thick from end to end. It was so thick that it covered his neck."

Then Ibn 'Abbas said, "If you had seen him while awake, you would not have described him better than this."[48]

The narration cited here offers a hadith within a hadith: the account of Muhammad's body related by Yazid al-Farisi and confirmed by Muhammad's cousin Ibn 'Abbas also includes Ibn 'Abbas's report of Muhammad having declared that because the Devil could not impersonate his form, anyone who saw Muhammad in a dream *really* saw him. Another tradition reports that the true dream or vision represents one forty-sixth of prophethood, the small share of prophetic experience that has been left in the world for non-prophets to access. Yazid's account of dreaming Muhammad's body achieves a double authorization, empowering Yazid as someone who had received a genuine visit from the Prophet in his dreams while preserving Ibn 'Abbas's privilege as someone who had seen the Prophet in this waking life and therefore wielded the authority to confirm or deny Yazid's vision.

We have no singularly authoritative account of Muhammad's physical appearance, but rather a considerable number of traditions attributed primarily to prominent male Companions, including 'Ali, Anas, Abu Tufayl, and Ibn 'Abbas. I pause here to consider that while multiple accounts of the prophetic body as a checklist of traits are traced to these figures, Muhammad's wives, despite their accounts on other topics, do not join them as primary reporters of his appearance. It seems that A'isha (or the network of scholars reporting on her authority) invested a different value in Muhammad's body than her political rival and Muhammad's biological cousin 'Ali (or Muhammad's and 'Ali's cousin Ibn 'Abbas, or sympathetic Companions such as Anas, or the networks reporting on them). As the wife of the Prophet, A'isha authorizes herself via reports of her intimacy with Muhammad's embodied

practices—giving accounts of eating meat from the same
bone as the Prophet, bathing in the same water, and so on—
but does not seem to treat the *material* of the prophetic body
with the same value as reporters who privilege Muhammad's
blood relations. Ninth-century scholar Ibn Sa'd designated a
chapter of his *Tabaqat al-Kubra* to "Attributes of the *Khalq*
of the Messenger of God"; Muhammad's *khalq* signified his
innate disposition and nature, and the reports compiled here
concerned accounts of Muhammad's physical appearance, as
in the hadith above. In the same chapter, A'isha only provides
a couple of narrations in which she describes his posture while
praying. In a more famous report, when A'isha is asked about
Muhammad's khalq, she does not recall his bodily details but
answers simply, "His khalq was the Qur'an," seemingly redi-
recting the question away from Muhammad's physical form
and instead conceptualizing his khalq as his ethics and moral
character.

The canonical hadith compiler Tirmidhi organized reports of the prophetic body, along with accounts of Muhammad's habits and personal possessions, into a special collection,
his *al-Shama'il al-Muhammadiya* (literally, "The Muhammadan Good Qualities"). While the depiction of Muhammad's physical form in visual art has been eschewed by most
Muslims (though certainly not all), textual representations of
Muhammad's physical attributes in hadiths such as the one
cited here were beautified with calligraphy and ornate design
in the *hilya* medium. Hilya works simultaneously negotiate
the legal problem of whether artists could draw Muhammad
(or, for that matter, *any* living things), present a visually pleas-
ing and pious artifact that celebrates the prophetic body, and

preserve the transcendent beauty of Muhammad's body by allowing it to remain abstract.

Comparing accounts of Muhammad's body in the hadith corpus, we can observe subtle variations. Descriptions of Muhammad having a medium height appear more or less consistently throughout the reports, along with accounts of his unique stride; he apparently seemed to walk as though descending from a height. Companions usually recall his hair as neither too lank nor too kinky. Accounts of Muhammad's skin color differ: reports attributed to 'Ali favor a description of Muhammad's complexion as white (or white mixed with red), while Anas traditions typically describe Muhammad as having had a medium complexion, neither too light nor too dark but a kind of brown. Given the ways in which Christian, Buddhist, and Muslim artists have often depicted Jesus, Buddha, and Muhammad as resembling the people in their own locales—Italian artists rendering Jesus as Italian, for example—perhaps these varying hadiths should be read in their specific settings. In this sense, we might interpret 'Ali's narrations as reflecting the phenotypical ideals popular in Medina, whereas the Basra-based transmissions of Anas's reports reflect conceptions of the body in Iraq.

Reports of Muhammad's physical appearance can also be examined alongside logics of the body that prevailed throughout Mediterranean antiquity. In the science of physiognomy, it was believed that one's inner character could be revealed by details of his or her external form. Physiognomic investments can be observed in the works of seminal Muslim intellectuals, such as the pioneering legal thinker Imam al-Shafi'i, who believed that people with blue eyes were naturally stupid.[49]

In premodern Islam, certain theories of bodies could prove Muhammad's status as a genuine messenger of God; reports of his appearance thus provided knowledge of tremendous truthmaking power. As hadith literature flourished in the post-Muhammad centuries, accounts of Muhammad's physical form would be found among stories of miracles in the literature of *dala'il al-nabuwwa*, "proofs of prophethood." The details of Muhammad's body told people something important about him, even providing evidence that could silence deniers of his station. His body itself was read as a miracle.

While pre-Islamic Arabs appeared to have practiced an indigenous tradition of physiognomy, they were not isolated from other logics of the body in nearby societies. In 555 CE, after Byzantine emperor Justinian closed the School of Athens and forced "heathen" scholars into exile, the Persian emperor Chosroes I (Anushirawan) established a new school for them in Jundishapur—near the future site of Baghdad—that included an academy of philosophy as well as a medical school.[50] The exchange of knowledge intensified with the 'Abbasid caliphate's endeavor to make vast bodies of Greek, Persian, Indian, and Chinese literature accessible in Arabic. Narratives about Muhammad, including his body, took shape within a changing world in which Muslims were in conversation with other cultures and traditions. Reports of Muhammad's body can read as reflections of these encounters. For example, accounts of Muhammad's body that place him repeatedly "between two men," meaning in a moderate position—a body neither too tall nor too short, skin neither too light nor too dark, hair neither too straight nor too curly—correspond to ancient Hellenic ideals of the superior body as one of perfect balance between extremes. Traditions that describe Muhammad's skin color as a mixture of white and red share resonance with descriptions by the Greek intellectual Polemon (d. 270 BCE) of the "pure Greek" body (which also happen to resonate with Polemon's reports of philosophers' bodies).[51] Polemon's *Physiognomy* circulated in Arabic early in the 'Abbasid translation project. Whether or not Polemon's treatment of bodies could have informed early hadith transmitters, we can at least say that various ideas about the body flowed throughout the setting in which the hadith corpus emerged. This might help to explain why narrators of Muhammad's body cared about some of the obscure details that they reported, such as the size of Muhammad's joints. It would certainly challenge simplistic narratives of a "clash of civilizations," which imagines a Muslim world locked in timeless conflict with a Western world, to consider that early Muslims imagined Muhammad with a "pure Greek" body!

The body is a social construction; even if our bodies appear to us as tangible things, the ways in which we think about them are learned. Popular ideas about gender, sexuality, reproduction, race, age, disability, health, hygiene, family, and personal space differ between one society and another; between two historical settings, we can even encounter irreconcilable ideas of where a body begins and ends. This means that bodies are both natural and cultural: we never encounter the natural matter of a body without some kind of cultural lens that informs what we see, whether that lens comes from a divinely revealed scripture or medical science. Muhammad's body as we access it today is entirely a product of culture, since we cannot make Muhammad's material being accessible to us (the politics of Muhammad's tomb being a whole other conversation). We know and understand Muhammad's body through the things that other people said about it; this remains important even in visionary experience, which does not eject us from questions about culture and language. The earliest reporters of Muhammad conceptualized his body through the lens of their own experience and the social milieu in which they learned about bodies. They upheld historically specific ideas of what made some bodies better than others, and represented Muhammad's body as a perfect one in accordance with those ideas. The "facts" of Muhammad's body, so far as we have them, change in their consequences and significance as these reports become meaningful beyond their point of origin.

8

PORTRAIT OF THE PROPHET AS
A YOUNG MAN

The image shown on the previous page, portraying Muhammad as a boy, circulated widely in Iran throughout the later twentieth century, and can read as a hadith in its own way. If you assumed that Muslims have *always* opposed the visual representation of living things and would absolutely *never* depict the Prophet, and that the opposition to painting Muhammad represents an inescapably foundational Islamic value, this picture offers a lesson: claims made in always/never language rarely hold up to closer scrutiny, and no one within a tradition speaks for everyone else.

Though debates over images of Muhammad refer to various sources, the Qur'an itself is silent on the matter of art. A number of hadiths portray Muhammad condemning visual representation of living things, but the diversity of Muslim interpretive traditions produces a multiplicity of views. No less an authority than Ayatollah Khomeini, leader of Iran's Islamic Revolution in 1979 and head of state until his death ten years later, had reportedly named this portrait of a youthful Muhammad as his favorite visual representation of the Prophet. In Iran, iterations of the image became widely available at stores and in numerous products, including postcards, full-sized posters, wall hangings, and key chains. It was only after a Danish newspaper's publication of offensive Muhammad cartoons that Iranian authorities banned this popular image. As Christiane Gruber explains, the Danish cartoon controversy provoked an "inversion of tidal proportions" among global Muslims, in which "Muhammad had to be reclaimed rhetorically in Islamic spheres and, in Iran most especially, reinverted and reinvented at an iconographical level."[52] In the case of Iran, taboos against depicting Muhammad's face were not merely representative of "traditional Islam," but just as much a modern response to a modern problem, emerging not in isolation from "the West" but in direct encounter with it. The question of drawing Muhammad's face thus reveals the ways in which tradition often finds its definition while engaging forces from *outside*.

This portrait authenticates itself with a hadith-style transmission history that traces its path to us: some prints of the image include a caption claiming that the artist had copied a painting by Bahira, a Christian monk who had seen Muhammad as a youth and recognized him as a future prophet. The original seventh-century piece is said to remain in an unnamed European museum.[53] Even if the painting itself is inescapably modern, its claimed linkage to Bahira grants its image of Muhammad's face with the power of an eyewitness; the painting authorizes itself in a way that mirrors the circulation of Muhammad's sayings and actions as oral tradition. Its supposed attribution to Bahira aside, this portrait of young Muhammad emerged as a copy of a photograph, which originated with Orientalist photographers in North Africa around 1905–1906, of an adolescent boy whose name happened to have been Muhammad.[54] Somehow, the image of this particular Muhammad became popular as *the* Muhammad.

While we see Muhammad here as an adolescent, the image behind him of a cave entrance covered in a spider's web refers to a miracle from much later in his life. The story goes that when Muhammad and his friend Abu Bakr fled from those who had conspired to kill him, they hid in a cave along the way from Mecca to Medina. A spider quickly spun its web over the entire cave entrance. When the conspirators' expert tracker arrived upon the cave entrance, he saw the intact web and assumed that no one could have recently gone into or out of the cave. Muhammad would have been roughly fifty years old (and Bahira was presumably long dead) at the time; our artist's reason for choosing this miracle as the background for a youthful Muhammad remains unclear, though it could have the effect of moving Muhammad's life out of worldly time.

Contrary to the notion that this image represents only an isolated departure from an otherwise universal Islamic norm, there does exist a tradition of Muhammad images, made as devotional material by Muslims for Muslims, notably in the domain of medieval Persian and Central Asian painted miniatures. Such works would often depict events from Muhammad's life. Several of the more striking examples portray Muhammad during his heavenly ascension; in some of these images, Muhammad's face is concealed, though numerous pieces depict his features in full.

Similar to visual representations of Jesus, the depiction of Muhammad's features invites the potential problem of racializing him. Classical miniatures coming from Central Asian contexts, for example, portray him as someone from the region. Likewise, Muhammad's descendents tend to look like the artists who paint them. Amina Inloes observes the "white and essentially Iranian" depictions of Muhammad's grandson Husayn in Iran, noting that contemporary Iraqi artists have sought to portray Husayn and the other Imams descended from Muhammad as more distinctly Arab. Inloes adds that these images neglect classical sources that identify the mothers of several of the Imams as African, including specifically Ethiopian/Somali, Egyptian, and Sudanese heritages.[55]

The Ansaru Allah Community (also known as the Nubian Islamic Hebrews), an African American Muslim movement prominent in the northeastern United States throughout the 1970s and '80s, regularly featured images of Muhammad and other figures of sacred history in its literature. These representations envision Muhammad, his family, and Companions as Black. Ansaru Allah pamphlets frequently presented an image in which Muhammad appears on his camel, holding the hooked staff that this community regarded as his inheritance from the Israelite prophets.[56] In the foreground, we see Muhammad's cousin and son-in-law 'Ali holding his famed double-bladed sword, and the first Companion to perform the call to prayer, Bilal, carrying the standard. However, the Ansaru Allah Community depicted Abu Bakr, whom it regarded as a usurper of 'Ali's natural right to the caliphate, as light-complexioned, marking what they perceived as Abu Bakr's ethical deficit in his skin.

9

MUHAMMAD THE ORPHAN

Sahl narrated:

The Messenger of God (God bless him and give him peace) said, "I and the one who looks after an orphan and provides for him will be like this in paradise," showing his index and middle fingers together.[57]

This hadith, appearing in Bukhari's section on manners and personal refinement (*adab*), is one of many in which Muhammad speaks on the treatment of orphans. We can think of these hadiths within a larger domain of Islamic ethics and Muhammad's instructions for being a decent human, particularly his concern for those less powerful ones whose rights and property are the most vulnerable. (In another hadith, Muhammad names orphans and women together as "the two weak ones" whose rights must be protected.) A second way of reading these hadiths invites reflection on Muhammad's own experience.

With so many ways of envisioning Muhammad—
prophet, ascetic, mystic, divinely guided warner to humankind and mercy to the worlds, statesman, jurist, general,
husband, father, grandfather, teacher of ethics and model for
the perfection of noble character—we might forget Muhammad the child, the Prophet before he was officially a prophet.
What can we say of Muhammad the child? Conforming
to literary conventions for recounting the lives of messianic
saviors, mighty kings, epic heroes, and other characters destined for future greatness, Muhammad's biography includes a
number of miraculous stories from his early years that provide
hints of what he will become.

Prior to Muhammad's conception, a woman offered herself to his father, 'Abd Allah. She explained to 'Abd Allah that
she had seen a blaze of light between his eyes; having heard
from her Christian brother that a prophet would soon appear in Arabia, she hoped that she could be his mother. After
'Abd Allah consummated his marriage with Amina, the blaze
between his eyes disappeared, and the woman lost interest.
She knew that Amina had conceived the future prophet.[58] As
a small boy, Muhammad's presence during a time of famine miraculously caused both women and animals to provide
milk in abundance.[59] Young Muhammad's future destiny
was recognized by multiple figures who operate by various
modes of knowledge, including Ethiopian Christians and the
learned Christian monk Bahira, as well as a soothsayer.[60] We
also read of an incident in which Muhammad's modesty was
protected by apparently angelic intervention. Local boys were
carrying stones and had wrapped their garments around their
necks, apparently to make the work easier, thereby exposing

themselves; young Muhammad followed suit until an invisible being struck him and told him to cover himself.[61]

In perhaps the most jarring episode from Muhammad's childhood, Muhammad undergoes a surgical purification at the hands of angels that apparently prepares him for his future prophetic mission. The earliest biography of the Prophet provides two versions of the incident. In the first, reported by Muhammad's wet nurse Halima, a boy ran to her screaming that two men in white had thrown Muhammad down, cut open his stomach, and were "stirring it up." They rushed to the scene and found only a traumatized Muhammad, who told them that the men were searching inside his torso but for what he did not know. Muhammad's mother, Amina (whose presence in this account suggests that Muhammad was younger than six at the time), reassures Halima that the boy will be okay, recounting the various miracles surrounding his birth. In the second version, young Muhammad was with another youth, shepherding lambs behind their tents, when two men dressed in white approached, carrying a gold basin filled with snow. The two men took hold of Muhammad and cut open his torso. They removed his heart, cut away a black portion from it, and then washed his heart and insides with the snow. They then weighed him against ten of his people, finding that Muhammad outweighed them, repeated the test with a hundred and then a thousand of his people, and deduced that "If you weighed him against all his people he would outweigh them."[62]

The story of Muhammad's angelic surgery appears in a variety of versions throughout the sources. In Sunni sources the narrative gradually appears to have been relocated from

Muhammad's childhood to his adulthood, specifically as a preparation for Muhammad's journey into the heavens.[63] One unusual version presents the chest opening as a prerequisite for Muhammad to start his mission as a prophet; it is only after the completion of the surgery that the angel Gabriel orders Muhammad to recite, thereby starting the revelation of the Qur'an.[64] In another outlier, the surgery is performed by two birds.[65] Shi'i sources, expressing a different investment in Muhammad's innate moral perfection (which remains inseparable from his bodily perfection), tend to omit this episode altogether.[66] The prime narrator for the incident in canonical hadith collections, Anas, was too young to have been present. He instead authorizes his account by telling us that he remembers the traces of stitching on Muhammad's chest.

In terms of historical veracity, the problem of our sources concerning Muhammad becomes magnified when we look at the forty years of his life prior to prophethood, when he was not yet someone whose biographical details would receive heightened attention. An important detail of his childhood, however, seems to bear some historical support: he was an orphan. According to Muhammad's oldest complete biography, his father, 'Abd Allah, died before he was born, and his mother, Amina, died when he was six years old. Muhammad was taken in by his paternal grandfather, 'Abd al-Muttalib, who died after only two years; Muhammad was then cared for by his paternal uncle, Abu Talib. While we can exercise caution in accepting every legend and even seemingly mundane details—some would question whether Muhammad's parents, living in a polytheistic milieu, were likely to have had names suggestive of monotheism, such as 'Abd Allah and

Amina[67]—our earliest source, the Qur'an, seems to support the notion that Muhammad had lost his parents as a child. In one of the presumably earlier revelations, the Qur'an asks him, "Did he [God] not find you an orphan and shelter?" (93:6).

The Qur'an's repeated mention of orphans bears a closer look. At various points throughout the text, the Qur'an mentions the vulnerability of orphans, commands kindness and equity for them (2:220, 4:8, 76:8), warns against the misappropriation of their property (4:2, 6:152, 17:34), condemns those who mistreat them (89:17, 93:9, 107:2), and promises that those who devour orphans' property are filling their own stomachs with hellfire (4:10). The Qur'an's only explicit permission for polygamy also includes the note that a man must refrain from marrying young orphans if he cannot treat them with fairness and justice (4:2–3). Surveying the Qur'an's concern for orphans within a broader condemnation of immorality and injustice in its own time, we could suggest that the exploitation and abuse of orphans was a fairly common problem in pre-Islamic Mecca. If one reads the Qur'an as a glimpse into Muhammad's own heart, with or without faith in the text's divine origin, the Qur'an could read as speaking from his firsthand knowledge.

The sources do not provide us with reports of adults mistreating the orphaned Muhammad, and by all accounts, Muhammad's uncle Abu Talib virtually adopted him as a son and devoted the rest of his life to caring for him. Our reflections on the Prophet's early years would be mostly speculative, but this is where the previous hadith's popular Iranian poster of a child Muhammad takes me. The Qur'an's declarations of orphans' rights and Muhammad's love for the protectors of orphans, along with the miracle stories, pour meaning into the image. The boy never knew his father. He lost his mother at six and his grandfather at eight, and seems periodically to have experienced the weirdness of random people promising his future greatness, either by observing signs on his body or finding references to him in their scriptures. Amid all of this, two angels tackled him to the ground and sliced open his chest in order to remove, wash, and reinstall his heart before his very eyes. When I look at the portrait of young Muhammad, I see none of this manifesting in the boy's face. An untouched lightness persists with his smile. I cannot know what the boy has seen, and his eyes give no hint that he grasps his unique circumstances—*no, child, not everyone gets cut open by angels*—let alone that he could know what's in store for him.

10

THE MOUNTAIN OF LIGHT

A'isha narrated:

The commencement [of prophethood] with the Messenger of God (God bless him and give him peace) was in true dreams. The angel came to him and said, "Recite, in the name of your lord who created, created the human being from a clot. Recite, and your lord is most generous."[68]

Arriving in Mecca two weeks before the start of pilgrimage season, I devoted one afternoon to visiting what tradition now calls the Mountain of Light (*Jabal al-Nur*), located just outside the city. It was on this mountain that the Qur'an's first excerpts entered the world; this is where Muhammad became the Prophet. At the foot of the mountain, a large sign sought to discourage me, warning that to visit this place was not a required part of the pilgrimage, and that there were no authentic religious practices associated with it; the mountain's historical significance did not justify superstitious or even idolatrous practices. This mountain stands in modern Saudi Arabia, and the sign reflects the government's position. At other sites throughout Mecca and Medina, wherever Muslims' popular values and practices run counter to the Saudi state's idea of Islam, we encounter a sign.

One of the uncles in my pilgrimage group had also tried to discourage me from hiking the Mountain of Light. "There's no reward in it," he said, insisting that I stay in Mecca. With limited days to spend in the holiest city, the uncle argued, anything that took you out of Mecca before the formal rites of hajj was a waste of time. He advised that instead I should spend the day at the Haram, the masjid that housed the Ka'ba, where each prayer would earn me as much as 100,000 times a prayer's normal reward. I tried gently to suggest to him that even if visiting the mountain did not come with a quantifiable reward, it could still be worth doing, but I'm not sure that he took me seriously.

Unfortunately for the Saudi state and disapproving uncles, the signs aren't convincing everyone. Pilgrims—women and men from every nation and some of advanced age—crowded the steep path up the mountain, just as they crowded various cemeteries and holy sites even as religious authorities claimed that such devotions strayed from true Islam.

It got busier as I reached the top and took my place in line, where people waited for their chance to enter a cave. To call it a cave might be generous, as there was barely enough room for two people to stand inside. When my turn came, two aunties were already performing prayers inside, without much concern for the people waiting behind them. I crouched my way into a space next to them and made a short prayer. In that space, the standing position of Muslim prayer wasn't really an option for me: apart from the placement of my hands, my prayer's moments of standing (*qiyyam*) would have been indistinguishable from the kneeling (*ruku*) portions. Physically uncomfortable and pressured by the fact that my prayer held up a line, I moved quickly and tried to have some sense of my location. This was the cave where everything started, this mass of traditions that we have named Islam and that calls us to the holy city. It was the kind of prayer that achieved its effect in my head only after it was already completed, as I walked back down the mountain.

As with other stories from the Prophet's life, there is no singular narrative of the first revelation. The episode comes to us through a number of reports, some more popular or supported by greater evidence than others. The popular outline presents Muhammad engaged in meditative retreats on what we now call the Mountain of Light. During one of these retreats in the year 610 CE, the angel Gabriel appeared to him and demanded that he recite. Muhammad pleaded that he was not a reciter; Gabriel responded by physically squeezing Muhammad, forcing him into submission. The angel's command has been recognized in hadith canon and traditions of Qur'an interpretation as comprising the first verses of the Qur'an. Because the Qur'an is not organized in the chronological order of its verses' revelation, these "first verses" appear near the end of the book, at the start of the ninety-sixth sura.

A rare version of the story, found in Tayalisi's *Musnad*, connects the beginning of Muhammad's prophethood with the usually unrelated story of angels performing surgery on him to cleanse his heart. (More canonical accounts of the

chest opening place this event either in Muhammad's childhood or prior to his later ascension into the heavens.) While
the angel Michael awaits at a liminal point between heaven
and earth, Gabriel opens Muhammad's torso and modifies
his insides as preparation for prophethood, then seals his
body closed and commands him to recite the ninety-sixth
sura. The report makes another notable departure from more
popular tellings in that it places Khadija, Muhammad's first
wife and the first believer in his mission, in the cave with him.
For Muslims who vet hadiths by the strengths of their transmission chains, this version bears weak support: it is traced
back to Abu Imran al-Jawni, who reports only from the authority of "a man" who had apparently attributed it to A'isha.
Al-Jawni receives good marks as a reporter from the premodern hadith masters, but because the link between al-Jawni
and A'isha remains anonymous, the chain is incomplete.[69]
Evaluation of the chain does not end there, however. Modern
critical analysis of hadith transmissions suggests that because
complete and well-evidenced chains gradually increased in
value for classical hadith masters, the development of chain-
based evaluation came with an unintended consequence: in
a bit of irony, hadiths with perfect chains are more likely to
reflect later fabrications and point to a forgery. This would
mean that if a chain of transmitters contains such a glaring
weakness as this anonymous "man," it might represent an
earlier, "truer" version of the story, speaking before flawless
chains of transmission became such a priority.[70] Older doesn't
always mean more authentic, but this still complicates our
assumptions about sacred history.

Remembering my visit to the cave and how cramped it

was for three people—two adults had room to stand, but a third was crouched over—I find myself drawn to the Tayalisi version in which Muhammad, Khadija, and Gabriel all share this cave and the encounter together. In a cave only five feet wide, the spatial limitations would have forbidden Khadija from remaining a passive observer; her presence radically changes the event. The inescapable intimacy between these three becomes even more amplified by the fact that Tayalisi's version also depicts Gabriel opening Muhammad's body and cleaning his insides. With no room to move, what could Khadija do at that moment? I imagine her holding her husband, consoling him through his surgery, perhaps even restraining his natural reflexes as Gabriel works upon him. Trying to find an earthly point of reference for this event, I can only come up with a context in which a woman giving birth, the baby's father, and the doctor are all stuck in a small closet or elevator together. This perhaps leads to a different way of thinking about Muhammad and his experience of prophethood.

11

THE ASCENSION

> *Abu 'Abd Allah narrated:*
>
> When the Messenger of God (God bless him and give him peace) was taken for the ascension, Gabriel took him to a place and left him there alone. He said, "Gabriel, why do you leave me in such a condition?"
>
> Gabriel said, "Go on. By God, you have stepped at a place where no human has ever stepped and no human has ever walked before you."[71]

In my Muhammad seminar at Kenyon College, I assigned students most or all of Kecia Ali's *The Lives of Muhammad*, Denise Spellberg's *Politics, Gender, and the Islamic Past: The Legacy of A'isha bint Abi Bakr*, and Frederick S. Colby's *Narrating Muhammad's Night Journey*. Each of these books, while sharing interest in the ways that stories change over time, examine the prophetic life with a different point of focus. Ali's work tracks the modern development of Muhammad's biog-

raphy as a literary genre that took shape in conversation between Muslim and non-Muslim writers, showing that as these
authors responded to one another's arguments, they uninten-
tionally collaborated toward a shared outline of what "really
mattered" in Muhammad's life. Spellberg charts the life of
Muhammad's wife A'isha as one endowed with meanings and
values that change over time, informed by sectarian debates
between Sunni and Shi'i authors as well as diverse notions of
what makes for an "ideal Muslim woman." Colby's *Narrating
Muhammad's Night Journey* focuses on Muhammad's ascension through the heavens, examining the story's development
in early and medieval sources from its primordial "first draft"
into multiple versions, reflecting the theological and sectarian
priorities of their narrators.

My students noted that Colby's book seems out of place.
Why did a scholar devote years to writing a dissertation and
book on such a seemingly minor detail in Muhammad's life—
literally a single night? And of course, the ascension didn't
"really" happen. If we're going to understand Muhammad as
a historical figure, shouldn't we focus on historical events?
Wouldn't it be more imperative to examine the concrete details, such as the shift from Muhammad's early preaching in
Mecca to his political career in Medina, his ethics, his marriages, or his battles? Perhaps what we need are the facts and
dates: Muhammad was born in 570, orphaned early in life,
married a wealthy widow named Khadija, began preaching a
message of monotheism, social justice, and imminent apocalyptic doom in 610 at forty years old, endured persecution
from his community, fled to Medina in 622 with his followers, married multiple women after the death of Khadija,

formed something like a state, signed treaties and collected taxes, conquered Mecca in 630, and then died in 632 as the most powerful human being in Arabia.

In today's imaginations of Muhammad, in which Muslims and non-Muslims argue over his legacy on an essentially secular field, his journey through the heavens does not appear as a priority. When we watch film representations of Muhammad's life such as the Anthony Quinn movie *The Message* or the Lebanese cartoon *Muhammad the Last Prophet*, the ascension doesn't even show up. In Muslim pamphlets and websites offering introductions to Muhammad for the curious non-Muslim reader, the night journey doesn't appear; while these resources call attention to the fact that the Qur'an praises Jesus and Mary, they're less interested in presenting the story of Muhammad actually meeting Jesus on another plane of existence. In modern biographies of Muhammad, authors either ignore the ascension or brush over it with a sentence or two. In the outline of Muhammad's life that Ali provides in her opening chapter—the basics as they appear consistently across the biographies that she examines—the ascension does not warrant a mention. Both his defenders and critics devote their energies to arguing over whether Muhammad was violent or peaceful, fanatical or tolerant, misogynistic or the world's first feminist. The empirical facts of wives and wars, rather than a fable of Muhammad flying through space and conversing with angels and dead prophets, are supposed to give us the means for judging Muhammad's ultimate value as a person who lived in real history.

Examining a wealth of Muslim philosophical, theological, mystical, poetic, and artistic traditions, however, it becomes clear that, historically speaking, Muhammad's ascension was far from insignificant. His miraculous journey confirmed his status as a genuine prophet. His interactions with other prophets—including their acceptance of him and his leading them in prayer—proved the truth of what Muhammad brought to the world, and the privilege of his community over others. His cousin Ibn 'Abbas narrated that Muhammad had said, "I saw Jesus, Moses, and Abraham. Jesus was kinky-haired, red-complexioned, and had a broad chest. Moses was dark brown, bulky, and had lank hair, like the men of al-Zut." When the people asked him to describe Abraham, Muhammad said only, "Look at your companion"—that is, Muhammad himself.[72] When compared to Moses and Jesus, both of whom might appear as stand-ins for the respective Jewish and Christian traditions that claim them, Muhammad is the one who bears the closest physical resemblance to their shared spiritual (and biological) ancestor, Abraham; Muhammad's din represents Abraham's din in its purest form.

The ascension not only stakes an Islamic claim over other traditions, but also becomes a template for any mystic's journey, telling us about the capacity for all humans to embark on quests for transcendent encounters and advanced knowledge. In proto-Shi'i tellings, 'Ali appears and becomes central to the story. In Sufi tradition, we find visionaries giving accounts of their own ascensions, recalling the various angelic, prophetic, or even divine figures with whom they interacted and the special secrets that they brought back to humankind. Depending on the version that one reads, the ascension provokes theological controversy for its suggestion that Muhammad might have seen God or even felt a physical sensation from the touch of God's hand. Some Muslims would celebrate this encounter, while others deny it outright or emphasize disclaimers that preserve God as beyond vision and touch (i.e., Muhammad saw with the eyes of his *heart*, not the eyes of his *head*; the touch took place within a dream; and so on). Muhammad's Companions themselves disagreed as to whether Muhammad could experience God in visible or tactile form (with his wife A'isha as a vehement opponent of the vision, and his cousin Ibn 'Abbas as its most prominent advocate). And while many non-Muslims (and Muslims too) assume that Islam so absolutely opposes the artistic representation of living things (especially prophets) that no Muslim would have ever produced an image of Muhammad, the Prophet's ascension enjoys prominence in the history of Muslim art. There are numerous images of Muhammad riding the Buraq through the heavens, escorted by angels and meeting the biblical prophets, and images of the Buraq—having departed long ago from the hadiths' mundane description of it as something like a white mule and appearing instead as a pegasus with human face and peacock tail—can often be found for purchase near Sufi shrines or gracing truck art. For many Muslims, the ascension would have been regarded as one of the central, definitive moments of Muhammad's prophetic career, at least as important as his first experience of revelation, the Meccans' persecution, the migration to Medina, or any of his battles.

In late antiquity, the mystical journey into other worlds was a popular narrative form that appeared in numerous traditions, including biblical traditions. Muhammad—or the tellers of Muhammad's story—confirmed his prophethood within the forms and structures of an established genre that also produced countless volumes reporting Muhammad's special bodily marks, his miracles of causing dried wells to overflow with water, and the foretelling of his appearance in the Bible, affirming Muhammad with the kind of qualifications that prophets need on their résumés. But in the modern world, something has changed. Among the same historical pressures and forces that popularly reconstructed Buddha as a rationalist freethinker and Jesus as a philosopher who might have hung out with Thoreau and Emerson, many readers (and writers) of Muhammad leave the mystical, magical, miraculous Muhammad behind.

12

"HIS CHARACTER WAS THE QUR'AN"

Sa'd bin Hisham narrated:
    I asked A'isha, "Inform me about the character traits of the Messenger of God (God bless him and give him peace)."
    She said, "Don't you read the Qur'an?"
    I said, "Yes."
    She said, "The character of the Messenger of God (God bless him and give him peace) was the Qur'an."[73]

In the Qur'an, regarded by Muslims as God's direct speech to Muhammad, God tells the Prophet, "You are of a great character" (68:4). In the canonical hadith sources, someone asks A'isha about Muhammad's character, to which she answers, "His character was the Qur'an." To develop one's personality and manners to be more Muhammad-like, therefore, amounts to a kind of Qur'an interpretation, an embodied engagement with the revelation.

Certainly, much of the literary corpus that presents us with traditions of Muhammad's sayings and actions offers prescriptions for correct belief and practice, the stuff that we might immediately classify as "religious." Hadith literature also provides a wealth of narrations in which Muhammad describes a way of being in the world that some might read as "secular" or humanist proverbs. In these narrations, Muhammad tells us how to behave with one another. He sometimes attaches his advice to matters of salvation, describing the personalities and habits that God loves and presenting the improvement of one's character as a mode of attaining God's mercy and blessings; but many of these narrations are also theologically minimalist. They do not rely on a sophisticated understanding of Muslim doctrinal positions or even faith in Islam in order to be useful. Instead, Muhammad appears in such narrations as a wise sage who gives life lessons.

Abu Hurarya narrated that Muhammad had said, "I was sent to perfect good character." Sufi traditions further report Muhammad saying, "Make yourself with the character traits of God."[74] The term used in these sources for "character," *khalq*, derives from a root that signifies the act of creation, representing one's character as an innate condition; the literary genre engaged with questions of ethics, *akhlaq* (the plural of *khalq*), essentially treats the question of how to live as fully human in accordance with the best elements of one's nature. The akhlaq literature, in addition to the related genre of works dealing with civility and personal refinement (*adab*), reflect not simply a straight line of transmission from revealed sacred sources to Muslim communities, but rather a harmonization between the sacred sources and various intellectual traditions that premodern Muslim thinkers engaged, such as Greek and Persian philosophical literatures, as well as the culture of high courts that patronized and commissioned such works. For the sophisticated premodern elites and bureaucrats who read akhlaq and adab literature in order to theorize statecraft or perform as educated ladies and gentlemen in polite society, there was not a conflict or tension between the ethics and manners learned from Aristotle and those found in the Qur'an and Sunna. Similar to the Muhammad-as-doctor who prescribes "prophetic medicine," itself a synthesis of hadith sources with the medical heritage of broader Mediterranean antiquity, the Muhammad of ethics and etiquette speaks as a doctor of souls in resonance with Greek philosophers.

Muhammad reportedly explains that after God created Adam, the Devil walked around Adam's body to inspect him from all sides (in less canonical versions, actually entering Adam through his mouth and exiting through his anus). From his examination of the first human body, the Devil learned that Adam was hollow and therefore easy to manipulate. In one version from eleventh-century scholar al-Tha'labi, the Devil exclaims, "This is a hollow creature that will not stand firm or remain in control of himself."[75] Needless to say, the Devil makes an assessment of the human condition that might seem pessimistic but not exactly invalid. This hollowness, and our desire to fill it, becomes our downfall. In a tradition that appears with slight variations throughout the Six Books, Muhammad tells us that if any of us were to possess two valleys of gold, we would desire a third, adding that nothing will satisfy our stomachs but dust.

In a considerable number of hadiths, Muhammad cautions us against losing ourselves to anger. Muhammad reportedly discouraged judges from making their decisions while angry, and said that an angry person should remain silent. Multiple hadiths praise the control of anger and offer rewards: the person who swallows his or her anger out of desire for seeing God's face has achieved the greatest swallowing; God keeps punishment away from the one who can restrain his or her anger. One hadith states that the person who restrains anger while having the power to act upon it experiences an increase in faith; another version holds that on the Day of Resurrection, God will first call such a man and offer him any paradisical maiden that he chooses. In perhaps the most famous example, a man who asks Muhammad for advice is told simply, "Do not get angry." Driving home the point, Muhammad repeats this advice two more times. After Muhammad defeated a local wrestler who was renowned for his strength, Muhammad reminded witnesses that true strength was not displayed in wrestling, but rather in control over one's own anger. He also suggested that when a standing person becomes overtaken with anger, that person should sit; if sitting does not help, the angry person should lie down. In other narrations, Muhammad prescribes the ritual washing that a Muslim would normally perform before prayer as a remedy for anger. Muhammad explains that since anger comes from the Devil, and the Devil is made from fire, water will put it/him out.

Muhammad consistently cautions against eating too

much, telling us that the son of Adam does not fill any container worse than his stomach, and warning a man who burped that the one who eats the most in this world will be hungry in the next. This does not exactly mean that it's a punishable "sin" to overeat, but Muhammad does describe the eating of whatever we desire as extravagance, and 'Ali told us not to make our stomachs into graveyards. This is the prophetic example: in the years after Muhammad's death, A'isha would cry upon remembering that he never filled his stomach twice in the same day with meat or bread.

From a particular Sufi point of view that would read human behavior as an expression of God's numerous attributes, the challenge of being human lies in our failure to express these attributes in their proper balance: God is the Creator as much as he is the Destroyer, the Exalter as much as he is the Abaser, and the Forgiver as much as he is the Punisher, but humans act out the divine attributes in gross disharmony and cause destruction to themselves and their world. The Prophet thus appears as a calming hand, guiding these hollow and unrestrained creatures to better self-regulation. Muslims engage the Sunna, the collective archive of the Prophet's habits and precedents, as a technology of Muhammadi selfhood in which even seemingly unimportant acts and disciplines remind us of him or condition us in his way of being.

For many of us, the issues hold greater stakes than Anas's effort to like the gourd that Muhammad put in his soup, and we find ourselves choosing between a degree of hadith skepticism (challenging the authenticity of a particular hadith or treating hadiths at large as unreliable) or an attempt to personally locate the essence of Muhammad's character for ourselves and then shed the troubled parts. While represented in the tradition as the paragon of perfected ethics and character, Muhammad was also a man who lived in a specific time and place. For many of us, tensions between our standards for locating "the good" and what we retrieve from the Sunna can pose a devastating challenge.

Gender-progressive Muslim intellectuals tend to prioritize the Qur'an over the hadith corpus as the prime site where reform can happen, but Muhammad's Sunna and the perfection of his khalq can become resources for thinking beyond the boundaries of the Qur'an's text. Many Muslims who struggle with verse 4:34 in the Qur'an, in which God appears to give a degree of permission for men to strike their wives, find solace in the behavior of the Prophet, who did not hit his wives. Remembering A'isha's statement that Muhammad's character was the Qur'an itself, they would argue that we should therefore look to Muhammad's life as the ultimate commentary on the Qur'an's message. Laury Silvers has argued that reading 4:34 through the lens of Muhammad's life moves us beyond a literalist treatment of the Qur'an's permissions and prohibitions, calling us instead to our ethical responsibility as human beings. If Muhammad, as a walking Qur'an, did not do what we think that the Qur'an tells us to do, then the Qur'an's real problem might be our reading of its words.[76] This approach might not easily settle every question; in some cases, readers face the opposite challenge, namely that we rely on the Qur'an to soften or reject what hadith sources present as Muhammad's statements and actions. Muslims who keep dogs as pets, for example, often consider the Qur'an more supportive on the issue than hadiths; while hadith texts portray Muhammad as disapproving of dogs in the home, the Qur'an refers to God protecting a group of Christians from persecution and specifically mentions a dog as their companion (18:9–26). Some Muslims would argue that the Qur'an, as God's perfectly preserved speech, reigns supreme over all other sources, including the imperfectly preserved speech of the Prophet. Others would counter that Muhammad's sublime precedent, the Sunna, reflects the ultimate mode of embodying the Qur'an and constitutes a divine revelation itself.

13

THE PEOPLE OF WUDU'

Abu Hurayra narrated:
The Messenger of God (God bless him
and give him peace) said, "You will return
to me beautiful and radiant from *wudu'*, the
sign of my community and no other."[77]

Under the contemporary rubric of "world religions," we often define traditions by their ingredients that most easily
resonate with globalizing norms of Western Europe and the
United States. The most crucial need-to-know aspects of a
tradition become those that correspond to a somewhat Protestant framework: faith, bible, church. Every world religion,
according to this template, should have important doctrines
and matters of faith concerning supernatural forces and the
ultimate purpose and destiny of human beings, a sacred scripture in which we can learn the doctrines and beliefs, and a
house of worship in which people express their commitments
to those doctrines and beliefs.

Muhammad was a man of prayer. At first glance, prayer obviously fits into a Euro-Christian conception of religion. In Arabic, *salat* is the term for ritual worship most straightforwardly translated as Muslim "prayer," though it also signifies "blessing." When Muslims recite prayers for peace and blessings upon the Prophet, for example, they say, *Salla Allahu alayhe wa salam*—literally "God blessed (did *salat*) on him and gave him peace." While Muslims engage in various acts of prayer or worship that would be categorized by different terms, *salat* refers specifically to the act that God commanded Muslims to perform five times daily. Salat is a function of the body: a series of prescribed movements and positions in proper sequence, accompanied by audible or silent recitations of formulas, while oriented toward the direction of Mecca. To properly perform salat, the body must also remain in a state of ritual purity, which is broken by various corporeal processes. When these bodily events occur, a Muslim restores ritual purity by washing in accordance with a specific script. The exact script for cleansing depends on whether the purity break was minor (such as farting or urinating) or major (such as sexual intercourse or menstruation).

Readers seeking an introduction to Muhammad wouldn't necessarily assume that ritual washing before prayer was the most important thing to learn about him. The canonical collections of Muhammad's sayings and actions, however, generally follow a standard arrangement in which the first chapters concern not theology or salvation, but the necessary knowledge for achieving and maintaining ritual purity. Before delving into matters of faith, the collections tell us first what exactly violates ritual purity, which violations require which kinds of washing, and the details of the Prophet's life as a ritual practitioner, drawing from his habits to address specific concerns. To the premodern hadith masters, scripts for washing the body amounted to a foundational question with the utmost priority.

Muslims are not alone in connecting prayer to the cleansing of the body; Jewish and Muslim traditions share significant overlaps in their concepts of ritual purity. Non-Muslims who come from traditions without ideas of ritual purity, however, might struggle to understand what a fart has to do with prayer. Isn't worship concerned only with the condition of the soul? Having become Muslim in a postcolonial age that had been shaped largely by globalizing Protestantism, I was taught that our physical acts of prayer had higher meanings or functions beyond the simple fact of God ordering us to do these things for our salvation. Various Intro to Islam pamphlets told me that ritual ablution offered a kind of mental preparation for worship: as I performed these specific acts with focused concentration, I refreshed my body and prepared my brain for the cognitive task of prayer. The specific acts of standing, sitting, and prostrating in the prayer itself were likewise less about the motions and positions than the mental process that they facilitated. While Muslim thinkers have historically valued the personal and contemplative dimensions of prayer, we can also say that in a changing world, the meanings of prayer change across different contexts, and in any given Muslim context, some resources for understanding prayer become more useful than others. Many Muslims treat salat as a meditative practice that incorporates both mind and body (in both premodern and modern contexts, we even find comparisons to yoga), while others treat salat and its prerequisite ablutions as God's prescription for physically removing sins from one's flesh. Though Muslims gather together in congregations and perform identical movements and recitations, following the same script, they can internalize its meaning—and the role of their bodies in its meaning—in profoundly divergent ways.

14

THE SEVEN OFT-REPEATED

Abu Hurayra narrated:
The Messenger of God (God bless him and give him peace) said, "The *umm* [mother or foundation] of the Qur'an is the seven oft-repeated verses and is the Mighty Qur'an."[78]

The Qur'an consists of nearly seven thousand verses; Muhammad's mention of the "seven oft-repeated" refers to its opening sura, al-Fatiha. How do a mere seven verses, just a hair more than one thousandth of the text, provide the mother or foundation of the entire revelation, and where does this lead as an introduction to Muhammad?

If you think of the Qur'an primarily as a source of law and divinely ordered regulation, al-Fatiha (literally "The Opening") would disappoint. It gives no concrete orders of how or when to pray, what to eat or not eat, when to fast, where to make pilgrimage, or how much one should give in charity.

It says nothing about punishment for crimes, the workings of a state, or interactions between gender identities. It does not name specific acts as deserving of God's punishment or reward. It does not tell its readers how to relate to people outside their own community; it does not even name a specific community or religion as its audience, providing us with no mention of "Islam" or "Muslims." Nor does al-Fatiha articulate a detailed catechism or path to salvation; in its seven short verses, it simply describes God as merciful, compassionate, lord of all worlds, and master of the day of judgment. It affirms that God is the only object of worship and source of help, and gives a plea that God guide us to the straight path of those whom he has favored—not the path of those who have earned divine anger or gone astray. That's the entire sura.

Who are these people that earn anger or go astray? This short sura doesn't tell us, but Muslims have certainly offered their opinions. The Hilali-Khan translation of the Qur'an promoted by Saudi state media, inserting its commentaries into the English verses, names these two groups of people as the Jews and Christians. The medieval Muslim shaykh Ibn al-'Arabi, however, named this verse's earners of wrath and strayed wanderers as Muslims who were so fixated on paradise as a lush garden of sensual rewards (drink, food, sex, nice furniture) that they forgot about God. The diversity of Muslim interpretations over this verse speaks to the reality that it gives us so little in terms of concrete information; we have to do the work ourselves.

Many of my students assume that every religion has its own "Bible," and that you can understand a religion simply by picking up its bible and reading it for yourself. This reflects the way that scholars often teach Islam in American colleges and universities. In its treatment of Islam, the basic "Intro to World Religions" course is far more likely to include short readings from the Qur'an than accounts of Muhammad's life. If one were to survey Islamic studies syllabi across the country, it would be much easier to find a course titled "Introduction to the Qur'an" than "Introduction to Muhammad." This was my own approach to Islam when I first began to explore the tradition as a teenager; rather than visit the nearest masjid or even meet a Muslim face-to-face, I read the Qur'an with confidence that it could grant me instant access to everything I needed. This kind of scripturalism has also become popular for many Muslims, who would argue in a Protestant *sola scriptura* fashion that the Qur'an alone provides the basis for Islam.

One can argue that a Qur'an-centered approach to Islam reveals the ways in which Western scholarship and global Protestant missionary projects treat a religion's scripture as the only legitimate key to its essence, and the ways in which modern printing (and modern print capitalism), rising literacy, and popular translation wrought profound transformations in Muslims' engagements of the Qur'an. Recognizing this point of rupture encourages us to consider experiences of the Qur'an that resist the label of "Muslim Bible."

Where does this get us with al-Fatiha? Due to its importance in prayer, we could make an argument for recognizing al-Fatiha as the most recited text in human history. In each of the five daily prayers, a Muslim performs cyclical units of bodily movement and textual recitation, called *rak'ats*, following the practice that Gabriel had taught Muhammad, who in turn taught his Companions. Each of the five daily prayers includes a particular number of rak'ats, and every rak'at includes a recitation of al-Fatiha. The pre-sunrise prayer, for example, consists of two rak'ats, meaning that a Muslim would recite al-Fatiha twice in that prayer; the post-sunrise prayer consists of three rak'ats, thus requiring three recitations of al-Fatiha. Moreover, at each of the five daily prayer times, a Sunni Muslim might supplement the required prayers with extra sunna prayers, which are not required but follow Muhammad's personal practice. The late-evening prayer, for example, consists of four required rak'ats, but a Muslim can also perform two sunna prayers at this time, the first consisting of four rak'ats, the second of two rak'ats, making a total of ten rak'ats—meaning that al-Fatiha would be recited ten times in this prayer alone. If a Muslim performs only the required prayers every day, this amounts to seventeen daily recitations of al-Fatiha; a Sunni Muslim who also performs sunna prayers would recite al-Fatiha thirty-five times a day. Shi'i Muslims also perform specific sets of recommended *nafila* prayers that would amount to thirty-four rak'ats daily if one did them all, producing a daily prayer regimen of fifty-one rak'ats. This does not include other categories of prayer—specific nighttime prayers based on Muhammad's habit, up to an extra twenty rak'ats each night in the month of Ramadan for Sunni *tarawih* prayers, and voluntary prayers that can be performated at virtually any time. Making a short prayer of two rak'ats for each of these forty hadiths means that I recited al-Fatiha eighty times to write this book. I cannot begin to guess how many Muslims in the past fifteen centuries regularly performed the five daily prayers, let alone these other special prayers. In an exceedingly conservative estimate, if only 1 percent of the world's 1.6 billion living Muslims performs the seventeen required rak'ats, not even considering the recommended "bonus" rak'ats, al-Fatiha would still have been recited 272 million times today.

This leads us to ask how the words operate in Muslim life—not only what the sura says, but what it does. Though there have been mountains of commentary written on al-Fatiha's exoteric and esoteric meanings (including the hidden truths in its specific words, letters, and even the dots under letters), treating the Qur'an exclusively as a text leaves out this dimension of embodied experience—the sense of what it means to stand in the prescribed posture of prayer and recite the sura, or hear an imam recite the sura and beautify the revelation with an oral calligraphy. It also gives us an incomplete picture of what the Qur'an could have meant in Muhammad's own life. Muhammad reportedly used al-Fatiha in healing practices, reciting it over the sick. For Muhammad as well as later Muslims, al-Fatiha (and the Qur'an) would offer not only a revealed message, but also technology—that is, you can do things with it and make change in material reality.

Beyond its short and perhaps imprecise message, the Qur'an's opening also opens us to the Prophet. Muhammad's character is the Qur'an, and the Qur'an is al-Fatiha, and al-Fatiha is not a theologian's dissertation or jurist's treatise. The Qur'an does not only exist as a book that makes arguments and truth claims. The Qur'an is both a site of personal reflection and communal relations. It is materiality, aurality, ritual, bodies, art, and magic.

15

FORGIVE HIS HANDS TOO

Jabir narrated:

Tufayl bin 'Amr went to the Prophet (God bless him and give him peace) and he said: "O Messenger of God, do you have a secure fortress?" The tribe of Daws had a fortress in the days of Jahiliyya. The Prophet (God bless him and give him peace) refused that offer, as God had reserved it for the Ansar. When the Messenger of God (God bless him and give him peace) performed the Hijra to Medina, Tufayl made the Hijra with a man from his tribe. They reached Medina and he became sick, and felt anxiety. He took iron arrowheads and cut through his finger joints, and his hands gushed out until he died. Then Tufayl saw him in a dream. His condition was good, but his hands were bandaged.

Tufayl asked him, "What did your lord arrange with you?" He said, "He pardoned me with my Hijra to his prophet, God bless him and give him peace." Tufayl asked, him, "Why do I see your hands wrapped?" He said, "It was said to me, 'We do not repair what you damaged.'"

Tufayl told the story to the Messenger of God (God bless him and give him peace).

The Messenger of God (God bless him and give him peace) said, "O God, forgive his hands too."[79]

After enduring harassment, boycotts, and violence from the Meccans for years, Muhammad and his community left Mecca for the nearby city of Yathrib, which would come to be known as Medinat al-Nabi, City of the Prophet, or simply al-Medina, "the city." It was in Medina that the Prophet began the statesman chapter of his life, negotiating treaties, mediating disputes, leading an army, and forming a new society defined by his prophetic leadership. Shortly after the death of the Prophet, the caliph 'Umar would designate this migration as the start of Muslim history, marking the rest of time thereafter in distance from the Hijra. (This writing, for example, takes place in year 1439 on the Hijri calendar.) When we talk about the Hijra today, something's often missing: recognition of the refugee experience. The Muslims did not arrive in Medina as triumphalist state-builders, but as an exiled, persecuted, rejected people. They fled torture and poverty for an unknowable future, and the Hijra did not mean an immediate end to everyone's pain.

Beyond the context of the Hijra, this hadith, found in

Muslim ibn Hajjaj's *Sahih* (generally recognized as the second most reliable source in the Sunni hadith canon, often placed on a virtual par with Bukhari's *Sahih* and occasionally even placed above it), highlights the compassion of both God and the Prophet. Though a number of hadiths criminalize suicide as a major sin with clear afterlife punishments, God brings this migrant into a realm of greater comforts than he had ever known in the world. But God leaves his wounds still in need of bandages, while the Prophet asks God to give more. Muhammad's prayer becomes a resource for those who might be unsure as to whether they can pray for loved ones who have taken their own lives. (I've been asked this question more than once.) The hadith establishes that God welcomed someone who had committed suicide into paradise, and also that Muhammad personally prayed for a completer of suicide, providing both divine affirmation and prophetic precedent.

If you're looking for "Islam's position on suicide," it's easy to skim the hadith corpus (particularly in today's world of searchable English-language hadith databases) and find statements attributed to the Prophet, some in which Muhammad directly quotes God, that unambiguously condemn the taker of his or her own life. Sadly, those hadiths are probably more familiar to most Muslims than this narration of divine and prophetic compassion for a suicidal refugee; whenever I share this hadith, my Muslim sisters and brothers are touched and often surprised. Muhammad also quotes God as saying that his wrath is overwhelmed by his mercy, and Muhammad himself appears here as one who intervenes with God for greater mercy upon those in unbearable pain.

16

HADITHS OF INTENTION

Nafi' bin Jubayr narrated:
The Prophet (God bless him and give him peace) mentioned the army that will be swallowed up by the earth, and Umm Salama said, "Perhaps they are forced?" He said, "They are resurrected according to their intentions."[80]

Describing a future apocalyptic war between good and evil, the Prophet refers to an army that sinks into the earth by God's intervention. When the Prophet's wife Umm Salama speculates that some soldiers in this cursed army might have been made to join against their free will, the Prophet assures her that even if they had found themselves in the wrong place at the wrong time, God would know the conditions of their hearts. They would be judged in the next world not for having aligned with the forces of evil, but for their inner motivations for doing so.

The Prophet's statement that God resurrects (that is, judges) people in accordance with their intentions actually appears in more than one hadith. Imam al-Nawawi, whose famous forty-hadith collection has enjoyed widespread circulation as an accessible primer to the basics of Muslim life, starts his collection with the famous "Hadith of Intention." Before walking his reader through the rest of what he presents as the path of Islam, Nawawi names proper intention as the journey's first step. We arrive at our destinies not only by the actions that we choose, but our reasons for choosing them and continued mindfulness of our purpose.

Nawawi's version specifically relates not to armies of the future apocalypse but to the Hijra, the Muslims' migration from Mecca to Medina. When Muhammad described the rewards that awaited those who took part in this epic flight, some members of the community complained that one man had only migrated for a woman in Medina whom he wished to marry. Like Princess Leia in *Star Wars*, who tells Han Solo, "If money is all that you love, then that's what you'll receive," Muhammad informed his Companions that God would reward the migrants based on their personal desires. If someone migrated for the purpose of marriage or a business opportunity, that would be his or her reward. If they migrated for God and the Prophet, then their reward would be God and the Prophet. The Qur'an derides those who pray only because they want others to see them praying. During my pilgrimage to Mecca, my hajj group's guide told us to remain focused on our intention. "If you want Allah," he said, "you get Allah. If you want show-off, you get show-off."

Just as someone might do the right things for wrong

reasons, there are also cases in which people engage in forbidden acts due to unavoidable necessity, as when extreme hunger forces someone to eat prohibited foods or steal. A friend of mine self-medicates with substances that an overwhelming majority of Muslim scholars regard as forbidden by God. While accepting the divine prohibition, she asserts that her personal use fulfills a compelling interest of health and wellness. My friend is not a reformist who seeks to change the rules, let alone a radical outlaw who would burn down the entire system; she remains conservative in relation to the law, even when she perceives herself as breaking it. In her reading, the Hadith of Intention allows her to assess personal choices beyond simple questions of *haram* (prohibited) and *halal* (permissible). "In terms of *shari'a*, I know that this is illegal," my friend tells me; "but that doesn't mean that I think of it as a sin." Another Muslim friend, cautious to approve or deny this perspective, simply remarked to me, "Allah knows best." While confident in his views on Islamic law as an earthly tradition of human interpreters, he felt less secure when it came to speculating on God's opinion. If God rewards and punishes based on the personal intentions behind our actions rather than outward appearances, we refrain from making claims upon someone's spiritual condition. These various hadiths of intention could call us to recognize that when humans act as judges over one another, they risk acting as imposters in God's role as *the* Judge (al-Hakam).

17

THE GREATER JIHAD

Jabir narrated:

The Messenger of God (God bless him and give him peace) returned from a military campaign. He (God bless him and give him peace) said, "You have arrived with a good arrival from the lesser jihad to the greater jihad."

They said, "And what is the greater jihad?"

He said, "The slave's battle against his passion."[81]

Concerned that my work remain accessible to non-Muslim readers, editors often ask me to translate my terms. It's perhaps my most enduring manuscript battle. I am repeatedly asked to turn *adhan* into "call to prayer," *wudu'* into "ablution," and *masjid* into its English equivalent, "mosque." Confident that my reader can survive an encounter with unfamiliar words, I often resist.

No editor, however, has ever asked me to translate *jihad*. No editor fears that this word will confuse or alienate the reader; no editor treats it as a word that the reader had probably never seen before. *Jihad* now operates effectively as an English word, instantly comprehended without requiring translation. But while this new English word, produced and circulated within English-language media, immediately evokes popular concepts of holy war, the usage of *jihad* attributed to the Prophet himself reflects a broader range of meanings. The English word *jihad* as it circulates in popular discourse is not simply the original Arabic left intact, but rather a translation of the Arabic into a new concept, and not always the best translation available.

The *j-h-d* root carries meanings of struggle and the exertion of effort. These root letters give us *ijtihad*, the term in classical Muslim thought for the arduous intellectual struggle undertaken by jurists to answer new legal problems with independent reasoning. The Prophet did engage his opponents in military conflict, and he did use the term *jihad* in reference to combat. But he also told his wife A'isha that pilgrimage to Mecca was the "most excellent" or "most beautiful" jihad (with some versions explicitly noting pilgrimage as women's jihad). In Abu Dawud's *Sunan*, one of the hadith collections in Sunni tradition's Six Books canon, the Prophet is reported to have stated, "The most excellent jihad is a just word to an oppressive ruler." Decades after Muhammad's death, when his granddaughter Zaynab stands in chains before the tyrant Yazid, surrounded by soldiers with the severed head of her brother Husayn at her side, she performs jihad with her words of defiance.

While our early sources present the battlefield as a fact of life in Muhammad's world, they also depict a Prophet who treats the interior combat against one's own soul as the more epic and demanding struggle. The various iterations of Muhammad's "greater jihad" hadith resonate with another episode in which he achieves success in a physical struggle with a literal opponent, only to then call attention to true strength as self-control. When Muhammad defeats the powerful wrestler Rukanah, he does not arrogantly celebrate his victory or flex his muscles, but instead reminds his Companions that the strongest man is the one who can defeat his anger.

Throughout premodern Muslim tradition, figures such as Ghazali have drawn from the greater jihad hadith for their pursuit of a perfected Muslim selfhood. Scholars such as the Shafi'i shaykh Bayhaqi (d. 1066) included the narration in his book on asceticism. The narration also enjoys prolific dissemination in Sufi traditions, but does not enjoy supreme canonical prestige in Sunni hadith evaluation. Fourteenth-century Hanbali jurist Ibn Taymiyya (d. 1328), living in an age in which Mongol invasions wreaked immeasurable destruction upon Muslims in the Persian and Eastern Mediterranean milieus, opposed Muslim scholars who might have cited the greater jihad hadith to justify their cooperation with their oppressors. However, Ibn al-Jawzi—one of Ibn Taymiyya's formative influences—employs the hadith in *Dhamm al-Hawwa* (Censure of Passion), his manual for combatting desires, and even notes Sufi claims of ascetic masters who so completely defeated their passions that they lived the rest of their days floating in the air.[82]

Today, the hadith circulates with considerable popularity

throughout Muslim discourses, touching the hearts of Muhammad's modern lovers as a reflection of his prophetic way,
which prioritized rigorous self-examination and self-critique
over material gains and political power. Beyond its value as
a resource for Muslim ethics, self-critique, and spirituality,
the hadith's circulation has proliferated in recent decades as
a counter to popular uses of *jihad* that provoke anti-Muslim
hysteria and racism. In representations of the lesser and greater
jihads, the Prophet's struggle for freedom, justice, and equality requires an internal, reflective dimension, while his project
of personal change also requires an effort to make change in
the world.

The leaders of justice movements, without denying the
urgency of material struggle, drew from the inner struggle
of the greater jihad. Sufi master Amadu Bamba (1853–1927),
founder of the Muridiyya order in Senegal, engaged French
colonial power with nonviolent resistance, supporting his
platform by making a distinction between the lesser and
greater jihads. The Khudai Khidmatgar, a Muslim movement dedicated to Indian independence from colonial Brit-
ain, worked with Mahatma Gandhi and shared his principles
of nonviolent freedom struggle. For the Khudai Khidmatgar
leader Abdul Ghaffar Khan (1890–1988), the path of nonvi-
olence did not reflect a departure from the ethics of jihad,
but rather expressed jihad's truest meaning as well as the
Prophet's own patience, compassion, and affirmation of life.
Even the twentieth-century Iranian revolutionary Ayatollah Khomeini (1902–1989), popularly associated in Western
imaginaries with violence, begins his forty-hadith collection
with a discussion of the greater jihad, and centers this hadith

as the foundation for his volume of mystical commentary, *The Greater Jihad or the Struggle with the Soul.*

My teachers and elders have told me many times that the key to a Muhammad-like existence lies in pursuing balance, in harmonizing opposites. The lesser and greater jihads find special harmony in the life of Muhammad's most complete follower, his cousin and son-in-law, 'Ali, whose achievements on the battlefield reflect both his courage and his grace. Fighting the fearsome 'Amr ibn Abd al-Wudd at the Battle of the Trench, 'Ali is said to have gained the upper hand and prepared to deliver the fatal blow when 'Amr spit in 'Ali's face. 'Ali then lowered his sword and refrained from killing 'Amr. 'Ali would later explain that he had been fighting selflessly in the cause of God, feeling neither a desire for glory nor enmity toward his opponents, but when 'Amr spit in his face, 'Ali suddenly became angry, which threatened the purity of his intention. Rather than kill for his own satisfaction, 'Ali withdrew from combat, at least until he could regulate his emotions and rededicate himself to God. At this moment, 'Ali simultaneously participates in both the lesser and greater jihads, prioritizing the greater and treating moral self-perfection as a more urgent goal than military victory or even his survival. Before defeating his external enemy with the mere swing of sharpened metal, the Lion of God conquered a more dangerous enemy within.

18

DEATH OF THE PROPHET

A'isha narrated:

The Prophet (God bless him and give him peace) died in my house, when it was my turn [among his wives to host him], and he was between my neck and my chest, and God mixed my saliva with his saliva. 'Abd Allah al-Rahman had entered with a siwak [toothbrush] and the Prophet (God bless him and give him peace) was weak, so I took it and softened it, then cleaned his teeth with it.[83]

If you could know only a single fact about Muhammad's life, some Muslims would be okay with this being the one: it's over. Muhammad is dead. This hadith won't immediately reveal the Prophet's character or answer questions that non-Muslims usually ask about him; it doesn't resolve any modern controversies. Nonetheless, for many Muslims who hold the oneness of God to be Islam's foremost concern, it's worth remembering that the Prophet's life ended in a mostly conventional human fashion.

Coming to Islam from a Christian background, I found Muhammad's humanity to offer a critical point at which I could divide my old and new worlds. Muhammad was not the Muslim Christ; he was neither a god nor the son of a god, nor a transcendent being with supernatural powers, and never the object of our prayers and devotion. He was conceived and born like humans, ate and drank and defecated, slept and had sex, and died. There was nothing corporeally exceptional about him, and he performed no miracles beyond his reception of God's speech, the Qur'an.

Of course, this is a fairly modern take on Muhammad, produced amid pressures for religions to prove their rationality and answer attacks from Christian missionaries. Classical sources abound with stories of Muhammad's special qualities and marvelous events from his life, including signs of his unique station at both his birth and death: water gushing out of his hands, ascension into the heavens, the night that he split the moon in half. At the same time we see tendencies toward a rather mundane Prophet: in one of our earliest biographical sources on the Prophet, Ma'mar ibn Rashid's *The Expeditions*, Muhammad's uncle 'Abbas insists after Muhammad's death that the Companions bury him soon, because his body will decay like any other body.[84] In Ibn Sa'd's *Tabaqat*, we also find narrations in which the Companions, apparently unsure as to whether the Prophet could really die, confirm his death by observing typical signs of early postmortem decomposition.[85] These narrations, while apparently uncontroversial for their earliest reporters and audiences, would later become unthinkable. Muslim imaginaries of the Prophet would come to favor assertions that the earth has been forbidden from consuming the bodies of prophets, and that Muhammad remains physically intact—and even sentient—within his grave.

The story of Abu Bakr reciting the Qur'an and reminding the community that Muhammad was never more than a mortal human being seems to stand at the intersection of these conflicting ideas. This account portrays a segment of the original Muslims, including no less revered a figure than the future caliph 'Umar, as unwilling to accept that Muhammad could have died in the usual human way. The narrative then presents Abu Bakr, Muhammad's father-in-law and closest friend, attempting to save Muslims from the same deification that Christians had imposed on Jesus. Muhammad was dead, he told them, but God would not die.

Because Muhammad's death sparked a crisis over political leadership that would contribute to lasting divisions among Muslims—in a somewhat simplistic read, it's the cause for our separation of Sunni and Shi'i traditions today—every detail of his death can become meaningful, even the question of which loved one held him during his last breath. A'isha tells us that the Prophet died in her arms, but competing reports place him in the arms of 'Ali, his cousin and son-in-law (and the rival of A'isha and her father). Wherever Muhammad died, his death was a moment at which the future of Islam could have been in jeopardy on both theological and communal levels. Reminding Muslims that even the greatest man of all time was still only a man, Abu Bakr intervened in both futures, protected God's exclusive right to be worshiped, and established himself as the voice of reason in a moment of controversy and chaos.

19

MUHAMMAD AS LIGHT

Abu 'Abd Allah narrated:

God, the most holy, the most high, has said, "O Muhammad, I have created you and 'Ali a light, a spirit, without body before I created my heavens, my earth, my throne, and my ocean. You continued to acknowledge me as your lord and speak of my glory. I then collected the spirits of both of you and made it one spirit. This spirit continued to speak of my glory, my holiness, and acknowledge me as the lord. I then divided it into two and two which became four: one Muhammad, one 'Ali; the other two, Hasan and Husayn." Then God created Fatima, peace be upon her, from a light beginning with a spirit that was created first without a body. He then wiped us with his right hand to allow his light to reach us all.[86]

There's the Muhammad who died like a normal human and even decomposed, but there's also the Muhammad from whom the stars and oceans were made, the Muhammadi Light, the Muhammadi Reality that existed before the universe as an emanation from God's name, ar-Rahman. Beyond his roles as ethical teacher, divinely guided legislator, and apocalyptic warner to his people, Muhammad appears in numerous hadith traditions as a cosmic principle that precedes not only the prophets before him, but in fact everything else in creation.

Not all Muslims accept the veracity of the *nur Muhammad* hadith or similar traditions that depict the Prophet as something akin to a hellenic Logos. Today, affirmation or rejection of the narration places you clearly on one or the other side of a line.

The notions of Muhammad as light preexisting the rest of humankind does not explicitly appear in the Qur'an, though Qur'an interpreters did find verses that could support them. The Qur'an describes Muhammad as a "light-giving lamp" (33:46); when parents name their son Lamp (Siraj), they name him with one of the Qur'an's honors for the Prophet. In 6:163, God instructs Muhammad to say, "I am the first of those who submit"; some readers interpret this to mean that Muhammad is not only the first submitter (*muslim*) in his own historical setting, but also that his act of submission precedes even that of Adam. Muslims have also read the Qur'an's mention of Muhammad's "movement in those who prostrate" (26:219) intertextually with hadiths in which Muhammad describes himself as traveling through the loins of his ancestors, moving between generations of pure and prophetic bodies, until the time of his birth.[87] Hadiths in which Muhammad states that he had been a prophet since the time that Adam was "between the spirit and the mud" appear in differing versions with subtle shifts in wording, some presenting Muhammad's pre-Adamic prophethood as simply a note on divine predestination—Muhammad's prophethood was *written* for him prior to Adam—rather than his literal preexistence.[88]

In various premodern commentaries, Muhammad's light not only precedes everything else in physical existence, but becomes the source from which the rest of creation emanates: God first creates Muhammad's light, and then from it creates the celestial Pen and Tablet, God's own throne, the heavens and earth, paradise and hell, angels, and humankind. In some narrations, God's first division of this primordial light produces the differentiation of Muhammad and 'Ali, presenting 'Ali as having preexisted Adam by upward of 40,000 years.[89]

For Muhammad to exist as timeless light means that he transcends the expected borders of his body: Muhammad does not begin or end with his skin, and his present existence cannot be confined to his physical remains. This offers meaningful social consequences in relation to the bodies that we privilege and authorize in the Prophet's absence. Shi'i scholars employed the Muhammadi light as a means of conceptualizing the special transmission between Muhammad and the line of infallible Imams descended from him, a linkage that was genetic but also something else. Through Muhammad's grandsons and their sons and so on through the Imamate, an element of his prophetic ontology travels through non-prophetic bodies. The Muhammadi light additionally provides a way to express the connection between

Muhammad and 'Ali beyond their biological relationship as cousins: they are connected before they have bodies. Sufi thinkers likewise theorized the Muhammadi light in ways that enabled the Prophet to remain present and accessible across time and space, continually guiding seekers in the centuries before and after his earthly life. Muhammad is the ultimate source of knowledge, guidance, and illumination for his prophetic predecessors: in a sense, Moses and Jesus become students or reflections of Muhammad. On the other side of his human lifespan, beyond the cessation of his bodily processes, Muhammad remains the Prophet. Muhammad continues to speak; he is still the source, guiding saints and advanced knowers.

20

THE CITY AND THE GATE

'Ali narrated:
> The Messenger of God (God bless him and give him peace) said, "I am the city of knowledge and 'Ali is its gate. Whoever seeks knowledge, enter through this gate."[90]

From this widely circulated hadith, one could suggest that the only proper introduction to Muhammad first requires an introduction to his cousin and son-in-law, 'Ali ibn Abu Talib. Apart from his patrilineal relation to Muhammad—both are grandsons of Abd al-Muttalib—and his devotion to Muhammad prior to and through the prophetic mission, 'Ali also became connected to Muhammad by his divinely ordained marriage to the Prophet's daughter, Fatima. It is only through the progeny from 'Ali's marriage to Fatima that Muhammad's line has continued into the present; to honor the tree of Muhammad today means also honoring the descendents of 'Ali.

Explorations of Islamic mysticism, Qur'an interpretation,

jurisprudence, battlefield ethics, and chivalry inevitably lead to encounters with 'Ali, and it would be impossible to comprehensively study Muslim traditions of art, poetry, and music without first knowing 'Ali. While it remains critically fraught to describe anything in the vast Islamic tradition as "universal," we could confidently present 'Ali as the figure most universally beloved and revered by Muslims after the Prophet himself. If we can say that Muslims have imagined, interpreted, and reconstructed Muhammad in countless ways, we should then recognize 'Ali as the gate to *many* cities.

The canonical Shi'i collection of 'Ali's sermons and wise sayings, *Nahj al-Balagha* (Peak of Eloquence), remains a foundational Muslim text, and his shrine in Najaf, Iraq, attracts more Muslim pilgrims than any site beyond the cities of Mecca and Medina. Though Sunni and Shi'i communities have often debated and condemned each other on the charge of misunderstanding 'Ali's true meaning and significance, we should also note the degree of historical overlap and intersection between Sunni and Shi'i ideas of 'Ali.

'Ali's biography weaves him into nearly every aspect of Muhammad's life. 'Ali's father, the Prophet's paternal uncle Abu Talib, took in young Muhammad after the death of Muhammad's mother and raised him virtually as his own son. As with Muhammad, 'Ali's extraordinary significance becomes apparent even at his birth: some sources report that he was born inside the Ka'ba. Muhammad, thirty years old when 'Ali was born, later repaid Abu Talib's compassionate care for him when, after Abu Talib's finances declined, Muhammad brought five-year-old 'Ali into his own home. When Muhammad received the call to prophethood, 'Ali—roughly ten years old at that point—became Muhammad's second believer (after Muhammad's wife Khadija), and the first male convert. 'Ali's young age at the time of his conversion undergoes a variety of interpretations. Some Sunni narratives, favoring Abu Bakr as the first grown man to convert, would discount 'Ali's conversion on the basis that 'Ali was still a child without the rational agency of a mature adult; in Shi'i readings, 'Ali's recognition of the truth while still a child constitutes a miracle comparable to the Qur'an's depiction of baby Jesus speaking from his cradle (19:30). 'Ali's youthfulness also establishes the sincerity of his conviction and his unflinching loyalty to the Prophet. When Muhammad gathered his kinsmen to publicly proclaim his divine mission, only thirteen-year-old 'Ali pledged his faith in Muhammad. As the men laughed and jeered at the self-proclaimed prophet and his boy disciple, young 'Ali remained firm in his position.

As Muhammad's prophetic mission met with rejection, mockery, and even physical harassment from the people of Mecca, 'Ali's father, Abu Talib, continued to stand by his nephew and advocate on his behalf with other clan leaders. However, the question of whether Abu Talib properly became a Muslim remains a controversial flashpoint between Sunnis, whose sources treat Abu Talib as remaining an unbeliever destined for a particular realm of the Fire, and Shi'i Muslims, whose sources portray Abu Talib as accepting Muhammad's prophethood even if he had not officially converted. Differing claims upon the fate of 'Ali's father reflect contested ideas about the family of the Prophet and 'Ali's own significance.

'Ali figures prominently in perhaps the definitive moment in narratives of the original Muslim community: its collective

migration from Mecca to Medina. The tradition reports that
when Muhammad and Abu Bakr made their nighttime escape from Mecca, 'Ali risked his life for the Prophet by remaining in his house and even sleeping in his bed, misleading
a pack of would-be assassins into thinking that Muhammad
was still in town. 'Ali later took part in the community's migration to Medina and the building of a new Muslim society.
When hostilities between Mecca and Medina turned to violence, 'Ali distinguished himself as not only a courageous
fighter, but a paragon of battlefield chivalry.

Upon the death of Muhammad, a committee elected
Abu Bakr, Muhammad's close Companion and father-in-
law, to lead the community. 'Ali was reportedly washing the
Prophet's body as the election took place, thereby excluded
both as a voter and as a potential candidate. At the time,
many would have considered 'Ali too young to take seriously
as a leader in comparison to the mature Abu Bakr. While
Sunni tradition would hold that Muhammad had not named
a successor prior to his death, Shi'i interpreters argue that
Muhammad had in fact named 'Ali with his proclamation
at Ghadir Khumm: "For whomever I am your *mawla*, 'Ali is
your *mawla*." The Ghadir Khumm decree appears not only
in Shi'i hadith canon but also in canonical Sunni sources.
However, Sunni scholars do not share the Shi'i view that
mawla in this context clearly means "master" and refers to
leadership over the community, instead reading the term to
express friendship, partnership, and patronage.

'Ali withheld his allegiance from Abu Bakr for six months
after the election. 'Umar ibn al-Khattab led a group to the
home of 'Ali and Fatima, demanding that 'Ali pledge; in Shi'i

sources, 'Umar's mob breaks down the door and tramples Fatima underneath it, forcing her miscarriage and eventual death. Prior to the incident, Fatima had experienced her own friction with the new order. When Fatima came to Abu Bakr to request the land at Fadak that she had inherited from her father, Abu Bakr denied her, asserting that Muhammad had said, "Prophets leave no inheritance." Abu Bakr not only shut down Fatima's claim to her father's land, but also implied that there could be no claim to political power based on familial relation to Muhammad.

Abu Bakr was succeeded after his death by his handpicked appointment, 'Umar ibn al-Khattab; 'Umar was succeeded in turn by 'Uthman ibn 'Affan, elected by a council in which 'Ali participated. 'Uthman was an unpopular ruler, his regime characterized by charges of nepotism and poor management. Moreover, 'Uthman's project of establishing a shared text of the Qur'an, prohibiting the use of alternative collections, alienated many Qur'an memorizers and compilers, including other Companions of the Prophet, who regarded their own archives as legitimate. After a mob stormed 'Uthman's house and killed him, 'Ali was elected Commander of the Believers, finally coming to power more than twenty years after the death of Muhammad.

For later Sunni tradition, 'Ali would represent the last of the "rightly guided caliphs," a roster of superior leaders in a lost golden age. For later Shi'i tradition, 'Ali would be remembered as the first infallible Imam in a chain of transcendent authority that passed from him to his sons and their sons. However, it would be somewhat naïve to assume that in 'Ali's lifetime—or even in the generations immediately after him—Muslims were clearly divided into Sunnis and Shi'is in ways that would resonate with our present categories. We would do better to consider these identities as having developed gradually into their recognizable forms. Sunni communal identity emerged in part through a shared interpretation of history that included a consensus regarding the "rightly guided caliphs." Proto-Sunni scholars came to recognize Abu Bakr, 'Umar, 'Uthman, and 'Ali as rightly guided, though it took some time and controversy before 'Ali made the roster.[91] For what we now recognize as Sunni historical memory, the four caliphs' chronology represents their proper and natural relationships; the caliphs' reigns correspond in descending order of their closeness to the Prophet. For Shi'i narratives, however, this sequence reads as a tragedy: 'Ali, the closest Companion to the Prophet and his explicitly named successor, was denied his just due and became the last to take office.

Even after his election, 'Ali's status as leader of the community remained contested. His first challenge came from none other than Muhammad's widow (and Abu Bakr's daughter) A'isha, who gathered supporters and actively opposed 'Ali's regime. At the Battle of the Camel, so named for the armored camel that A'isha rode to the scene, 'Ali's forces prevailed. A'isha was taken prisoner, pardoned, and sent to Medina, after which she retired from politics and withdrew to life as a scholar. Though Sunni Muslims in tenth-century Iraq attempted to establish a ritual commemoration of the Battle of the Camel, complete with dramatic reenactments and a woman on a camel portraying A'isha, the incident did not become a popular component of Sunni public memory.[92] Sunni popular consciousness, rather than emphasize this military struggle between two of Muhammad's most beloved Companions and the history of tensions and rivalries between their families, would define the original Muslim community as one of selfless cooperation and mostly uncompromised unity.

Numerous hadiths, however, reflect the anxiety and heartbreak felt by many Muslims after the Battle of the Camel. For those who would read the Prophet's Companions as the greatest generation in human history, the Battle of the Camel potentially offers a devastating crisis: If this was the society that we should all seek to emulate, how did its heroes become so divided that Muhammad's own family waged war against itself? How can those of us belonging to later, inferior generations begin to analyze this history, or even make judgments upon its participants?

A number of statements attributed to Muhammad express clearly partisan verdicts on behalf of one side or another. Some hadiths, while not addressing specific political conflicts or denouncing rival parties, can read as politically loaded in their praises for Abu Bakr, A'isha, 'Ali, or Fatima. The hadith in which Muhammad names Fatima the master over all women in paradise, for example, becomes particularly compelling when we see that the hadith's reporters attribute this report to A'isha, thus portraying A'isha as a confessor of Fatima's superiority. Some hadiths offer less than glowing representations of these figures, such as narrations in which A'isha speaks with a sassy tone to the Prophet, or 'Ali angers his father-in-law by attempting to marry a second wife and Muhammad humiliates 'Ali by proclaiming that whoever hurts Fatima has hurt him. Other hadiths appear to offer reconciliation, such as the tradition in which Muhammad lists ten men who have been promised paradise: the list includes Abu Bakr, 'Umar, 'Uthman, and 'Ali, as well as A'isha's two major allies against 'Ali in the Battle of the Camel, Talha and Zubayr. Proto-Sunni hadith collections would often include *fada'il* (virtues, excellences) sections, in which one could investigate Muhammad's endorsements of specific Companions, reading Muhammad's kind words for A'isha alongside his praises of 'Ali. These compilations of prophetic praises for Companions who had bitterly opposed one another smooth over the tensions and present a vision of history that would become foundational for Sunni Muslim identities.[93]

Opposition to 'Ali's rule continued after the Battle of the Camel. Mu'awiya ibn Abi Sufyan, the governor of Syria (and a member of the same clan as 'Uthman), challenged 'Ali on the basis of justice for 'Uthman. When 'Ali agreed to arbitration with the rival party, 'Ali's most zealous supporters became disillusioned and abandoned him, forming an extremist third party that would be known derisively as the Khawarij (Outsiders). A member of the Khawarij assassinated 'Ali with a poisoned sword while 'Ali's head was lowered in prayer at the masjid in Kufa.

From the perspective of those who regarded 'Ali as *the* legitimate successor to Muhammad, who could follow him? 'Ali's supporters understood that his sons would inherit his authority. Though Muhammad ibn al-Hanafiya, the son of 'Ali and a concubine, briefly gathered a movement centered on his own claim to power, pro-'Ali camps gradually crystallized into Shi'i tradition around an investment in 'Ali's sons with Fatima. This line, after all, descended not only from 'Ali but the Prophet himself. In what would become Shi'i tradition, 'Ali is the non-prophetic inheritor of Muhammad's prophetic legacy, followed by his sons Hasan (believed to have been poisoned by Mu'awiya) and Husayn (brutally murdered by the forces of Mu'awiya's son Yazid); the fourth Imam was Husayn's son Zayn al-'Abidin; Zayn's son Muhammad al-Baqir became the fifth Imam, and so on. Disagreements over the successor to the sixth Imam, Ja'far as-Sadiq, caused a splintering in the lineage between followers of different sons; those who favored Ja'far's son Isma'il as the true seventh Imam became known as Isma'ilis, following the lineage that proceeded from Isma'il and continues today with the Agha Khan. The largest community of Shi'is, known as Ithna Ashari (Twelver) Shi'is, follow Ja'far's son Musa and the line from him; this roster concludes with the twelfth Imam, al-Mahdi, who disappeared as a child and is awaited to return at the end of the world. In the Ithna Ashari vision of history, each of the eleven Imams preceding al-Mahdi underwent varying degrees of persecution, including imprisonment and torture, and ultimately martyrdom. To accept 'Ali as Imam means recognizing injustice as this world's normative condition; the poor and righteous suffer while tyrants enjoy a fleeting illusion of victory and power.

While it is most associated with Shi'ism, praise for 'Ali appears throughout both Sunni and Shi'i traditions, often in overlapping narrations, though a slight change in details can shift their meanings. In some sources, a story of Muhammad healing 'Ali's eye infection by spitting into it becomes more than a medical miracle of the Prophet, but evidence of a special transmission between the Prophet and his closest Companion:

when Muhammad's saliva enters 'Ali's eye, 'Ali receives transcendent knowledge. For emphasizing 'Ali's privileged relationship to Muhammad's prophetic knowledge, considerable overlap also exists between Shi'ism and the traditions of Sufism. Often carelessly defined as Islam's "mystical dimension," Sufi tradition took shape in classical Islam through initiatory lodges that authorized themselves with master-disciple lineages tracing back to the Prophet. The overwhelming majority of Sufi orders, whether Sunni or Shi'i in their orientation, trace their connection to the Prophet through 'Ali, the exemplary disciple and recipient of higher knowledge. To join a Sufi order and pledge to its master, in most cases, means pledging to the student of the student of the student, and so on down the chain of initiated masters, each a student of the previous master, ending with the greatest student of the Prophet.

Muhammad had said, "'Ali is with the Qur'an, and the Qur'an is with 'Ali." Reportedly the first memorizer of the Qur'an, 'Ali also appears throughout the tradition as an authority on its hidden meanings. As God's uncreated speech, the Qur'an is more than ink and paper, but 'Ali is also more than flesh and blood, and the two entities are linked on a cosmological level. In one apocryphal tradition, 'Ali names the heart of the Qur'an as its first sura, al-Fatiha; 'Ali then explains that the heart of the first sura is its first verse, *bismillahir rahmanir rahim*, "in the name of God, ar-Rahman, the Merciful"; the heart of the first verse is *bismillah*, "in the name of God"; the heart of the first word is its first letter, *ba*; the heart of the *ba* is the dot underneath it; and that dot is 'Ali himself. As the secret of the first syllable that one pronounces at the start of the Qur'an, 'Ali opens the revelation's gate for us.

21

THE PEOPLE OF THE HOUSE

Abu Sa'id al-Khudri narrated:
The Messenger of God (God bless him and give him peace) said, "I will be taken, and I have left you with two heavy things: The book of God and my family. You will never go astray after them."[94]

Despite hadiths in which Muhammad names the love for his kin, literally the "People of the House" (*ahl al-bayt*)—especially his daughter Fatima, paternal cousin 'Ali, and his descendants from Fatima's marriage to 'Ali—as a definitive feature of Islam, books in the contemporary Intro to Islam genre do not typically treat the Prophet's family as crucial for non-Muslims who want to learn about the tradition. *The Cambridge Companion to Muhammad*, designed for college courses (with fourteen chapters devoted to specific themes, providing a chapter/topic for each week of a semester), offers us readings such as "The Prophet as lawgiver and legal authority" and "The Prophet Muhammad in ritual," but no chapter that gives focused attention to Muhammad's family. When introductory works on Islam do discuss Muhammad's family, they tend to present it as meaningful only for Shi'i Muslims, who in turn are portrayed as a sectarian periphery. However, to leave out the Prophet's family not only marginalizes Shi'i Muslims; it also ignores a historically prominent dimension in Sunni traditions.

In the sitting position of each of the five daily prayers, Muslims recite a prayer for Muhammad *and* his descendants. For Sunni and Shi'i jurisprudential traditions alike, failure to recite it means that the obligations of prayer have not been met. As part of the celebration of the two annual Eid holidays, Muslims recite a prayer that includes asking God to bless the family of the Prophet. Though practices of commemorating the tragic martyrdom of Muhammad's grandson Husayn developed primarily within Shi'i communities, we can point to multiple settings in which Sunnis also took part in these observances.

Love for the Prophet's family transforms the landscape, dotting the map with a proliferation of sites at which believers can plug into the beneficent energies (*baraka*) associated with Muhammad. The most prominent examples would be the shrines of 'Ali and Husayn in Iraq, which attracts upward of a million visitors every year. Shrines for the Prophet's family are not only found in Shi'i-majority societies; in the city of Lahore in Sunni-majority Pakistan, a shrine believed to house the graves of several women from the Prophet's family receives visitations from both Shi'i and Sunni Muslims. In Cairo and Damascus, two shrines that make opposing claims of housing the severed head of Husayn exist inside the precincts of Sunni masjids, and receive visitation from both Sunni and Shi'i Muslims. In Egypt and Syria, shrines dedicated to the Prophet's family often reflect Shi'i histories, as the region was once home to the Fatimid empire, a Shi'i caliphate; but these were not abandoned after the Fatimids' fall. Later Sunni empires such as the Mamluks and Ottomans also embarked on projects of establishing and maintaining tombs and shrines related to the People of the House. Such sites remain popular destinations for Sunni as well as Shi'i pilgrims. Some of these sites, such as the grave of Muhammad's granddaughter in Cairo, bear particular associations with the fulfillment of prayers and forgiveness of sins.

The hadith of the "two heavy things," pairing Muhammad's family with the Qur'an, appears in Sunni literature. We find variations in collections such as Ibn Hanbal's *Musnad*, Hakim's *Mustadrak*, the *Sunan* works of Darimi and Bayhaqi, and Nasa'i's *Sunan al-Kubra*. The specific version cited here appears in a collection by Sunni scholar Muhammad al-Kattani (1858–1927). Having collected forty (actually forty-two) hadiths exclusively from Sunni works that demonstrate love for the Prophet's family as an obligation for *all* Muslims, al-Kattani notes in his epilogue, "The narrations on this subject are numerous without limit."[95] Among the narrations that al-Kattani saw fit to include in his arba'in, we read of the Prophet comparing his family to Noah's ark: "Whoever boarded it was saved and whoever stayed behind drowned."[96] The Prophet tells his uncle 'Abbas that belief will not enter someone's heart until that person loves 'Abbas for the sake of God and the fact of his kinship to the Prophet.[97] Muhammad promises his assistance in the next world for those who love and support the people of his house,[98] while promising a future of divine wrath and fire for those who hate them.[99] For al-Kattani and the Sunni scholarly authorities whose opinions he cites as evidence, failure to love the People of the House amounts to a rejection of Muhammad's unique status and the divine favors bestowed upon him:

> Know that when God most high especially chose his Prophet, God bless him and give him peace, over all of creation and distinguished him with all the unique attributes, privileges, and miraculous powers, through his blessing he gave his descendants a high rank, elevated the position of those related to and dependent on him, made love for him a serious matter for all creation, and made it an obligation to love his entire family and progeny.[100]

One way of distinguishing Shi'i from Sunni articulations of Islam would represent Shi'i tradition as defined by an investment in the family of Muhammad as both the authentic guides to his prophetic knowledge and material traces of Muhammad's miraculous body. This investment expresses itself in the concept of the Imamate, a chain of master teachers that starts with 'Ali, passes to his sons Hasan and Husayn, and then continues through Husayn's progeny. In contrast, Sunni tradition would be defined by its valorization of Muhammad's Companions, a more expansive category that privileges Muslims (family or not) who had personally met Muhammad, accepted him as a prophet, and died as Muslims; Sunni intellectual tradition formed on the basis of the Companions' supreme authority as sources of Muhammad's teachings and precedent-setting behaviors. Some of the hadiths that al-Kattani includes in his arba'in reconcile this possible tension, showing Muhammad as having prescribed love for both the Companions and his progeny.[101] Linking the Companions and the People of the House in shared privilege could heal some historical pain from conflicts between the People of the House and certain major Companions—including Muhammad's wife A'isha, who had her own claim on the prophetic "House" and was a rival and opponent to both Fatima and 'Ali. A variation of this hadith names Muhammad's wives as a *third* special category requiring Muslims' love and loyalty.

Aware that some of his Sunni readers would regard the arba'in's subject matter and thesis as too close to a Shi'i orientation, al-Kattani argues in his introduction that devotion to the Prophet's family was the practice of the Companions, including caliphs such as Abu Bakr and 'Umar whom Shi'i traditions regard as opponents of the ahl al-bayt.[102] In the most canonical Sunni collection, Sahih al-Bukhari, Abu Bakr calls upon Muslims to protect and revere the people of Muhammad's house; during a time of famine, 'Umar took the hand of Muhammad's uncle 'Abbas and prayed for rain through him: "O God, we seek a means to you through the uncle of your Prophet, to ask that you drive the drought away from us and send down the rain."[103] In other Sunni hadith collections, we read of Muhammad disclosing that his daughter Fatima will reign as master over all women in paradise (with some versions exempting the Virgin Mary and others from Fatima's lordship), and naming his grandsons Hasan and

Husayn the leaders of paradisical youths. Al-Kattani, perhaps strategically, does not include these hadiths, as the specific mentions of Fatima and her sons could read as too overtly inclined to Shi'i alignment; he does, however, report a hadith in which Muhammad names himself their paternal protector and guardian.[104] He also cites scholarly giants of the early post-Companion generations, such as Malik and ash-Shafi'i, to present his project as fully in line with Sunni intellectual tradition, and finally argues that the text of the Qur'an itself exalts the Prophet's family.[105]

Writing in the early decades of the twentieth century, al-Kattani makes a case that devotion to the People of the House traditionally stands at the very heart of Sunni consciousness. But whether due to trends of Sunni revivalism that draw sharper contrasts between Sunni and Shi'i identities, or trends of modernist reform that deemphasize traditional ideas of Muhammad as a superhuman figure with extraordinary properties, something has changed. Devotion to the People of the House faces increasing opposition, as demonstrated in the almost predictable Sunni attacks on Shi'i observances in Iraq and elsewhere.

Jannat al-Baqi, the cemetery in Medina that serves as the resting place for numerous members of the Prophet's family and various prominent Companions, reflects these tensions. Throughout Muslim history, Sunni rulers and social elites funded the construction and maintenance of shrines in the cemetery, but in the twentieth century these practices fell out of line with the brand of Sunni revivalism favored by the new Saudi state. The Saudi government destroyed the shrines, rendered Jannat al-Baqi an empty brown field, and blocked access to the graves of Shi'i Imams (and the alleged grave of Fatima). But the rise of the Saudi state does not amount to a pure revival of "Sunni tradition," even if this is what the state claims for itself, but rather a resurgence of one particular way of thinking about Sunni tradition, drawing from a specific intellectual heritage associated with fourteenth-century scholar Ibn Taymiyya. It is not, historically speaking, the only or even the predominant version of Sunni tradition.

I converted roughly seventy years after al-Kattani passed away. As a teenager first reading about Islam from introductory books and pamphlets written by apologetic Sunni scholars, often produced with relationships to a globalizing Saudi media matrix, I did not learn that loving Muhammad's family could be a foundational duty for Muslims and definitive marker of Islam. Nowhere in the Sunni literature and communities through which I first found myself as a Muslim did I learn about the significance of Fatima or her children. This could mean that al-Kattani's arba'in did not shift the momentum in Sunni discourses. Al-Kattani compiled his arba'in prior to the full crystallization of the anti-Shi'i Saudi state, and generations before the especially brutal anti-Shi'ism of entities such as al-Qaeda, the Taliban, and ISIS. If anything, as the border between Sunni and Shi'i traditions has grown more concrete in many contexts, some Sunni Muslims would feel more anxiety about overstepping their communal bounds in devotion to the Prophet's family than in al-Kattani's lifetime. This highlights problems of describing Islam in terms of having "orthodox" or "mainstream" positions that may appear timeless, unchanging, and easily identifiable against inauthentic "heterodoxy." Love for the ahl al-bayt can seem "universal" in one context and "sectarian" in another. What one generation finds acceptable and even foundational does not necessarily meet the needs of the next. The division between Sunni and Shi'i treatments of the Prophet's family appears as the point of separation between the ocean and the beach; while we might perceive a clear difference between them, we also recognize that the tide constantly goes in and out, moving the point at which one begins and the other ends.

22

THE LADY OF LIGHT

Abu 'Abd Allah narrated:

When Fatima (peace be upon her) conceived Husayn, Gabriel came to the Messenger of God (God bless him and give him peace) and said, "Fatima (peace be upon her) will give birth to a son. Your umma will murder him after you die."

When Fatima conceived Husayn, she was unhappy, and when she gave birth, she was unhappy. No mother has ever been seen in the world to bear a child that she would not like. But she was unhappy. She knew that he would be murdered.

It is for this that the verse of the Qur'an came: "And we have enjoined the human being to be kind to his parents. His mother carried him with hardship and gave birth to him with hardship, and his weaning is 30 months . . ." [46:15][106]

As Sunni and Shi'i traditions developed with competing models of exemplary feminine piety, Sunni hadith canon privileged Muhammad's beloved wife A'isha. In Ibn Hanbal's *Musnad*, A'isha's compiled hadiths weigh in at 2,433 reports, no less than 554 pages in the edition on my shelf. The sheer volume of A'isha's corpus speaks to the significance of the Prophet's widow in the preservation of his teachings and legacy. In contrast, the *Musnad* cites Fatima as the source for only nine hadiths across fewer than four full pages.[107] Though no less a hadith giant than A'isha herself recalls Muhammad's praise for his daughter, including famous reports in which Muhammad says, "Fatima is part of me, and whoever hurts her hurts me" (in its original context, a jab at Fatima's husband, 'Ali) and names Fatima as master of women in paradise, Fatima's own voice does not meaningfully survive in the Sunni hadith corpus.

The most immediate explanation for A'isha's prominence and Fatima's virtual absence lies in the difference in their life spans. According to hadith sources, Muhammad told Fatima from his deathbed that she would be the first of his family to join him; true to the Prophet's word, she lived less than three months after her father. She spent that time in constant grief and isolation, mourning in a "House of Sadness" that 'Ali had built for her, rather than disseminating her legal opinions or answering questions about her father. In a culture in which the most powerful media was oral tradition, Fatima left the battlefield of historical memory decades earlier than A'isha, who retired to Medina after her failed war against 'Ali and developed a significant teaching circle. A'isha's memories and interpretations were privileged by the fact that she survived long enough to train younger generations of scholars. We thus find a transmission network that gives powerful signal boosts to A'isha's teachings, but nothing comparable for Fatima.

In Shi'i tradition, however, Fatima takes on a cosmic significance that more than makes up for her lack of historical opportunity. As the Shi'i Imamate begins with Fatima's husband, 'Ali, and then passes through their sons and then *their* sons and so on, Fatima becomes the node that connects her father to a chain of transcendent authorities who, while not prophets themselves, carry the bodily baraka of their prophetic genealogy. Whereas Sunni hadith methodologies privilege the Companions as reporters with unquestionable reliability, Shi'i hadith sciences regard the members of the Imamate as infallible authorities on their grandfather Muhammad.

In Shi'i sources, Fatima becomes a transcendent figure, existing as an emanation of light prior to the creation of all things, a being of supernal majesty witnessed by Adam and Eve, a material trace of paradise in this world, an eternal mourner over the tragedies of her family, intercessor for those who share in her grief, and a revolutionary judge in the afterlife who hangs Husayn's bloody clothes upon the throne of God and calls for justice upon the oppressors. The fifth Shi'i Imam, Muhammad al-Baqir, narrates that his great-grandmother Fatima will stand near the gates of hellfire. As people are marked on their foreheads with the labels of *mu'min* (believer) or *kafir* (unbeliever) and assigned to corresponding fates, Fatima reads a third designation: *muhibb* (lover), reflected in the person whose long record of sins had earned him or her the fire, but who nonetheless enters paradise by virtue of loving Fatima.[108]

While Fatima's earthly life identifies her always in relation to men—she is Muhammad's daughter, 'Ali's wife, and mother of Hasan and Husayn—she exists outside the world as something more. As cosmic principle, she holds power beyond the constraints of her historical positions to such a degree that the honorific title "Mother of Her Father" becomes coherent.

When Adam and Eve become arrogant over their status, confident that they are the greatest of God's creations, God shows them Fatima in her palace of red rubies. When Fatima is born, she is washed and wrapped by none other than the Virgin Mary, Pharaoh's righteous wife Asiya, and a host of paradisical virgins.[109] After the Prophet dies, Fatima regularly receives visits from Gabriel, who comforts her with knowledge of her father's condition in the next world. Gabriel also informs Fatima of her family's future destinies, and 'Ali writes down Gabriel's communications to her in a book that would become three times as large as the Qur'an.[110]

The honors that Fatima receives in these narratives of supernatural encounters and existence outside of time appear in severe contrast to the degradation that she receives in her short life. She was born just before or during the persecutions that Meccans would heap upon her father; she knew a short period in which her father had become the most powerful man in the Arabian Peninsula, but the family still lived simply; then her father died and her household was perceived as a threat to the new state. She was deprived of her inheritance by the first caliph, Abu Bakr, and reportedly slapped in the face by the second caliph, 'Umar (or struck in the stomach by 'Umar's slave), during an intrusion upon her home that resulted in her miscarriage. Canonical Shi'i sources tell us that during this assault, Fatima pulled 'Umar by his garment and told him, "By God, O son of al-Khattab, had I not disliked inflicting calamity upon innocent people, you would have learned how my swearing could bring swift response."[111] Less than three months after the loss of her father, Fatima herself received martyrdom through her injuries. In this world, she was a young wife and mother with blisters on her hands, living in poverty, dying at roughly fifteen to eighteen years old, and asking on her deathbed that her husband bury her at night so that her grave cannot be known. But in the next world, she rides a camel made of jewels into paradise, escorted by Gabriel and 140,000 angels, wearing a crown of light. Fatima herself is light, both as an emanation from her father and the source through which prophethood and imamate flow.[112]

While A'isha won in a certain sense by becoming a master teacher who often corrected the Prophet's male Companions, a legal authority for seminal jurists of early Medina, a narrator of thousands of prophetic traditions, and an interpreter of the Qur'an, it is perhaps ironic that the classical center of Sunni knowledge production, al-Azhar University in Cairo, is named not after A'isha but rather Fatima (taken from her title al-Zahra, the Radiant). Of course, the school had been founded not by Sunnis but by Isma'ili Shi'i Muslims under the Fatimid Empire, so named because its rulers claimed descent from her. Though A'isha is now remembered for her scholarly prestige, she never became a transcendent figure like Fatima. Karen G. Ruffle reports that during her ethnographic work in Hyderabad, she heard accounts of Fatima visiting individuals and communities, appearing at mourning assemblies and visiting believers in dreams and mystical visions.[113] I myself have experienced Fatima in this way. In my psychedelic goddess quest, *Tripping with Allah*, I drink ayahuasca (a hallucinogenic tea used in Amazonian shamanism) and receive a visit from the Lady of Light. My Fatima vision, even as it goes far beyond the pale of responsible "orthodoxy," can be located within a tradition, but I can't recall having ever heard of an A'isha-centered dream or vision. For Shi'i Muslims, Fatima becomes present whenever they gather to mourn for Husayn; she witnesses their grief and collects their tears. Ruffle describes Fatima in the context of Hyderabadi communities as "endowed with a vernacular form of feminine power" (which she names with the Devanagari term *shakti*).[114] Though Muhammad's praises of his daughter in hadith literature as "Master of the Women of Paradise" often exempt the Virgin Mary from her authority, popular tradition also recognizes Fatima with the honorific title Maryam al-Kubra, Greatest Mary.

References to Fatima became prominent in the ideologies of sacred resistance to tyranny that culminated in the Iranian Revolution, exemplified in the revolutionary intellectual 'Ali Shari'ati's book *Fatima Is Fatima*. She can stand outside the state but also become the state, though one wonders how the Fatima who throws her son's blood-soaked clothes onto the throne of God would respond to her appropriation by modern Iranian statecraft. Her power also flows through other channels: the *khamsa* (hand-shaped amulet), ubiquitous throughout Middle Eastern contexts and popular among Muslim and Jewish communities alike as a protection against the evil eye, has been interpreted by many Muslims to represent the hand of Fatima. Neither the charm nor its reading as Fatima's hand find support in canonical texts, but Islam has never been only a shelf of canonical texts. When Fatima's power exists on the ground rather than the page, when she appears most manifest in amulets and at shrines that a certain idea of "orthodoxy" condemns, it only repeats her position in the Muslim social order during her own life.

Writing within the bounds of the critical study of religion, I recognize that people experience their traditions in different ways. Not only might two Muslims disagree as to what constitutes Islam's essence; even if they agree on a reasonable and popular essence, such as *tawhid* (monotheism), they could still disagree over that center's definition and limits. When I'm wearing my academic hat, I resist essences. As a Muslim body in the world, however, I have to locate cores and essences for myself. There have been moments throughout my Muslim experience that Fatima seemed to offer one possible center, whether at a commemoration of her son's martyrdom or in my own encounter with Fatima during an ayahuasca vision. Sometimes I feel as though I could know nothing about Islam apart from Muhammad's daughter Fatima, and that this *muhibb* path might be sufficient.

23

MUHAMMAD THE GRANDFATHER

Ibn 'Abbas narrated:

I saw the Prophet (God bless him and give him peace) in a dream in the middle of the day. He was disheveled and covered in dust. In his hand was a bottle filled with blood.

I said, "My father and mother for you, O Messenger of God. What is this?"

He said, "This is the blood of Husayn and his companions. I have been collecting it all day."

I calculated that time and found that he was killed that day.[115]

Accounts of Muhammad's tenderness toward his grandchildren offer a vital window into the character of the Prophet, and also serve to punctuate the tragedies that fall upon them in the years after his death. As we read of Muhammad kissing his grandson Husayn on the neck, we remember that the tyrants of the world would cast their swords upon that same blessed spot. As we read of the Prophet letting his grandchildren climb on his back as he prayed, we confront their later fates at the hands of his community.

When Syrian governor Mu'awiyya triumphed in his revolt against 'Ali's caliphate, the caliphate changed in two profound ways: the center of caliphal power shifted from Medina to Damascus, and the caliphal office itself became a conventional monarchy, in which Mu'awiyya would be succeeded by his son Yazid.

History does not remember Yazid with kindness. He lived as the prototypical spoiled prince, constantly drunk, making animals race or even fight each other for his amusement, and was reported to spend time with "beardless young men," which in Mediterranean antiquity expressed an implication about one's private life. Yazid was even alleged to have had sex with his favorite drinking buddy, his pet monkey Abu Qays, to whom Yazid also taught the ritual movements of Muslim prayer so that the monkey could lead Friday congregations in the mosque. While Yazid's father, Mu'awiyya, was a polarizing figure—recognized as a Companion of the Prophet, but one who violently opposed 'Ali's caliphate—Yazid made for an even harder sell as a righteous ruler of Muslims. The controversy intensifies as we go further back into Yazid lineage. In the days of the Prophet, Mu'awiyya's parents had done everything in their power to destroy Islam; Yazid's grandfather Abu Sufyan was a prominent clan leader whose supporters harassed and persecuted Muhammad's followers in Mecca, and his grandmother Hind was such a vicious enemy of the Prophet that she chewed the liver of his martyred uncle

Hamza on the battlefield. The two became Muslims only after Muhammad's conquest of Mecca, when it was clear that they had lost.

While 'Ali's elder son, Hasan, waived all rights to the caliphate during the reign of Mu'awiyya, his son Husayn refused to pledge allegiance to Yazid's regime, and found support for resistance against Yazid among the earlier partisans of 'Ali. In 680 CE, Husayn and his small camp met the caliphal army at the plain of Karbala, in what is now Iraq.

When Husayn's flag bearer and half brother, 'Abbas, son of 'Ali and Umm al-Banin, attempted to retrieve water at the Euphrates for their camp's suffering children, the caliphal forces ambushed him and severed both of his arms. 'Abbas continued on his mission, carrying the bag of water with his teeth. Before an enemy arrow put out his eye, 'Abbas saw another arrow pierce his waterskin, causing the water to pour into the sand. Desperate to save his children, Husayn brought his infant 'Ali Asghar before the enemy soldiers, begging them for water, pleading that the children were not combatants and posed no threat. A soldier sent an arrow into the baby's neck.

At the mass murder that we now call the Battle of Karbala, Husayn and his dozens of fighters were slaughtered, decapitated, mutilated, trampled under horses, and left to rot in the sun. The women in Husayn's camp, including his sister Zaynab bint 'Ali and four-year-old daughter Sakina, were forced to march five hundred miles to Damascus while in chains and a state of humiliating exposure, vulnerable to the stares and taunts of men in every town along the route. Leading the way, Yazid's soldiers carried the heads of Husayn and his companions on their spears.

In Shi'i remembrances of Karbala, the event overflows with accounts of selflessness and sacrifice exhibited by Husayn and his companions, and the depraved brutality of the caliphal force. Every detail opens a dozen new chapters for reflection and mourning: 'Abbas at the river, refusing to satisfy his own thirst before bringing water to the children; John bin Huwayy, an elderly Ethiopian Christian who recited praises of Husayn even as the soldiers struck him down; al-Hurr, a warrior in the caliphal army who experienced a change of heart and joined Husayn, knowing that it would cost him his life; a soldier of the caliphate brutally ripping Sakina's earrings; the defiant and devastating speech that Husayn's sister Zaynab gives to Yazid in his palace, perhaps Islam's greatest "truth to power" moment. Shi'i depictions of Karbala also place Husayn's mother, Fatima, at the center of the tragedy. Fatima knows what will happen to her son, and knows that she will not be there to help him. She asks Zaynab to kiss Husayn's neck—where Muhammad kissed him, and where the soldier Shimr would cut him. Though Fatima died more than five decades before the events at Karbala, she is present as a transcendent witness to her son's suffering. We envision all of this happening in front of his mother's eyes.

As a critical moment in the unfolding of divine plan and human salvation, Husayn's stand at Karbala takes on a meaning beyond earthly time. The event represents injustice throughout all of history. Husayn's great-grandson (thus the great-great-great-grandson of the Prophet) and sixth Imam of Shi'i tradition, Ja'far as-Sadiq, would later reportedly name every land Karbala and every day Ashura, the day of the tragedy. We inhabit a world that constantly repeats Karbala.

Karbala becomes a lens through which we read the struggles that mark our own historical moment. Karbala gives a name to every exploitation of undeserved privilege, every act of violence in service of unjust power, every torture of the innocent.

Depending on the gravity that various Muslim historical memories give to the martyrdom of Husayn, Muhammad's own life and mission undergo dramatic reinventions and shifts in meaning. In Sunni treatments of post-prophetic history, Muhammad and his Companions achieved a society distinguished by greater justice and equality than the world had ever seen, or would see again; the rest of human history reflects a decline from that perfect generation. According to Shi'i traditions, the generations of the Companions and their successors did not make a world of perfect unity, peace, and justice, but rather one of chaos, war, and oppression, in which the forces that opposed Muhammad's prophethood during his life stole his legacy, became the dominant order, and rewrote their claim to power in his name. Rather than deny Muhammad, they co-opted him for their own brand, even while cutting the bodies of his family to pieces.

Before I embarked on my pilgrimage to Mecca, a loved one gave me this advice for moments of stress and irritation: "Remember that no one was treated worse by the people of Mecca than the Prophet himself." The mistreatment of Muhammad did not end with the Meccans' acceptance of Islam. Wherever his loved ones traveled, they endured persecution at the hands of those entrusted to defend his legacy; no family was treated worse by Muslims than the Prophet's own family.

24

LIKE THE STARS

Jabir narrated:
    The Messenger of God (God bless him
and give him peace) said, "My Companions
are like the stars. Whoever among them
you use for guidance, you will be rightly
guided."[116]

Neither Sunni nor Shi'i tradition arrived fully formed the
day after Muhammad died. Both traditions developed gradually. In early Islam, not all 'Alids (supporters of 'Ali and his
family) considered themselves members of one community;
nor did the legal schools that now recognize one another as
Sunni always imagine that they shared the same tradition.
The imagined category of Sunni Islam includes Ibn al-'Arabi,
the Andalusian mystic known to his admirers as Shaykh al-
Akbar, the Greatest Shaykh, as well as Ibn Taymiyya, the severe Hanbali jurist whose followers would deride Ibn al-'Arabi
as Shaykh al-Akfar, the Most Unbelieving Shaykh. The net-

works associated with master scholar Ibn Hanbal derided followers of master scholar Abu Hanifa as hopeless innovators, though now the Hanbali and Hanafi schools named after these men can more or less coexist within a shared rubric of "Sunni tradition." Even today, however, not all Sunnis accept all other Sunnis as legitimate members of *ahl al-sunna*. Likewise, Shi'i Islam has been characterized by internal heterogeneity, most prominently in the question of the Imamate, the succession of religious authority from Muhammad to 'Ali and then to 'Ali's sons. Throughout the history of the Shi'i Imamate, we see the death of an Imam provoking factional disputes among his followers over which son would become the next Imam. For the most part, these brief schisms did not become lasting divisions, leaving us today with just three prominent Shi'i traditions: the Ithna Ash'ari (Twelver), who follow a line of twelve infallible Imams; the Isma'ilis, whose line splits from Ithna Ash'ari Shi'ism after the death of the sixth Imam; and Zaydis, named for the completion of their line with the fifth Imam, Husayn's grandson Zayd. However, each of these traditions can in turn be divided into multiple communities, legal and theological schools, and sectarian movements.

Beyond internal diversity, we should also note the overlaps. Early Shi'i authorities, such as Ja'far as-Sadiq, the sixth Imam, appear as reliable transmitters in Sunni hadith collections and teachers of Sunni legal scholars. The Sunni hadith corpus recognizes all of Muhammad's Companions as trustworthy sources, and thus by definition includes both sides of what we retroactively term the Sunni-Shi'i schism.

Many Sunni Muslims as well as non-Muslims would

simply define Sunnis with a quick glance at their name: they are Muslims who follow the Sunna, the sublime customs and precedents established by the Prophet. But the messiness of history and the instability of our categories force me to pause. Not only does this definition raise the problem of how and where we get the Sunna (a question to which Sunni Muslims have given more than one answer), but it risks implying that non-Sunni Muslims don't care about the Sunna. Shi'i Muslims also love the Prophet and strive to follow his Sunna; the issue here is not whether a Muslim holds a stake in the Sunna, but the specific assumptions, commitments, authoritative experts, and traditions of interpretation that determine where a Muslim goes to learn the Sunna.

With these disclaimers in place, we might begin to construct an idea of Sunni Islam by looking at the Companions. The schools of thought that would eventually crystallize into Sunni identity did so in part by sharing an investment in the Companions as authoritative transmitters of the Sunna. In contrast, Shi'i hadith methodology would privilege the holders of the Imamate as unquestionable narrators, and assess Companions on a case-by-case basis to classify them as defenders or opponents of the Prophet's family. For Sunni hadith scholars, the Companions were not only trustworthy for their status as eyewitnesses to the Prophet, but also stood beyond reproach as moral reporters. This means that if a hadith presents itself as A'isha quoting the Prophet, and hadith critics can vet the chain of reporters and confidently state that the hadith does come from A'isha, then we also know that the Prophet said these words. For Sunni hadith scholars, it would have been unthinkable to suggest that perhaps A'isha or any

Companion had lied. In their eyes, to disparage a Companion's integrity would take you out of Sunni Islam—which, for many, would also mean taking you out of legitimate Islam altogether.

This commitment to the Companions—as well as a theoretical conversation in which the scholars had to define "Companion" as a category—produces a particular body of knowledge. But within that archive, there are tensions. The Companions were all authoritative as reporters of what they saw and heard from Muhammad, but nonetheless disagreed with one another. Fourteenth-century scholar al-Zarkashi (d. 1392) compiled various narrations in which A'isha criticized hadiths from the Prophet's male Companions. In one of the more famous examples, A'isha denounces a misogynistic hadith from Abu Hurayra in which the Prophet allegedly placed women, donkeys, and dogs in the same category as interrupters of a man's prayer. A'isha also strongly rejects the popular claim that Muhammad had seen God, deriving her opinion from her personal interpretation of the Qur'an.[117] This positions her against a number of Companions such as Anas and Muhammad's cousin Ibn 'Abbas, who assert that Muhammad had explicitly claimed to have seen his lord either physically or with the "eyes of his heart." In matters of practice, Companions express differing opinions on when they witnessed the Prophet's sayings and actions (one Companion might report an earlier teaching that had since been updated or abrogated without his/her knowledge), or what they perceived as the consequences of a prophetic act (i.e., whether Muhammad intended with a particular action to set a precedent for all cases, or considered it a onetime decision).

Reflecting the subjectivity of his or her own encounter
with Muhammad, each Companion's life can potentially
shine a unique light on the life of the Prophet. Abu Dharr,
for example, stood up against the reigning powers of his
time, including other Companions of Muhammad. He criticized Muslims for their greed in hoarding war plunder and
condemned Mu'awiya for blowing the state's treasury on his
palace, for which the caliph 'Uthman banished him from
Damascus to Medina, where he suffered a second exile and
spent the rest of his days in the desert.[118] Abu Dharr then
freed his Ethiopian Christian slave John, who would die as an
elderly man some three decades later while defending Husayn
at Karbala. In the twentieth century, thinkers such as Iranian
revolutionary philosopher 'Ali Shari'ati saw in Abu Dharr an
Islamic voice of justice and radical resistance, a Companion
of the Prophet who could walk out of seventh-century Arabia
into 1968 Paris. Facing a new age of tyranny and inequality,
many intellectuals found Abu Dharr a helpful star to follow.
For Muslim socialists, Abu Dharr even provided a resource
for locating socialist ideology at the origins of Islam. Similarly, the Prophet's Companion Bilal ibn Rabah (or Bilal
al-Habishi, Bilal the Ethiopian), who accepted Islam while a
slave and later became a leading figure in the original Muslim community, found special prominence in modern Muslim media as an illustration of Islamic antiracism and social
egalitarianism. In the 1970s, when the Nation of Islam re-
oriented itself toward Sunni identity, members were briefly
renamed Bilalians, with the figure of Bilal providing a discursive bridge between the NOI's reading of sacred Black history
and the larger Sunni tradition. Salman al-Farisi (Salman the

Persian), who identified Muhammad as a prophet by intuition and from observing the signs on Muhammad's body, became a major figure in Isma'ili gnosticism and Sufi initiatic lineages. As Sarah Bowen Savant observes in her examination of early post-conquest Iran, Salman's origins also became significant in the formation of Iranian Muslim identities.[119] Ibn 'Abbas might tell you that Muhammad had seen God with his physical eyes and felt the touch of God's own hand, and A'isha might tell you that this claim is absurd at best and blasphemous at worst, but neither of their positions lead you astray. Each Companion opens a path.

In opposing the charge that Islam is uniquely patriarchal and misogynistic, Muslims often present Muhammad's first wife, Khadija, as an example of an empowered Muslim woman, emphasizing her financial independence and the fact that she was older than the Prophet. (Sources give her age as anywhere from twenty-eight to forty at the time that she married Muhammad in his mid-twenties.) She not only hired him to work for her, but also asked for his hand in marriage. Kecia Ali explains that as a strategic counter against Islamophobic media, Muslim thinkers employ the story of Khadija to prove that Muhammad "was not consumed by lust and that he was comfortable with a powerful woman."[120] Likewise, the life of A'isha provides an example of a woman unafraid to challenge and even tease the Prophet, who was also a legal scholar, custodian of oral tradition, and leader of armed resistance against the caliphate. When we focus our attention on any particular Companion, it changes what we see in the Prophet's legacy. Not all stars are equal in brightness, but every star is a star.

This hadith also helps to restore an idea of sacred history that had been injured by the Companions' literally waging war against one another. Ibn 'Abbas did not only disagree with A'isha as to whether Muhammad's eyes could perceive God; he also served in 'Ali's army to oppose her forces at the Battle of the Camel. Sunni hadith methodology would develop to imagine a unity that had never been there. Muhammad comes to us through these broken and grafted histories, his presence mediated by those who had known him and who opposed each other in their claims upon him. To paraphrase Walt Whitman's "Song of Myself," Muhammad can contradict himself, given the multitudes that he contains.

25

MOTHER OF THE BELIEVERS

A'isha narrated:
I wish that when I die, I am completely forgotten.[121]

These words come from Ibn Abi Shayba's *Musannaf* and represent a narration from later in A'isha's life, decades after the deaths of her husband and father. She speaks as an old woman living near their graves but far from the new center of power, rehabilitating her social position as a teacher of the Qur'an and the law, a custodian of sacred memory for younger generations. She remembers her failed revolution, for which she will be blamed and which will be used for centures as proof that women are impulsive, irrational, and destructive. She has retired from a life of political resistance, but the turmoil continues without her. In another narration from the same section of the *Musannaf,* she tells us, "I wish that I was a leaf from this tree."[122]

Examining A'isha's wish to be "completely forgotten,"

Nadia Maria El Cheikh has observed something remarkable in A'isha's precise wording, *nasyan mansiyan*: with this lament, A'isha perfectly repeats the Virgin Mary's words as they appear in the Qur'an. Clinging to the trunk of a palm tree during the pains of her labor, Mary cries, "I wish that I had died before this and that I was completely forgotten" (19:23). El Cheikh reminds us that both Mary and A'isha were falsely accused of sexual misconduct.[123] When given word of her miraculous pregnancy, Mary pleads to the angel, "I am not a whore"; as a sectarian mascot and polemical target generations after her death, A'isha would also undergo branding as a "whore" by her critics.[124] Analyzing the story of Mary as an example of "subversive births" in the Qur'an, Aisha Geissinger notes that in the nineteenth sura, Mary appears "strikingly . . . painfully alone and outcast."[125] A'isha maintains a circle of students in Medina and tells stories of the Prophet to her nephew 'Urwa, but also feels alone and lost, a childless old widow and defeated dissident living under house arrest. A'isha appears to have located her own experience as an echo of the Qur'an's portrayal of Mary as an unjustly scandalized woman, forced by her unwanted role in the fulfillment of the divine plan to withdraw from society and endure her pain alone.

Rather than engage the Sunni-Shi'i schism only as a power struggle in which 'Ali and Abu Bakr become the central contestants, I find it helpful to present the early community's divisions in terms of competing gendered triangles. This borrows from queer theory scholar Eve Sedgwick's notion of triangulation, which calls attention to the role of women's bodies in mediating relationships between men.[126]

Once you start looking for triangulation, you see it everywhere, repeated in countless movies in which an adventuring group of friends includes two men and one woman. The two men are closely bonded, and in turn bonded to the woman: one is her sexual partner, the other her family, a literal or figurative brother. Perhaps the paradigmatic example appears in the original Star Wars trilogy's dynamic among Luke, Han, and Leia; we can also find it in Harry Potter, Ron Weasley, and Hermoine Granger. The story of early Islam can also be read as the story of two triangles. One triangle consists of Muhammad, his daughter, Fatima, and her husband, 'Ali. In the opposing triangle, Muhammad's most important male Companion is Abu Bakr, and their special relationship becomes intensified by Muhammad's marriage to Abu Bakr's daughter, A'isha. The question is not simply whether 'Ali or Abu Bakr will succeed Muhammad in political office, but rather which triangulation should be given priority as a heart of the tradition.

While it appears at first glance that A'isha finds significance in this triangulation entirely as a prop of patriarchy, her body transferring privilege and authority from one powerful man to another, from a different perspective she is the last living member of that triangle, and makes choices that have an impact on Islam forever in innumerable ways.

A'isha was born in Islam, meaning that both of her parents were Muslims at a time when the movement was still new and comprised of adult converts. Her father was a wealthy man whose conversion to Muhammad's movement, otherwise characterized by its appeal to slaves and the poor, had provided valuable support. (In one famous instance, Abu

Bakr bought freedom for a Muslim slave, Bilal ibn Rabah, who suffered torture at the hands of his polytheist owners.) At the age of six or seven, following a revelation by the angel Gabriel, A'isha was contracted in marriage to the Prophet, and joined him as his wife at the age of nine. Because she was the only virgin among the Prophet's wives, her father became known by the honorific Abu Bakr, Father of the Virgin.

Her marriage was characterized both by accounts of tenderness—A'isha tells stories of racing her husband, sitting on his shoulders to watch Ethiopians dance, and sleeping between her husband and the direction of Mecca as he prayed—and stories of sassy exchanges. A'isha did not display the verbal filter with her husband that some would have expected for the Messenger of God. She insults his other wives, deriding Khadija, Fatima's mother, as "a toothless old woman that God replaced with one better."[127] When Companions remark on the beauty of her co-wife Safiyya, A'isha remarks that when she looks at Safiyya, she sees only "a Jew like any other Jew." Also jealous of her co-wife Zaynab, A'isha insults Muhammad's breath whenever he comes back from Zaynab's home. When Muhammad and A'isha contemplate what each of them would do if the other passed away, A'isha snaps that if she died, Muhammad would just sleep with another one of his wives. When Muhammad describes the maidens of paradise, the *hur*, as endowed with eternally renewing virginity, A'isha shouts, "Ouch!"[128] A'isha shrugs at Muhammad's fabulous descriptions of the hur, who never get sick, become pregnant, menstruate, defecate, or blow their noses. The hur boast of their beauty and immortality: "We are the eternal ones, we do not disintegrate; we are the soft ones, we do not cause suffering; we are the pleased ones, we do not get angry. Blessed is he who belongs to us and to whom we belong." A'isha promises that the women of this world will answer, "We are the ones who prayed and you never did, we are the ones who fasted and you never did, we are the ones who made wudu' and you never did, we are the ones who gave charity and you never did." By virtue of their superior claim, A'isha swears by God that the women of earth will win.[129]

At fourteen, A'isha's riding a camel alone with a young man in the community provoked rumor and innuendo that she had been adulterous. A'isha's status remained insecure until God sent a revelation that declared her innocence. When the Prophet welcomed A'isha back and Abu Bakr rejoiced, she defiantly told her father, "Praise to God, not to you or your friend."[130]

By this timeline, A'isha was roughly eighteen years old when her husband, the Messenger of God, passed away in her arms. Because prophets are reportedly buried where they die, what had been A'isha's chamber became Muhammad's grave. Her father succeeded her husband as leader of the Muslim community, but died just two years later, and was buried next to her husband.

A little over twenty years after the deaths of Muhammad and Abu Bakr, Muhammad's cousin and son-in-law, 'Ali, was elected to the caliphate. A'isha and 'Ali shared long-standing enmity; many years earlier, when A'isha was accused of adultery, 'Ali had encouraged the Prophet to divorce her. Disagreeing with 'Ali's lack of interest in pursuing justice against the killers of the previous caliph—and, according to her later critics, desiring to be caliph herself[131]—A'isha and two relatives staged a revolt against 'Ali's regime. Their forces met 'Ali at the Battle of the Camel in Basra. A'isha lost, became 'Ali's prisoner, and was taken back to Medina. She retired from the political sphere, and the textual tradition portrays her as broken by regret, wishing that she could have died long before that day.

Spending the rest of her life under house arrest in Medina, A'isha became a teacher, sharing her legal opinions and interpretations of the Qur'an with young scholars who had not known her husband. To expand her teaching circle, A'isha skillfully navigated legal restraints on interaction between women and men. To loosen the bounds of gender segregation, she instructed men to be "nursed" by her sister—to swallow a few drops of her milk from a dish—which in the logic of milk kinship turned them into her legal relatives and deregulated their interaction. Prominent male Companions such as 'Ali disagreed with A'isha's argument, but she nonetheless abided by her independent ruling. While her take on milk kinship loosened gendered constrictions, her opinions on other issues were employed by men in later eras to opposite effect. Marion Holmes Katz writes that A'isha's reported statement, "If the Messenger of God had lived to see what women have innovated, he would have forbidden them from visiting the masjid, as the women of the Israelites were forbidden," would become "the most widely cited authority statement condemning women's mosque attendance." With A'isha's judgment as their support, male jurists cited women's "swiftly deteriorating moral standards" as grounds for placing further restrictions on their public life than Muhammad had imposed in his own lifetime.[132]

A'isha again became the subject of controversy when she refused to allow the Prophet's grandson, the son of 'Ali and Fatima, Hasan bin 'Ali, to be buried next to her husband in her home. Hasan was instead buried in the neighboring Jannat al-Baqi cemetery. A'isha herself died several years later, having taught well into her late sixties, and was also buried at Jannat al-Baqi. If we accept the hadiths regarding her age, she would have been younger than twenty when Muhammad died, but she survived him by nearly five decades, during which she lived a remarkable life and became a maker of tradition.

Like her husband, A'isha remains an enormously complex figure that can be reimagined and reconstructed in numerous ways. She remains contested terrain in polemical exchanges both between Muslims and non-Muslims and also in conversations within Muslim communities. Anti-Muslim voices erase virtually every detail of her life beyond her wedding, presenting her as forever a scared child bride. Sunni responses focus on narrations of A'isha's married life and the nature of her relationship to the Prophet, as well as her venerable scholarship: in Ibn Hanbal's monumental hadith collection, his *Musnad*, A'isha contributes more than two thousand narrations, making her one of only seven Companions to have reported more than a thousand hadiths and the fourth most prolific reporter overall. In contrast, Shi'i sources tend to portray her as a vindictive enemy of the Prophet's family; a fringe Shi'i media personality, Shaykh Yasser al-Habib, even celebrates her death anniversary (complete with a cake reading *A'isha fi-l-Nar*, 'A'isha is in the Fire) and has accused her of conspiring to murder the Prophet. A'isha connects to so many questions in Islam—how to understand the early history, which sources to trust as reliable, and where we should locate the scholarly tradition that can guide our lives as Muslims—that a Muslim's relationship to A'isha can conceivably change everything about his or her religion. A'isha remains, in this sense, a "founder" of Islam, even if her preference would have been to disappear from our memory.

26

PROPHETIC SEXUALITY

Tawus bin Kaysan narrated:
The Prophet (God bless him and give him peace) was given the power of forty or forty-five men in sexual intercourse.[133]

Muhammad liked sex, and he apparently had a lot of it. The Companion Anas recalls that Muhammad was the greatest of men in "generosity, courage, fierceness, and frequency of intercourse."[134] For early Muslim communities, his sexuality was nothing short of miraculous. Throughout canonical hadith collections and the *dala'il al-nabuwwa* ("proofs of prophethood") literary genre, in which Muslim scholars compiled reports of Muhammad's extraordinary nature to confirm his prophetic station, we find accounts of Muhammad possessing superhuman sexual vigor. The hadith corpus tells us in varying reports that his sex drive equaled that of twenty or thirty men or sometimes forty or fifty, and that in the years that he practiced plural marriage (when he was in his fifties and sixties), he had sex with each of his wives every night. In one tradition, Gabriel even brings Muhammad a bucket of food that enhances his performance.[135] While the hadith literature often describes paradise in highly sexualized terms, with penises never becoming soft and orgasms lasting for centuries, Muhammad's own sex afterlife remains privileged: in one narration, he tells A'isha that God had married him in the next world to the sister of Moses, the wife of Pharaoh, and the Virgin Mary.[136]

Reading pamphlets and Intro to Islam literature early in my teen conversion, I never encountered these canonical boasts of Muhammad's sexuality; instead, I learned more diplomatic treatments of his sex life. Muhammad did not marry multiple women out of an interest in sex, these authors insisted: rather, in a society based on linkages of tribe and clan, his marriages performed a necessary alliance-building service in the formation of a new Muslim society. Additionally, his marriages set precedents for Muslim men, since he married women that they might not have sought as partners: Jewish and Christian women, for example, or widows with children of their own, or women older than himself. Finally, the authors reminded me that Muhammad practiced monogamy in his marriage to Khadija, never engaging in plural marriage until after her death. Accompanied by reminders that the Qur'an discourages (without prohibiting) polygamy, Muhammad's exclusive devotion to Khadija demonstrated that Muhammad felt the kind of "soul mate" connection with Khadija that we often prioritize in modern ideas of marriage, and that Muhammad personally viewed monogamy as the most developed marital arrangement.

How did things change? Ze'ev Maghen observes the first
shift taking place in medieval Islam, after Muslim thinkers'
engagement with Greek philosophy had become so embedded
in the tradition that even the staunchest anti-philosophers such
as Ibn Taymiyya could not avoid it. In this period, Maghen
notes, we see some movement toward deemphasizing prophetic sexuality, observable in treatments of Zaynab, who di-
vorced Muhammad's adopted son Zayd and then married the
Prophet. The notion that Muhammad felt an intense physical
attraction toward Zaynab when she was still married to Zayd
became problematic to later Muslim scholars, who carefully
navigated around the issue.[137] An even more profound transformation of Muslim thought occurred in modernity, when
nearly the entire world's Muslim population fell under colonial
domination by various European empires. European colonial-
ism came with Christian missionary projects and a globalizing
regime that promoted new ways of thinking about bodies. Informed by Christian traditions of celibacy and the model of
Christ as apparently uninterested in sex, the operative assumption seems to be that if Muhammad loved sexual intercourse,
he could not have been genuinely spiritual. Between Christian
evangelists' presentation of a celibate, seemingly asexual Christ
as the pinnacle of spiritual development, Cartesian binary op-
positions of soul versus body, post-Enlightenment notions of
disembodied rationality, racializing Orientalist depictions of
Muslim men as lascivious harem lords, and the broader sexual milieu of Victorian culture in the nineteenth century, the
sexuality that had once proven Muhammad's prophethood became a potential mark against him.

Anti-Muslim writers increasingly used Muhammad's

sexuality as a weapon to portray Islam as monstrous and barbaric, though they differed in the points that they found most objectionable. Nineteenth-century American writers, more urgently concerned with the threat of polygamous Mormons than Muslims, found Muhammad's chief offense to have been his practice of plural marriage. In contrast, writers at the end of the twentieth century zoomed in on A'isha's young age to portray Muhammad as a pedophile. Reading the Prophet's attackers across multiple historical contexts, we find that while Muhammad always has opponents, the resources and strategies that they find useful against him remain in flux. In one age, Christian writers disparaged Muhammad's claims of divine revelation by insisting that he was possessed by demons; in a later era, Islamophobes diagnosed Muhammad as prone to seizures and mental illness, discrediting him through contemporary diagnostical terms and ableist prejudices rather than claims of a dark supernatural power.

These changing rules also apply to Muhammad's defenders. Modern Muslim intellectuals and pamphleteers have advocated for Muhammad on a radically different terrain than that of the classical dala'il writers. Rather than celebrate a prophet who loved sex, they found discomfort in accounts of Muhammad's passion, and sought to reconstruct Muhammad as what Maghen terms a "quasi-Christ-like figure" and "flaccid philosopher-king."[138] The question of sex therefore becomes a worthy introduction to Muhammad for the ways that it highlights historical change. Our diverse readings of Muhammad's flesh render his body as another text, bringing with it all of the problems of texts.

27

THE A'ISHA QUESTION

A'isha narrated:
   The Messenger of God (God bless him and give him peace) married me when I was a girl of six years old, and he consummated with me when I was a girl of nine years old.[139]

After reading Denise Spellberg's discussion of A'isha in her *Politics, Gender, and the Islamic Past,* one of my students remarked that the book was undermined by Spellberg's "excessive feminism." Because Spellberg focused on ways that medieval Muslim historians mapped their constructions of gender upon the figure of A'isha, writing their own gendered prejudices and values into the significance that they saw in A'isha's life, this student argued that Spellberg had unfairly imposed "modern" and "Western" assumptions and values onto premodern and non-Western texts.

While questioning how one can precisely measure feminism to determine the point at which it becomes "excessive," I had to recognize the student's concern. Whenever we read the sacred past, we do so with our present eyes, and our own historical moment will inevitably inform the questions that we ask of our sources. Spellberg's scholarship on A'isha absolutely reflects an expression of its own world, just as the premodern texts she examines represent their world. Even deciding to write about A'isha in the first place, regardless of the specific author's intentions, reflects a time and place in which A'isha matters a great deal to significant numbers of people. Considering the importance of Spellberg's contribution, I wish that we had similar books on numerous other Companions of the Prophet: there is not yet a definitive study in this vein on 'Ali, Fatima, Khadija, Abu Bakr, Bilal, or Salman al-Farisi. Why A'isha? She is also the only Companion whose life has inspired multiple prominent novels by non-Muslim authors, and that she is far and away the Companion most likely to appear in anti-Muslim cartoons that depict the Prophet. In a search for Muhammad images online, the first page of hits will often provide not only classical Persian miniatures of Muhammad's mystical ascension, but also drawings of A'isha as a terrified or helplessly unaware child, a victim captive to the Prophet—who himself appears in these images as a leering, depraved, and sometimes fanged predator.

According to narrations in the Six Books canon attributed to A'isha herself, her marriage to the Prophet was contracted when she was six years old, and she began to live with the Prophet as his wife when she was nine. I do not have the confidence of an eyewitness in making a claim on their marriage. Some Muslims have reexamined traditional timelines to argue that A'isha must have been in her late teens when she married the Prophet. Hadith skeptics can dismiss the historical reliability of troubling narrations, but, as Kecia Ali points out, such a move comes with the price of treating even the most canonical of Sunni Islam's Six Books canon, Bukhari's *Sahih*, as unreliable.[140] Some Muslims are more willing to pay that price than others; the problem of A'isha's age could read as primarily a Sunni problem, since A'isha is the source for her own age and Shi'i hadith scholars do not face the same obligation to accept A'isha as a reliable narrator. Critically engaging the hadith corpus also calls us to question the possible sectarianism in Sunni sources that portray A'isha as a childlike figure, since this portrayal accompanies a virtual silence regarding Fatima's childhood. Pernilla Myrne has suggested that the hadiths' highlighting of young A'isha and erasure of young Fatima serve to privilege A'isha as almost more "daughterly" in relation to Muhammad than his actual daughter, thereby doubling the prestige for Sunni tradition's feminine ideal over her Shi'i counterpart.[141]

Historicity aside, A'isha's marriage has become an increasingly sensitive issue in conversations both inside and outside Muslim communities, as anti-Muslim voices have increasingly focused on A'isha as a means of pathologizing Muhammad—and, by extension, all Muslim men. There is no neutral way of talking about A'isha. In the classroom, A'isha's life provokes a tension between my feminism and my antiracist commitments. I will not resort to pious apologetics for ways that gender and sexuality were constructed in the seventh century CE; that's not my job. Nor is it my sense that a simple "Things were different in that time" should end the conversation. Nonetheless, presenting sexuality as a cultural construct does point to the instability of our own judgments and the norms that we presume to be universal.

In the earliest American-authored biography of Muhammad, George Bush (1796–1859, also a distant relative of the presidents) does not hold A'isha's age against him, acknowledging her youth only with a remark on "the surprising physical precocity peculiar to an eastern climate." Washington Irving (1783–1859) similarly notes that while A'isha married young, "the female form is wonderfully precocious in the quickening climates of the east," and John Davenport (1789–1877) describes A'isha as Abu Bakr's "young and beautiful daughter."[142] They noted that A'isha had married at an unusually young age, but her age wasn't so unusual as to be unthinkable in their world.

As Nicholas L. Syrett points out in his history of American child marriage, the meaning of age has changed dramatically even within the relatively narrow frame of American history. Prior to our contemporary reliance on birth certificates, many Americans did not know their precise ages, which meant that there was no magical birthday at which a person suddenly passed from child into consenting adult. Before our school systems arranged children into distinct grades that were organized by age, a child's exact age could not have had the same significance for defining his or her social identity or presumed cognitive abilities. Particularly in rural environments, children became adults when they could perform the tasks expected of adults: when you were grown enough to work the field, you worked the field; when you were grown enough to have babies, you had babies. From the beginnings of the colonial period, in which children could marry at the age of seven and Catholic law in French and Spanish colonies placed the minimum age of marriage at eleven for girls and thirteen for boys, throughout the nineteenth century and into the twentieth, child marriage remained considerably widespread.[143]

In early American history, Syrett argues, the regulation of child marriage had less to do with children's welfare than with parents guarding their estates and ensuring a girl's successful transfer from her father's control to her husband's. As American ideas of childhood changed over the course of the nineteenth century and opposition to child marriage escalated, representations of child marriage sometimes involved racist tropes. In the 1868 novel *The Child Wife* (authored by a man who married a fifteen-year-old), the male protagonist is derided for marrying a fourteen-year-old girl with the insult "You are turning Turk!"[144] Writers condemned child marriage in the "uncivilized" American South through unflattering comparisons to "dark" and "heathen" lands such as Turkey, China, and India.[145] It was only in the later twentieth century, after decades of changing American notions of childhood and activism against child marriage, not to mention the emergence of "pedophilia" as a diagnostical category (which originated in 1886), that non-Muslim writers began calling attention to A'isha as a child bride and sometimes applying the new term *pedophile* to the Prophet. It was likewise in this period that Muslim writers began to treat A'isha's age at her marriage as something to defend, contextualize, or deny. Even so, Spellberg's study of A'isha's image in classical sources, published in 1994, does not acknowledge the "pedophilia" trope in contemporary discussions of A'isha. Though Spellberg does discuss A'isha's age, her silence is telling. Scholars rarely pass up the chance to connect their studies of premodern texts to modern controversies; this is part of how we claim "real world" relevance for our work in dusty archives. But as late as the 1990s, A'isha's age was not yet firmly established as a necessary point of anti-Muslim arguments.

None of this means that the A'isha question is not worth our time. It does mean acknowledging that history looms over our conversations. While discussing A'isha's marriage, I cannot help but remain mindful of the palpable Islamophobia on American college campuses. My first time talking about A'isha in a classroom setting was during my doctoral work at the University of North Carolina at Chapel Hill, in the same semester that three young members of the local community were murdered within a few miles of the campus. For Muslims whose communities were already wounded by countless threats, intimidations, physical attacks, acts of vandalism, and the mainstreaming of anti-Muslim hate speech in American media, the Chapel Hill tragedy became a national and international trauma. My roster of students included several of the victims' friends. Amid ongoing conversations about Islamophobia and the ways in which our campus sadly became a laboratory for examining the kinds of prejudice and violence that we discussed in class, the air in the room changed when A'isha's age became a topic. I am wary of the hard reality that what students retain or forget after leaving the classroom is not entirely subject to my will; a year after taking my course, it's possible that a student might jettison all of the nuance and critical theorizing and remember only that Muhammad married a child. While my solution is not to omit challenging elements of the prophetic biography (indeed, it's only worse when a teacher edits history and students later uncover the "forbidden secrets" on their own), my academic position also includes a commitment to the classroom being a safe space both in terms of gender and race.

Without denying anyone's right to feel personal difficulty with A'isha's life, I also want my students to examine their own positions and the ways in which all of our concepts, including sexuality and childhood, reflect social constructions that change over time, rather than universal truths and self-evident facts of nature. In resistance to racism and Islamophobia, and also in accordance with what it means as academics to be careful with our terms, we can examine the polemical charge that Muhammad was a "pedophile" and the problem of reading modern diagnostical concepts into premodern sources. Meanwhile, recognizing the widespread crisis of American college campuses as rape cultures, I would not carelessly and pseudo-critically dismiss consent, as one scholar had, as a modern "fetish." I do not know all of my students' experiences. Subjecting A'isha's life to our interrogation, I potentially risk interrogating students about their own lives.

Should A'isha's biography come with a trigger warning, or does this grant some power to well-funded, networked, and institutionally privileged forces of anti-Muslim bigotry and white supremacy? Is it possible to confess personal difficulty when facing the A'isha question without indulging Islamophobia? Can competing commitments be satisfied in one move? After several attempts at the A'isha conversation, I don't have supreme confidence that I've ever done it right. It sometimes feels that I've leaned too hard in one direction, for which I'd compensate next time by leaning on the other side. For my student who had raised objections to Spellberg's "excessive feminism," who happened to be a white non-Muslim man, none of this posed a serious problem. I don't know everything about the world that he inhabits, but he might have the option of simply throwing out both the interest in gender and sensitivity to Islamophobia and going on with his life. Not everyone is so advantaged.

28

MUHAMMAD THE LAWGIVER

Abu Hurayra narrated:
  The Messenger of God (God bless him
and give him peace) said, "Avoid the *hudud*
when you find uncertainty with it."[146]

Though this meaning does not appear with such legal preci-
sion in the Qur'an, Muslim jurists would eventually come to
define the *hudud* (plural of *hadd*, "limit") as prohibited acts
with specific and nonnegotiable punishments commanded
by God.[147] Through the lens of legal tradition, Muhammad's
command to avoid the hudud in the case of uncertainties
would mean that a judge should search for any conceivable
way of refraining from severe punishment whenever possible. In a famous case examined by Scott C. Lucas, a man
came to Muhammad and confessed that he had committed
fornication, which warranted a hadd punishment of death.
Desperate to spare the man's life, the Prophet gave him multiple outs, asking repeatedly, "Perhaps you only kissed her?"

until finally accepting his confessions and carrying out the penalty. For Lucas, a "contrapuntal reading" of the episode provides opportunities to consider the ethical dimensions of Islamic law and even argue against the validity of stoning as a punishment for illicit sex.[148]

In 1935, when the new building housing the Supreme Court of the United States was completed, its north wall frieze presented eighteen of history's greatest legislators. The figures stand in chronological order, starting with Menes and Hammurabi, moving on to biblical prophets Moses and Solomon and Greek figures Lycurgus, Solon, and Draco, followed by Confucius, and progressing through Western history to Napoleon. Standing between Justinian and Charlemagne, we find the frieze's last lawgiver from outside Europe and America: Muhammad. Some Muslims found the Prophet's portrayal inappropriate; not only would many find discomfort with the visual depiction of Muhammad, but the frieze also enforces popular Orientalist cliches by depicting Muhammad with an open Qur'an in one hand and a sword in the other. Despite protests from Muslim civic organizations in recent decades, Muhammad remains in the frieze today. The Supreme Court's official website now offers disclaimers stating that the image was a well-intended tribute, that it does not actually resemble Muhammad, and that Muslims generally don't like images of the Prophet.

Objections aside, the engraving of Muhammad's face into the Supreme Court of the United States of America points to a change in broader American perceptions of Muhammad (and his law) between 1935 and our present. In FDR's America, Jim Crow ruled throughout the South and Japanese Americans were on the verge of being incarcerated in internment camps. America's well-funded, networked, and highly politicized Islamophobia industry, however, was still half a century from development into its recognizable form; in the 1930s, there were no anti-Muslim activists to scream "creeping shari'a" over the Supreme Court's tribute to Islamic law.

Contrary to both the Supreme Court frieze and contemporary anti-shari'a hysteria, however, Muhammad did not provide the world with his own immutable code of law. As the head of something that we could cautiously describe as a state, he did implement policies regarding such topics as taxation, punishment for crimes, family law, and the rights of religious minorities. Muhammad's personal precedent, his Sunna, also holds the status of divine revelation and thus operates with lawgiving power. But Muhammad did not come down from the mountain with a detailed and comprehensive legal system. Nor did the authoritative generation of Muhammad's Companions act as though there was a singular model of an Islamic state with a divinely revealed legal code to regulate all of its policies. The early caliphates did not impose a holistic "Islamic law" upon newly conquered Sasanian and Byzantine territories, but rather incorporated those territories' preexisting models.

Early in Islam's history, Muslims encountered issues that had not been addressed by the Qur'an or Muhammad. A popular example would be the question of a grandmother's inheritance. Without a clear command from the Qur'an or reported precedent from Muhammad's lifetime, legal experts had to employ analogical reasoning to find an answer. Most of what we call Islamic law, therefore, comes neither from the Qur'an nor the Sunna but from centuries of jurists' elaboration. Like translators rendering a text into new languages, they understood their effort to render sacred sources into a coherent system of earthly law as at least partly a project of speculation. While Muslims conceive of shari'a (literally meaning "road" or "way") as a divine revelation, what Muslims actually follow is *fiqh*, jurisprudence, the thoroughly human effort to understand and implement shari'a.

Muslim intellectuals' development of fiqh was often regional in nature: scholars in Medina would have reached different conclusions on certain questions than scholars in Basra. These local networks contributed to the formation of numerous competing schools that often disagreed with one another. While early scholars agreed that the Qur'an forbade the consumption of grape-based wine, for example, they disagreed as to whether this prohibition applied to all intoxicants. While the Maliki school held that the Qur'an's mention of *khamr* referred to any intoxicating drink, early Hanafis objected that the prohibition applied only to fermented grape juice. The school's namesake, Abu Hanifa, allowed the consumption of non-grape-based intoxicants, as long as the consumer avoided getting drunk, but his own school eventually overruled him and moved toward conformity with the Maliki position.[149] The legal conversation over drugs became increasingly complex when Muslim scholars encountered new substances, such as nonfermented drinks that had dramatic effects on their consumers' personalities (such as coffee) and intoxicants that did not primarily come in beverage form (such as cannabis). The schools also offered differing opinions on the legal consequences of *liwat*, anal sex between men; while they agreed that it was a prohibited act, they disagreed about its nature and penalty. Because the Hanafis did not regard liwat as a form of fornication (for the Hanafis, fornication was defined strictly by the illicit penetration of a vagina by a penis), they did not treat anal sex between men as subject to a divinely revealed punishment, and therefore left the matter up to judges' personal discretion.[150]

In 1265, Malik az-Zahir Baybars, sultan of the Mamluk state, introduced a reform that would leave a lasting impact on Muslim legal tradition forever: rather than authorize only one school and exclude others, he appointed chief judges from four schools (Hanbali, Hanafi, Maliki, and Shafi'i), theoretically granting them equal authority.[151] This policy determined the four schools that would hold "mainstream" status even into our present, establishing them as shareholders in a mutual "Sunni" legal tradition. It also further defined and enforced a Sunni-Shi'i border by not including the Ja'fari school, named for the sixth Shi'i Imam, the Prophet's great-great-great-grandson Ja'far as-Sadiq. The establishment of four imperially supported schools achieved both an expansion and constriction of legal possibilities, denying that there could be only one authentic school of law while excluding other Sunni schools and Shi'i law as conceivably "mainstream."

In modern legal discourses, we have seen an escalation of old tensions between advocates of *taqlid*, the concept of faithful adherence to one legal school or authority, and *ijtihad*, independent reasoning without allegiance to a school. Coming from the same j-h-d root as jihad, ijtihad implies an arduous intellectual struggle with textual tradition. In the twelfth century CE, Almohad caliph 'Abd al-Mu'min bin 'Ali so vehemently opposed taqlid as "blind" adherence to the legal schools that he ordered the burning of their jurisprudential texts.[152] In the nineteenth and twentieth centuries, ijtihad became a frequent theme of revivalist and reformist discourses, as Muslim thinkers sought to return to the righteous ways of the earliest Muslim community or reconcile Islamic tradition with modern rationality (and many Muslims saw these two projects as fundamentally compatible). Supporters of ijtihad represent a wide ideological spectrum: hard-line Saudi clerics who rule that women cannot drive cars and progressive reformists who hold that women can lead men in congregational prayer might appear to represent polar opposites in contemporary Muslim thought, but both could claim ijtihad as the basis for their positions. Enabling Muslim thinkers to reconfigure or even sidestep the legal tradition and draw on only the Qur'an and Sunna to guide their judgment, ijtihad thus can lead to both a scripturalist "fundamentalism" and also a kind of post-Enlightenment rationalist individualism.

By calling attention to diversity among (and within) the schools, and to the historical contexts in which classical legal opinions emerged, we can ask new questions of and conceivably find new answers in Muslim legal tradition. In her masterful comparative study of sexual violence as a legal concept between the Hanafi and Maliki schools, Hina Azam confronts the limits of the tradition for answering modern needs, but adds that these schools did not reach their conclusions simply through the Qur'an and Sunna. Rather, "they each reflect an array of socially and culturally rooted ideas about the nature of legal agency, gender, and sexuality." The classical jurists were human beings inhabiting a world, who engaged

sacred law through the lenses that their world provided. For
Azam, recognizing this serves to unfreeze the tradition:

> Studying the history of Islamic laws concerning sex-
> ual violence reveals creativity as much as it reveals
> constraint, and encourages us to regard the interpre-
> tation of Islamic moral law more as an ongoing pro-
> cess than as a predetermined or static collection of
> doctrines and directives.[153]

At the turn of the twentieth century, Muslim jurists debated the permissibility of mass-printing copies of the Qur'an,
of performing the call to prayer with microphones, and of
using the telegraph. Near the end of the twentieth century,
Ayatollah Khomeini, supreme leader of the Islamic Republic
of Iran, ruled that sex-reassignment surgery for transgender
individuals was Islamically acceptable. Today, scholars give
fatwas (nonbinding legal opinions) as to whether one needs to
be in a state of ritual purity before using a Qur'an phone app.
Islamic legal tradition has never existed as an uncarved block
incapable of change, but rather survives as an ongoing process of mediation, interpretation, and negotiation. Contemporary scholars invested in reform still look to the Prophet as
a spiritual and ethical center for legal thought, but recognize
that their conversation about the purpose, principles, sources,
methods, and limits of Islamic law is never a one-on-one encounter with the Prophet alone.

29

DELEUZIAN FINGERNAILS

Bara' bin Zayd narrated:
    The Prophet (God bless him and give him peace) was in the house of Umm Sulaym on a mat, and he sweated. When the Messenger of God woke up, Umm Sulaym was rubbing the sweat. He said, "O Umm Sulaym, what are you doing?" She said, "I take this for the *baraka* that comes from you."[154]

In his *Tabaqat*, ninth-century hadith scholar Ibn Sa'd provides an account of the caliph Mu'awiya ordering that when he dies, he is to be buried with Muhammad's hairs and fingernail clippings, placed in his mouth and nose, for the *baraka* in these items.[155] Even hadith master Ibn Hanbal, whose modern heirs are seen as passionately opposed to material relics, owned three hairs of the Prophet, and asked to be buried with them in his mouth and on his eyes.

    To introduce Muhammad with a discussion of baraka—a concept not immediately recognizable in popular non-Muslim imaginations without translation, though translation might not be fully possible—forces a rethinking of Islam's assumed center and the structure by which Islam undergoes ordering by many Muslims and non-Muslims alike. We're not starting with the Qur'an, its theology, law, or politics. Naming an alternative center and point of entry into the Muhammadi rhizome, we start with baraka, often clumsily rendered in English as "blessings."

Baraka might be of particular salience for engaging questions of religion more broadly in light of twentieth-century philosopher Gilles Deleuze. Throughout the small but growing body of literature that places Deleuzian thought in conversation with "religion"—which tends to really mean "theology" in these projects, and almost exclusively Euro-American Christian theology at that—we encounter the suggestion that for Deleuze, the meaningful problem is not exactly theism, but transcendence, the attractions of our hopes and fears to imaginary worlds outside our own. To believe in an unseen creator god up/out there is to take our imaginations away from lived reality. Deleuzian scholars interested in theological openings have suggested rethinking theology in terms of immanence: the problem is not God but rather God's otherworldliness.[156] Such scholars, searching for God in this world, are not typically interested in Muslim contexts, which would refer us to a different set of traditions, resources, and tensions.

Informed by Deleuze, we can observe two broad tendencies in the ways that Muslims have historically conceptualized baraka, one emphasizing transcendence, the other immanence. I describe them as "tendencies" in order to avoid the assumption of a zero-sum dualism in which every Muslim who takes part in one must be imagined to absolutely reject the other, or the presence of one requires the absence and denial of the other. These tendencies are not mutually exclusive or necessarily incompatible, though in any given articulation of baraka, we might find one prioritized over the other.

The tendency toward transcendence presents baraka chiefly as an economy of credits that God distributes as reward for obedience. Baraka enters the world from above in a downward flow. God commands that you perform certain acts, names other acts as not exactly required but still worthy of reward, and also marks off a category of actions as expressly forbidden. For performing the actions that God requires or likes, as well as avoiding the actions that God prohibits (these abstentions themselves counting as good acts), you earn baraka points. Any assertion that a particular act earns someone baraka needs the qualification of insha'Allah, "if God wills," because God alone remains the owner and distributor of baraka and ultimately gives as much baraka as he wants, when and where he wants, to whom he wants.

In recognition of God's absolute power over baraka's flows and stoppages, Muslims can specifically ask God for baraka. Muhammad himself prayed for baraka, and to imitate these prayers—repeating Muhammad's words, and performing these prayers in the same manners and contexts in which Muhammad performed them—can achieve not only the acquisition of baraka via a direct request to God, but also the baraka earned by following the specific practice of the Prophet. As Muhammad, too, depends on God for baraka, it is additionally a meritorious act for Muslims to pray that

God sends baraka upon the Prophet—both as *sunna*, meaning that Muhammad personally authorized and encouraged Muslims to do so, and *fard*, meaning that this practice even appears within required actions: In each of the five mandated daily prayers, the portion spent in a sitting position (*julus*) includes a silent appeal, "Give/do baraka to Muhammad and the family of Muhammad as you gave/did baraka to Abraham and the family of Abraham" (*wa barik 'ala Muhammadin wa 'ala ali Muhammadin kama barakta 'ala Ibrahima wa 'ala ali Ibrahima*). Muslim prayers for baraka extend not only to the Prophet and his family, but the rest of our fellow humans: everywhere in what we call "the Muslim world," Muslims greet each other with "Peace be upon you, and the mercy of God and his baraka" (*As-salamu alaikum wa rahmatullahi wa barakatahuh*).

When Muslims conceptualize baraka with an emphasis on transcendence, translating the word into English as "blessings" is less of a problem. God is the maker, owner, and distributor of blessings. But the tradition offers another model for thinking about baraka, one in which baraka appears less as an economy of points or credits that God hands out and more as an energy field that becomes accessible in the world. This model starts with Muhammad's body, the conduit through which baraka flows to other bodies.

The most obvious flow of baraka through Muhammad's body into the world would be the Qur'an itself, the revelation of which occurs as a physical event that produces observable signs in Muhammad's body—sweating, a dramatic increase in body weight, etc.—and becomes accessible to the rest of humankind exclusively through its recitation from

Muhammad's own lips. The Qur'an also describes itself as *mubarak*, a site or object of baraka (6:92, 6:155).

Imagining Muhammad's body as a conduit of baraka does not undo baraka's relationship to transcendence, especially in his own lifetime, as baraka enhances his own authority. In the post-Muhammad Islam, however, this way of thinking about baraka as a flow between bodies threatens to decentralize the tradition, scattering baraka in shrines and relics as a force that can be located in physical space. While this relation of baraka to material things does not exactly deny the idea of Islam as a textually driven tradition, shrines do provide a possible alternative to the Islamic sciences of theology and law, as well as the trained professional scholars whom we trust to regulate them.

How did the idea of baraka as a flow between bodies emerge? In his description of *ziyarat*, the historically popular practice of visiting holy peoples' tombs with belief that such sites operate as locii of baraka, Shahab Ahmed asserts, "The idea of the cosmic economy of *barakah* proceeds directly from the Neo-Platonic logic of emanation that underpins the Avicennan cosmos."[157] This attribution of a singular and arborescent genealogy for baraka serves Ahmed's broader narrative (establishing philosophy's impact as fully "Islamic" in the daily lives of Muslims), but erases the complexity of Muslim lives on the ground—particularly when considering the vast scope of his project, covering what he terms the "Balkans-to-Bengal complex." Ahmed cautions that we should not read him as suggesting that norms and ideas move exclusively from "high" to "low" culture, advising that we "should keep our eyes open not only for 'trickle down' but also for 'trickle up,'" but does not heed his own counsel in the case of baraka.[158] A less arborescent view of baraka would not require that this notion "proceeds directly" from *any* singular source. Rather, when we consider the internal heterogeneities that characterize Ahmed's "Balkans-to-Bengal complex" and take into account his notion of the "Pre-Text of Revelation"— the truth upon which the revelation's truth depends, which necessarily differs among Muslims of varying orientations— we become open to baraka as something more rhizomatic, a notion of baraka that defies genealogy. As Islam spread—or, to put it more precisely, as *people* decided that these resources were useful for navigating their own lives and thus adopted these resources as their own—they not only inherited genealogies but contributed to them. This means that baraka does not have a singular set of roots.

Considering individuals and communities in various settings that consciously came to accept the Qur'an as true, let's acknowledge that they did so without erasing their prior notions of how the world worked and without becoming blank slates that passively received a new system. Rather, the Qur'an demonstrated itself as true in accordance with what they already accepted as true; it proved its truth within their own pre-Islamic frames of reference. When Deleuze and Guattari state that "in certain regions of Senegal, Islam superimposes a plane of subordination on the old plane of connotation of animist values,"[159] or when Shahab Ahmed asserts that baraka "proceeds directly" from Neo-Platonism's Islamic legacy, their arborescent claims leave out much of what's happening on (in) the ground. One genealogy of baraka can certainly reflect Neo-Platonist roots (not only for Muslims, but also in Jewish traditions as observed in Kabbala's emanationist treatments of berakhah), but this is not baraka's only lineage. When we look closely at the ways in which baraka appears as a beneficent energy or force that can be transmitted between bodies and inanimate objects, it reads as a concept that could easily find analogues in settings that have encountered neither Islam nor Neo-Platonism. Different locales can have their own answers to baraka, and these concepts become tangled in one another. If the first Muslim converts in the steppes of Central Asia or mountain villages in Iran or the deserts of the Sudan held on to their local ideas of special energies and forces as they learned about baraka, incorporating baraka into their pre-conversion modes of engaging the world, then baraka's history is not reducible to a singular Avicennan tree with Neo-Platonist roots. Rather, baraka emerges rhizomatically, characterized by multiplicities and local connections. Baraka does not have any origin that can be *the* origin. It is not necessary that all of the local articulations of baraka and the people or sites that appear as local conduits of baraka reflect the same intellectual transmission. The Chinese Muslim notion of bairekati/bailekati, signifying concepts such as "blessing," "happiness," "luck," and "good omen,"[160] for which people paste scraps of the Ka'ba's cloth cover (kiswa) between the eyebrows of their deceased loved ones in the practice of zhan bairekati,[161] might reflect a different set of ingredients than the experience of baraka produced in other Muslim contexts.

Learning about baraka within the particularities of my own experience, I came to perceive baraka not as a force, but the Force, conceptualizing baraka through an imagination informed by the Star Wars universe. If I express this notion of baraka as the Force to other individuals who had deeply internalized the mythos of Star Wars, and it contributes to their understanding of baraka, which then leads them to communicate the idea of baraka in this way, then we have produced a new genealogy and can even claim that baraka "proceeds directly" from a Hollywood space fantasy franchise.

*

The historical tension between transcendent and immanent conceptions of baraka plays out on a small brown field in the holy city of Medina, in the modern kingdom of Saudi Arabia: Jannat al-Baqi, the cemetery neighboring the Prophet's Masjid. The cemetery holds a number of Muhammad's most prominent Companions and family members, as well as famed Muslims of later generations. Early sources even provide room to speculate that Muhammad himself was buried in this cemetery, rather than in his masjid.[162]

In the Ottoman era, the culture of shrines and pilgrimage to local holy places was entirely part of what Muslims then recognized as "mainstream" and "orthodox" Islam. The Ottoman Empire, though officially Sunni, did not suppress Shi'i veneration of holy sites such as Karbala and Najaf, and Sunni and Shi'i Muslims alike performed pilgrimage to special tombs. But in the Hijaz region that includes Mecca and Medina, the end of the eighteenth century saw a Sunni revivalist movement, led by scholar Muhammad ibn 'Abd al-Wahhab (1703–1792), that condemned popular Muslim practices at graves as idolatrous betrayals of the Prophet's authentic practice. Roughly a decade after Ibn 'Abd al-Wahhab's death, adherents to his ideology (now pejoratively labeled "Wahhabism") invaded Karbala, slaughtered as many as five thousand people, destroyed the dome that covered the tomb of the Prophet's grandson Husayn, and plundered the shrine's treasures of gold, carpets, and cash. The so-called Wahhabiyya also took Mecca and Medina, in the process destroying domes, burning unacceptable books, and looting. They flattened Jannat al-Baqi and nearly tore down the dome over the Prophet's own masjid, but decided against it after men fell to their deaths early in the process. With the Ottoman reconquest of the holy cities, the shrines in Jannat al-Baqi were restored. Photographs from the nineteenth century preserve communal memory of the domed shrines that were once sprinkled across Jannat al-Baqi.

The 1920s saw the disintegration of the Ottoman Empire. Soon after, the Ottoman vision of orthodoxy would undergo erasure from the Arabian Peninsula. In 1926, following the success of an alliance between Ibn Sa'ud and followers of Ibn 'Abd al-Wahhab that led to the formation of a nascent Saudi state, Jannat al-Baqi's landscape was again flattened, the shrines razed. In the tearing down of these structures, the graves that many Muslims had regarded as holy pilgrimage sites were marked only with uninscribed stones, rendered virtually anonymous beyond the memories of those who could recall where specific domed shrines had once stood. In the Saudi state's position, the bodies buried at Jannat al-Baqi held no significance for their personal identities; any baraka associated with the cemetery became accessible strictly as a reward for ritual obedience, rather than a flow of energy directly from the Companions' corporeal remains.

Deleuze can inform our analysis of Jannat al Baqi and baraka in another way. The Deleuzian model of the assemblage imagines a graph in which one axis marks at one end the assemblage's "content" (the material artifacts of the assemblage), and at the other the assemblage's "expression" (the linguistic or symbolic construction of the assemblage and "order words" imposed upon the content). The second axis represents the opposing tendencies of (re)territorialization and deterritorialization, the ways in which the assemblage becomes stabilized or destabilized, stratified or liberated.

In Jannat al-Baqi, the material content most obviously consists of bodies; this is, after all, a cemetery. But the content also includes living bodies, such as visitors to the cemetery who come from all over the world and bring with them an enormous diversity of ideas about how to understand the lives of Jannat al-Baqi's buried residents and how to properly engage their bodies. Throughout Jannat al-Baqi, these visitors encounter other living bodies, scholars who patrol the cemetery to correct them on behalf of the Saudi government's position, which condemns numerous Muslim practices regarding graves as beyond the limits of Islam. The scholars, regardless of their national origins, wear Saudi dress of white thobes and red keffiyas, which, while not exclusively their uniform, tend to mark them against the international population of visitors, who may or may not also be wearing clothing that reflects their homelands. The often antagonistic encounters between visitors and cemetery scholars, aurally unavoidable to passersby, contribute to the broader affect of Jannat al-Baqi. These encounters between bodies, it should be said, take place on gendered terms. Although women's bodies lie buried in Jannat al-Baqi, living women cannot enter. The assemblage thus includes bodies outside the walls: the women who offer their salam to these bodies through the fence, and the uniformed guards who control access to the inside.

In addition to the organic matter, Jannat al-Baqi's material content includes the stark brown field in which the bodies rest, and the unmarked stones that show where bodies are buried, but do not identify them. Jannat al-Baqi's spatial boundaries were redefined in the twentieth century when King Faisal expanded the cemetery and constructed concrete walls to designate those boundaries, closing off this quiet empty field from the active and modern city outside. Outside the cemetery, large signs—white text on blue, stylistically resembling highway signs—give instructions as to the precise manner in which Muhammad visited graves and the modes of grave veneration that he had prohibited. Smooth cement paths, also a product of modern renovation, provide specific routes through the cemetery. Brick arrangements that surround particular graves mark them as special even without an inscription of names, such as that of 'Uthman, third caliph in the Sunni historical narrative. A fence blocks access to the graves most valued by Shi'i pilgrims, those of the second, fourth, fifth, and sixth of the twelve Imams (and possibly their matriarch, Muhammad's daughter Fatima, whose precise burial place remains unknown). The assemblage can also consist of artifacts that exist outside the walls but nonetheless become part of Jannat al-Baqi as a sensory experience, such as the green dome and minarets of Masjid al-Nabi, the mosque and resting place of the Prophet, visible from within Jannat al-Baqi's walls.

The expressive dimension of the assemblage consists of the modes by which the material content becomes subject to incorporeal transformations. These modes are most straight-forwardly discursive, such as the proclamations on the big blue signs telling visitors in English: "Graves are to be visited for introspection and learning a lesson . . . The Prophet has forbidden supplications to the dead, and asking them to procure for us what is good and ward off what is evil." The official discourse inscribed upon the cemetery denies its special importance; the visitors will find no special energies flowing out of the ground. If there is any baraka to be obtained from visiting Jannat al-Baqi, it is only the baraka that one could obtain from any cemetery: the baraka of following in Muhammad's example, visiting graves in accordance with his personal practices and prescriptions, and reflecting on the graves in order to cultivate a change in one's inner condition. The graves are valuable only because the Qur'an says that visiting graves will remind you of your own mortality, not because they are magical. The cemetery scholars repeat the signs' arguments to whomever they perceive as violating the limits of acceptable practice. The signs and the scholars, both citing statements attributed to the Prophet to make their points, contribute to the assemblage's form of expression and its production of concepts. Here, walking among the bodies of the original Muslim community's most prominent figures, and in the shadow of the Prophet's own mosque/tomb, Muslims engage a particular classification of Islam defined by claims to the origins, Islam as characterized by the oppositional concepts of Sunna and Bida' (innovation). These terms, presented in this zero-sum dualism, carry enormous power and serve to reorder the meanings of the graves and the significance of what people do at graves. In the narrative of the blue signs and the patrolling scholars, either one adheres to the practices and prescriptions of Muhammad (as located within a textual canon recognized by the Saudi state), or one departs from Muhammad's Sunna and indulges in unacceptable departures from Islam.

Though the Saudi state has demolished the shrines and worked to strip away Shi'i-positive strata, many visitors continue to territorialize the theoretically smooth space by smuggling in their own private maps. Whether entering Jannat al-Baqi with a folded-up sheet of paper or a website on one's phone, the map must be examined with discretion, since the map's very presence defies Saudi de/reterritorialization of Jannat al-Baqi. The contraband map provides a transmission of officially suppressed knowledge. I have never seen a map of Jannat al-Baqi that labels every grave; the purpose of the map is to preserve what the Saudi state had found most threatening, namely the representation of specific graves as sites of extraordinary power. Of course, while the identification of some graves depends on the contraband map, the state's blockading of the area in which four of the twelve Shi'i Imams and possibly Fatima are buried continues to ironically mark that space as significant and preserve the power of the graves. During my own visit to Jannat al-Baqi, I first noticed this area by the crowd of Shi'i pilgrims assembled in front of the fence, getting as close to the graves as the state allowed.

Other expressive components of the Jannat al-Baqi assemblage circulate outside the physical boundaries: not only the Sunni revivalist discourse of the Saudi state, but also the international outcry over the state's destruction of historically meaningful and even sacred sites throughout the holy cities and surrounding areas. This is not exclusively a Shi'i outcry, though Shi'i communities feel special wounds with the destruction of shrines dedicated to Muhammad's family, and weave these demolitions into a larger narrative of oppression and degradation across time. At a recent commemoration of the Battle of Karbala in 680 CE, at which Muhammad's grandson Husayn and his supporters were brutally slaughtered by the Umayyad caliphate, I heard the imam relate a story of a woman in Islam's early centuries whose right arm was chopped off by the caliphal soldiers when she made the pilgrimage to Husayn's tomb in Karbala; the next year, she came back and gave them her left arm. The imam seamlessly wove this episode into a story of a man who lost four sons fighting ISIS and could not bury them because their bodies were gone. He went to the ayatullah whom he followed and asked if he could dig four empty graves just to have a place to mourn his sons. The ayatullah answered, "No, that is not permissible. Go to Karbala and visit the companions of Husayn, because your sons are with them." This discourse of endless persecution and degradation connected with love for the Prophet's household writes an incorporeal transformation upon the flattened shrines of Jannat al-Baqi. Just as the Umayyad caliphate abused the body of Husayn, marching his head on a lance from Karbala to Damascus, and the nineteenth-century followers of Ibn 'Abd al-Wahhab inflicted mass slaughter, looting, and destruction at Husayn's tomb, the twentieth-century Saudi state purged all traces of veneration for Husayn's mother and their family. These events weave together into one story, characterized in Ja'far's famous statement, "Every day is Ashura, every land is Karbala."

"Every assemblage is basically territorial," Deleuze and Guattari tell us. "The first concrete rule for assemblages is to discover what territoriality they envelop."[163] In relation to baraka, multiple territorialities can be mapped upon the dusty field of Jannat al-Baqi, depending on ways that space is controlled and contested among various forces. The space is changed by Ottoman imperial patronage of holy sites and the Saudi state that purged its land of Ottoman traces; by sectarian conflicts between Sunni and Shi'i Muslims, as well as between "Wahhabis" and other Sunnis; by modern conversations in which the immanence of baraka in material things receives mockery from traditionalists for being "idolatrous" and by rationalists who call it "superstition" (with these criticisms often overlapping).

In the tension between transcendent and immanent thoughts of baraka, we also find competing ideas of the Prophet. There's Muhammad the lawgiver and receiver of divine speech, but also Muhammad the body, supreme locus of baraka's flows. At the question of baraka, it becomes unclear where Muhammad's body begins and ends. Many Muslims would insist that even if his Companions obtained baraka through his sweat, his bodily remains are now useless, unable to help or harm anyone. Others, however, continue to experience baraka at sites and artifacts associated with the Prophet's body, expanding his body beyond the borders of his flesh. By no means do I suggest that Muslims who favor baraka's immanence are deniers of God's transcendence and supreme agency over baraka, somehow less pure in their monotheism, or neglectful of divinely revealed commands and prohibitions. These are precisely the charges levied against many such Muslims by the razers of shrines. Muslims who conceive of baraka in transcendent and immanent modes share many of their sources in common, and Deleuze would point out that territorialization and deterritorialization each contains a tendency toward the other. Both tendencies appear in the legacies of the Prophet. Depending on the diverse ways that Muslims open or deny possible connections to him, Muhammad himself can appear as a centralizing, authoritarian tree or a scattering, rootless rhizome.

30

MUHAMMAD AND THE ANIMAL

'Abd Allah bin Ja'far narrated:

The Messenger of God (God bless him and give him peace) seated me behind him one day and he said a hadith to me that I will never report to anyone.

When the Messenger of God (God bless him and give him peace) relieved himself, he liked to cover himself with a small hill or a cluster of date palms.

One day, he entered the garden of a man from the Ansar when a camel came to him, dragging along, tears flowing from its eyes [Bahz and 'Affan, transmitters of this hadith, said that when the camel saw the Prophet, he felt compassion as tears flowed from its eyes]. The Messenger of God (God bless him and give him peace) wiped its tears and head, and it became calm.

He said, "Who is the master of this

camel?" A youth from the Ansar came and
said, "It is mine, O Messenger of God."

He said, "Do you not fear God with this
animal, that God has given you? It complains
to me that you starve it and wear it out."[164]

A multitude of hadiths present Muhammad as condemning
cruelty to animals: he forbids tying up an animal for target
practice, mutilating animals, or burdening them with labor
for which they had not been created. In a famous narration,
Muhammad told the story of a woman who had tied up a cat
and refused to feed it; for starving the cat, the woman was
condemned to hellfire. According to one version of the story,
Muhammad personally witnessed the woman in hell, getting
scratched by a cat. In a mirror of that story, Muhammad also
spoke of a sex worker whose sins were forgiven when she res-
cued a dog that was dying of thirst. The hadith traditions
provide reports of Muhammad demanding that his Companions reunite captured baby birds with their mother, as well as
stating that if someone plants a tree from which animals obtain their nourishment, God rewards this as an act of charity.

'Abd Allah bin Ja'far, the witness to Muhammad's compassion for the starved and overworked camel, also tells us
that the final time that he ever saw Muhammad, the Prophet
held dates in one hand and a cucumber in the other, taking alternate bites from each before telling him, "The best
part of the sheep is meat from the back."[165] Muhammad was
a meat eater, and his community adhered to divinely revealed regulations that categorized animals as allowed (*halal*)
or prohibited (*haram*) to consume. The status of an animal

could be made clear by its mention in the Qur'an, as in the revelation's explicit prohibition of eating pork, or in hadith traditions, which tell us of various animals that Muhammad ate, forbade, or refused to eat without banning for others. Yet some animals' status remained ambiguous. Muhammad is portrayed in some narrations as forbidding the consumption of lizards, while others reported him giving permission; still other accounts suggest that while Muhammad personally disliked lizards, he did not expressly bar others from eating them. As legal schools crystallized in the early centuries after Muhammad, each operating by its own logic, methods, and sources, they sometimes disagreed on whether the meat of a particular animal was permissible. The Hanafi school upholds a prohibition on most seafood, such as lobsters, crabs, eels, and shrimp, but regards fish as properly halal, due to the Qur'an's expressed allowance of fish. But what makes a fish a fish? Premodern legal debates on seafood lead us to a postmodern exposure of "fish" as an unstable social construction. In the view of other legal schools, everything found in the water counts within the category of "fish" and thereby falls into the Qur'an's permission. In globalized modernity, in which Muslims live all over the planet and have access to the cuisines of every locale, Muslims employ the logics of tradition to classify animals that would not have been available in Muhammad's setting. The permissibility of alligators, for example, depends on whether they are classified as land animals (in which case, as predators, they would be haram) or as a kind of "fish."

Alongside ongoing legal questions of what Muslims *can* eat, many Muslims today raise the ethical "beyond halal" question of what (and how) Muslims *should* eat,[166] offering an Islamically driven critique of food practices in modern capitalism. Muslims find an alternative to the torture and mutilation of animals in factory farms by slaughtering animals in accordance with Muhammad's practices and the prescriptions of Islamic legal tradition, and following strict regulations for their treatment. Some Muslims advocate vegan or vegetarian diets, making a case that while Muhammad authorized meat consumption in his own historical context, it is no longer necessary to consume animal products to live healthy lives; in this argument, Islamic legal traditions regarding food remain intact, but a sense of Islam as an ethical tradition takes priority. Muslim vegans and vegetarians offer readings of tradition that speak to modern problems and conversations about animal cruelty. Muslim veganism and vegetarianism can also draw from Sufi Muslim traditions, which provide numerous accounts of premodern saintly figures who abandoned hunting and meat consumption as antithetical to their spiritual callings.[167]

The tradition does not present Muhammad as regarding all animals as sharing in the same character or essence. Bees are protected creatures, for example, but even a pilgrim in Mecca—existing in a state of ritual purity that otherwise forbids the killing of any animals—may kill "mischief" animals, such as rats and scorpions. Muhammad permits the killing of geckos, a pest in his own setting, with a narrative that when animals attempted to save Abraham from being burned alive, only the gecko refrained from attempting to put out the fire.

In popular tellings of Muhammad's grandson Husayn and his murder in Karbala, both Husayn and the bloodthirsty despot Yazid are characterized in part by their relationships to animals. Narrations emphasize the nobility and selflessness of Husayn's white horse Dhul-Jannah, who receives countless arrows from Yazid's army into its own flesh, informs Husayn's family of his death, and in various oral traditions reacts to Husayn's martyrdom either by continuing to fight enemy soldiers, disappearing into the wilderness, or committing suicide by smashing its own head into a rock. Yazid, in contrast, binds his pet monkey, Abu Qays, to a saddle on a donkey and makes it race, dresses it in red and yellow silks with an embroidered cap, trains it to be both his drinking buddy and the leader of congregational prayer, and reportedly fulfills his sexual appetites with the monkey until he dies from it. According to popular traditions, a lion rushes to the body of Husayn to shield him from further mutilation and desecration, while stray dogs are alleged even today to single out the cursed Yazid's grave as a place to urinate.

In the eternal divide between dog lovers and cat lovers, Muhammad by all accounts would have sided with Team Cats. While hadith literature depicts Muhammad regarding cats as natural companions to humans (and affectionately naming one of his friends Abu Hurayra, Father of Kittens, in honor of the cat that always accompanied him), this same literature reviles dogs as ritually polluting, associated with the Devil, and repellant to angels. A popular tradition that circulates with some variation portrays Muhammad as wanting to kill all dogs, but then realizing that dogs are a nation unto themselves, and reducing his order to the killing of black dogs. When asked to explain the difference between black dogs and red or yellow dogs, Muhammad answers that the black dog is a devil (*shaytan*). In still another tradition, the angel Gabriel no-shows a scheduled meeting with Muhammad, later explaining that angels will not enter a house in which there is a dog. Muhammad then discovers that one of his grandsons had smuggled a puppy into the house and hid it under his things. Notably, such treatments of dogs are absent from our oldest source, the Qur'an. In contrast to these hadiths, the Qur'an's story of the "Companions of the Cave"—a group of Christians who were miraculously saved from Roman persecution by sleeping in a cave for 309 years—includes a dog as one of the divinely protected sleepers (18:22).

The demonization of dogs (especially black dogs) in hadith literature could have served to mark a border between Muslims and Zoroastrians, in whose traditions we find positive representations of dogs (especially black dogs),[168] as Muslim territorial domain spread into Zoroastrian lands during the early post-Muhammad generations, the same era in which the hadith corpus emerged. At the time, many communities practiced both Islam and Zoroastrianism: the hadith master Ibn Hanbal's grandfather, for example, was believed to have been a Zoroastrian convert to Islam. Given the cultural codes that humans inscribe upon the animals in their lives, a community's symbolic relationship to a particular animal can define and secure its borders. A modern example can be found in the development of taboos against eating beef in Hinduism, which intensified during British colonial rule as an identity-making wall between Hindu and Muslim communities.[169]

The hadith of a crying camel can take us into new terrains of critical reflection: according to Muhammad, what makes a human *not* an animal? If being human means assuming a firm border between human and nonhuman, where does Muhammad draw his border, and does the border ever become perforated?

Similar to critical studies of race, gender, and sexuality, a growing body of scholarship theorizes the human—defined in binary relation against its opposite, the animal—as a social construction. This means that the difference between human and animal, rather than an obvious fact of nature, exists instead as a produced fact of culture. Humans must decide where to locate the boundary that separates them from animals. They draw this boundary at different points, in conversation with their culturally learned worldviews, perhaps naming features such as rational thought, free will, language, or possession of a soul as the essence of being human. A society reveals its values and prejudices in part through the ways in which it chooses to distinguish humans from animals. Philosopher Giorgio Agamben describes this ongoing process of defining and enforcing the human-animal divide as the "anthropological machine."[170] Humans contribute to the anthropological machine whenever they insult other humans in animalizing terms. The anthropological machine can be wielded to label some humans as less human than others. Through comparisons of human groups to monkeys, or marking them as "animalistic" with stereotypes of irrationality, unrestrained sexuality, and propensity for violence, the anthropological machine has been exploited to legitimize slavery, oppression, and genocide.

Muhammad took part in an anthropological machine during his lifetime and could also be imagined as producing his own unique anthropological machine, or contributing to countless anthropological machines across the centuries after his death. Muslim thinkers throughout history would engage the sacred sources to form their own constructions of "human" as a category. For instance, Ibn al-'Arabi theorized that all created things operated as expressions of God's Names, that human beings were uniquely privileged in their capacity to express *all* of God's Names—and that Muhammad (along with Ibn al-'Arabi himself) represented the template for an advanced human who achieved this comprehensiveness in pure truth and harmony. His position can be read to supremely privilege humans or unsettle human exceptionalism, depending on his readers' priorities. Anyone who perceives Muhammad as the most perfect and complete human of all time has entered into a set of concepts in which Muhammad—in his definition as the perfect human—represents the most *non-animal* someone can become. To call him the best human, in other words, means first knowing what makes "human" a desirable status.

It could be suggested that the Prophet's task is to define humanity not in relation to animals, but rather to God. Humans realize their humanity in this case not by looking down to the inferior other, but instead by looking up at their superior. Because God exists far beyond any comparison to his creation, humans and animals are equally non-God. Like humans, animals take part in submission (*islam*) to God; the Qur'an describes birds as joining David in the praise of God (21:79), serving alongside humans and jinns in Solomon's kingdom (27:17), and protecting the Ka'ba against an army that sought to destroy it (105:3–4). The Qur'an even refers to God's communication to the bees as *wahy*, "inspiration," a term also used to describe the experience of human prophets (19:47). But positioning humans in relation to God also constructs and enforces a human-animal border: humans become human through a particular connection with the Lord of All the Worlds, a connection from which animals are mostly excluded.

For many, the question of Islam's relationship to animality would hinge on how one reads verse 2:30 in the Qur'an, which reports that prior to the creation of Adam, God announced to the angels, "I will place a *khalifa* on the earth." As the word from which we get the English "caliph" and "caliphate," *khalifa* might read at first glance as a term of dominion, similar to popular readings of biblical tradition: God has granted humankind mastery over the earth. In a chain-of-command model, humans exist to serve God, and animals have been put on the earth for humans' benefit and service.

But what, exactly, might it mean to be khalifa? This becomes a historical problem. Even as the divine revelation's exact words remain unchanged, their meanings are subject to the instability of human language: the same word can mean multiple things when traveling across generations. The Arabic *kh-l-f* root signifies a state of following or succession. In her scholarship on animals in the Qur'an, Sarra Tlili traces the history of commentary on 2:30, arguing that for the earliest interpreters of the Qur'an, God's plan to appoint a khalifa meant that God would make Adam to succeed the jinns, a species of spiritual beings who were created prior to humans. Tlili demonstrates that interpretations of khalifa changed over time, largely in relation to the development of the caliphate as a human political office. While the earliest political successors to Muhammad, starting with his father-in-law Abu Bakr, were retroactively termed "caliphs" in later generations, it does not appear that Abu Bakr or any of the first four leaders actually used the title for themselves. During the Umayyad caliphate, the meaning and significance of "caliphate" changed, and in turn informed classical commentators of post-Umayyad generations, such as al-Tabari. In the interpretive tradition, Adam's role as God's earthly khalifa thus came to increasingly signify government and the implementation of decrees.[171] Today, translations and commentaries of the Qur'an in English typically interpret *khalifa* as "vicegerent," further endowing humankind with both the supreme privileges and ethical responsibilities of administrative lordship over the earth.

A well-circulated tradition represents Muhammad forbidding humans from striking each other on the face, on the basis that God had "created Adam in his form." Amid the flourishing of Islamic theology in the early 'Abbasid centuries, Muslim scholars argued over how to properly understand the narration's ambiguous language: who did the "his" in "his form" refer to? Because Arabic does not have capital letters, it remains unclear as to whether the pronoun reflects a human "his" or the divine "His." At a time when Muslim intellectuals grew intensely sensitive to their peers' charges of anthropomorphism, some found discomfort with the notion of God creating Adam in God's form. They instead read the "his" as a reference to Adam, meaning that God created Adam in Adam's form. For traditionists such as Ibn Hanbal, such rationalizing efforts were ridiculous: Ibn Hanbal insisted that God had created Adam in God's form, even if the precise implications of that statement eluded human understanding.[172] Meanwhile, other narrations did portray God as appearing in corporeally anthropomorphic form, specifically as a beautiful boy, and even touching his physical hand to Muhammad's body. However one chooses to engage such hadiths—many traditionists preferred versions in which Muhammad clarified that the encounter had happened in a dream, or interpreted the vision as possible through the eyes of Muhammad's heart, not the eyes in his head; others favored A'isha's uncompromising rejection of claims that Muhammad had seen his lord, regardless of sleep or wakefulness—the canon of sacred sources does not present a similar problem of God taking on a zoomorphic appearance. Traditionists, theologians, and philosophers wrote countless volumes wrestling with verses in the Qur'an that mentioned God's hands and his sitting on a throne, but did not have to contend with the Qur'an making references to God's feathers, horns, or tail. God never portrays himself in the Qur'an or hadith canon as a camel or an elephant. In the double bind of scriptural monotheism, caught between the failure of words to represent the Absolute and the right of this Absolute to describe itself in the confines of a book, God exists beyond the limits of human comprehension—far above any semblance to bodies or forms—yet articulates his self-description with language of *human* body parts. While humans and animals share membership in the category of created things, thereby definitively *not-God*, animals are barred from a certain ontological intimacy shared between God and humans.

Beyond the sacred sources, however, we do find an exception among Sufi traditions in which the attributes of God can become knowable in both human and nonhuman physical creations. When Abu al-Husayn Nuri heard a dog barking, he recognized it as the voice of God and answered the dog with the recitation of pilgrims in Mecca, "Labbayk" ("Here I am, Lord").[173] And it might also be worth noting that Muhammad's prohibitions against striking humans in the face are paralleled by similar commands against striking animal faces or unnecessarily marking them. Does this shut down humanity's theomorphic privilege found in "God created Adam in God's form"? Or could it expand the theomorphism to let animals in? What does it mean to be made in the form of the formless? Sufi traditions might further complicate the anthropological machine by praising dogs as exemplary and selfless companions, superior lovers of their masters and worthy models of imitation for humans on the path, while also deriding dogs as metaphorical stand-ins for the ugly human personality.[174] As a bit of insider Sufi humor, an order that I had joined posted a "Beware of Dog" sign in front of its lodge—warning us not of any creature waiting inside the house, but rather the ego that we brought with us.

The corpus of stories and statements attributed to Muhammad is vast enough to provide materials both for affirming human exceptionalism and undermining it. Stories of disobedient humans becoming metamorphosed into monkeys and pigs, for example, present animality as a clear demotion. But Muhammad's description of martyrs, who become occupants of paradise prior to the proper resurrection of their bodies, as enjoying paradise with the bodies of green birds offers a different take on human-animal transformation. At various points in the hadith corpus, many of our standard modes for distinguishing humans from animals fall away. Like humans, animals appear in the sources as *muslims*, submitters to the divine will, at the very least in a lowercase sense. Animals are said to form nations; they express themselves with language; in their communications with Muhammad, they exhibit not only the ability to convey their grievances to him, but also the necessary intellect to recognize him as an exceptional human who will understand and care for them. Before crying to the Prophet, the camel seems to know that Muhammad is, after all, the Prophet. To follow Muhammad's sublime example means engaging God's creation—humans and nonhumans like—with humility and compassion. Humans and animals share in their status as created things and servants of the Creator. Whatever meanings and values humans might invest in their special position as khalifa, the privileged human relationship to God comes with a call to act as agents of divine mercy.

31

THE BAG OF MEAT

Yunus ibn Bukayr narrated on the authority of Ibn Ishaq:

I was told that the Messenger of God (God bless him and give him peace), while speaking of Zayd ibn 'Amr ibn Nufayl, said, "He was the first to blame me for worshiping idols and forbade me to do so. I had come from al-Ta'if with Zayd ibn Haritha when I passed by Zayd ibn 'Amr on the high ground above Mecca, for Quraysh had made a public example of him for abandoning their religion, so that he went forth from among them in the high ground of Mecca. I went and sat with him. I had with me a bag of meat from our sacrifices to our idols which Zayd ibn Haritha was carrying, and I offered it to him. I was a young boy at the time. I said, 'Eat some of this food, O my uncle.' He replied, 'Nephew, it is a part of those sacrifices of yours which you offer to your idols, isn't it?' When I answered that it was, he said, 'If you were to ask the daughters of 'Abd al-Muttalib, they would tell you that I never eat of those sacrifices and I want nothing to do with them.' Then he blamed me and those who worship idols and sacrifice to them, saying, 'They are futile: they can do neither good nor harm,' or words to that effect."

The Messenger added, "After that, with that knowledge, I never stroked an idol of theirs nor did I sacrifice to them until God honored me with his messengership."[175]

The notion of *'ismah*, God's protection of prophets from sin and error, appears throughout Muslim traditions as a crucial dimension to understanding Muhammad. The Prophet's life and words, after all, hold such moral authority and transcendent truth that Muslims are to follow them for the rest of time. Muhammad was the most perfect human, and it would make sense to believe that God had granted him some kind of protection from normal human failings.

Depending on the various ways that Muslims articulated belief in Muhammad's infallibility, his perfection stood in possible friction with the fact that he only attained prophethood at the age of forty. For most of his adult life, Muhammad lived without divine guidance in a chronological and spatial location that sources characterize as *jahiliyya*, "ignorance." Before he was a morally and spiritually perfected prophet, how did Muhammad live? Before having a religion of his own to teach, did he practice the religion of his community, even venerating a plurality of gods and goddesses via images that had been fashioned by human hands?

In various places throughout the early sources, we encounter a tension between the supposed "ignorance" of pre-Islamic Mecca and the veneration of Muhammad and his family. Muhammad's parents reportedly lived in a bastion of polytheism but nonetheless had names in harmony with monotheism: his father's name, 'Abd Allah, translates to "Servant of God"; his mother's name, Amina, means "faithful." Hadiths also present Muhammad insisting that throughout the jahiliyya generations that preceded his birth, none of his ancestors had been born from fornication.

A number of contemporary scholars, tracking change in the ways that Muslim sources depict events from Muhammad's life, argue that the concept of prophetic 'ismah intensified during the early centuries of Islam. In his study of the "Satanic Verses" tradition that depicts the Devil momentarily tricking Muhammad into praising pre-Islamic goddesses, Shahab Ahmed demonstrates that the earliest Muslim sources reflect no discomfort over the Devil's temporary win over the Prophet. Opposition to the Satanic Verses story developed alongside the ascendance of the Hadith Folk as makers and owners of orthodoxy. Narratives of the Satanic Verses incident may stand beyond the pale of *modern* Muslim "orthodoxy," but the story was nonetheless entirely "orthodox" for early Muslims.[176]

M. J. Kister likewise notes that the story of Muhammad possibly eating meat that had been slaughtered for goddesses (or even slaughtering the meat himself as a full participant in so-called jahiliyya religion) is "undoubtedly an old one" that only becomes troublesome to Muslim sensibilities as the tradition develops over time.[177] He tracks shifting attitudes between versions of the "bag of meat" story, with some versions and commentators downplaying the degree to which Muhammad personally becomes implicated in polytheism and sanitizing its representation of the pre-prophetic Prophet. In its variations, the "bag of meat" story reflects anxieties concerning Muhammad's pre-prophetic life. Even if he is not yet the Prophet, one would still expect him to be Muhammad; but how do we imagine him without his prophetic vocation? What should we want from him in his four non-prophetic decades, and what changes if he had once participated in the religion of his community?

As with other prophetic traditions, the full significance of Muhammad eating meat that had been slaughtered for a goddess depends as much on our context as his own. Today, we might be less likely to focus on the materiality of the meat itself; the meat's power becomes symbolic. For readers in another setting, however, you really are what you eat, and the integrity of Muhammad's body operates as one of the most salient reflections of his station. The *dala'il al-nabuwwa* or "proofs of prophethood" literary genre abounds with reports of Muhammad's bodily excellence. The transcendent supremacy of his illuminated face, stride, soft skin, the Seal of Prophethood between his shoulders, the perfect balance of his complexion and height, the smell of his sweat, and even his sex drive all demonstrated that this body was special. The question of whether Muhammad ate meat from the altar of a stone goddess relates not only to his intellectual condition, private faith, and protection from moral error; the polytheists' food itself, absorbed into Muhammad's body, *becomes* Muhammad and therefore threatens to change him from within. We find our own logics of the body transforming the meaning and implications of the story.

32

MUHAMMAD THE SHAMAN

Ibn 'Abbas narrated:

A woman came to the Messenger of God (God bless him and give him peace) with her son. She said, "O Messenger of God, my son is possessed. It seizes him during our breakfasts and dinners and acts wickedly on us." The Messenger of God (God bless him and give him peace) rubbed his chest and prayed. He vomited and then something like a black puppy came out of his mouth.[178]

Our words come with problems. The concepts of "shamanism" and "shamans" were constructed by white scholars in the seventeenth century, who took the term from a specific kind of indigenous practitioner in Siberia. While the term *shaman* was inadequate even for representing the diversity of Siberian practitioners—only Tungusic-speaking communities used the word—Europeans turned "shamanism" into a catch-all category for whatever they saw "primitive" peoples doing in

South America or Pacific islands or Central Asia or anywhere in Africa. Sometimes, treatments of shamanism were rife with racist judgments of irrational "superstition" and "magic," positioning these traditions as inferior to evolved Christian religion. In other contexts, shaman-friendly Orientalist scholars imagined shamanism as a more "spiritual" alternative to the problems of text-based and church-based religions, a kind of paint-with-all-the-colors-of-the-wind deeper communion with the earth. In both cases, it was Western observers deciding the terms by which these shamans would be measured.[179]

Having given a cautious disclaimer about the necessity of undoing shamanism as category, let's take this hadith as a portal into considering Muhammad as a shaman. In some academic treatments, Muhammad's ascension into the heavens has been compared to shamanic vision quests and journeys into worlds of the unseen. James Porter, for example, notes similarities between Muhammad's steed during his ascension, the Buraq, and the "extremely common" theme in shamanic contexts that "the shaman rides up to the sky on the back of some animal."[180] Do these similarities mark Muhammad as a shaman? Or would we find a more productive framework for thinking about Muhammad's ascension using the "ascension narrative" as an established genre in his context? Or were all ascensions cases of shamanism?

Another question is what distinguishes shamans from prophets. Writing about shamanism in Bangladesh, Anwarul Karim defines the shaman as a "kind of healer who makes use of supernatural powers and magic for various healing or curing of disease. A shaman specializes in spirit illness and spirit possession, deals with good as well as evil spirits, and is a mediator between the supernatural and the community."[181] Under Karim's definition, Muhammad performed all the duties of a shaman. He interacted with angels and jinns. He exorcized demons from the human bodies that they occupied. And the Qur'an establishes that Muhammad certainly mediated between supernatural forces and his community.

Perhaps the presence of a book separates shamans from prophets. Not every prophet produces a scripture, however; in Muhammad's lifetime, the Qur'an wasn't even a scripture in the sense that we'd normally use the term, and there are also shamans who write books (and host podcasts, for that matter). Maybe "shaman" is what we call a prophet in religions that don't have names. The challenges of thinking about prophets as shamans today reveals more about the coding of these terms by our prejudices and assumptions than about prophets and shamans themselves.

Across what we now call the Muslim world, in places like Bangladesh and Kazakhstan and Senegal and Indonesia, new Muslims understood Muhammad's prophethood—and prophethood as a concept—through their culturally specific lenses. Coming to Islam in the mid-1990s, I grew confident in Muhammad's prophethood through a litany of arguments that were mostly secular: Muhammad strove to build a better society, sought justice and equality, preached antiracism, and encouraged the pursuit of knowledge. I would not have been impressed by special birthmarks, heavenly ascensions, or miraculous healings, the proofs that could have attracted converts in another time and place. The Muhammad that I embraced as a prophet corresponded to my preexisting notions of what a developed human being should be: having been inspired by

Malcolm X, I wanted the kind of Muhammad that Malcolm would embrace, and Malcolm wasn't into shamans.

Because I first learned about the Prophet through twentieth-century Muslim writers who were interested in things like Islamic theories of economics and the state, he looked to me like a perfect nation-builder; but to shamans, he would have looked like a shaman. If Muhammad did shamanish things in the canonical hadith sources, we don't have to think of shamanism's interactions with Islam in terms of "syncretism" or a conscious blending of otherwise separate traditions. Shamans could organically become Muslim shamans by incorporating whatever they understood as "Muslim" resources and concepts—Muhammad, the Qur'an, angels, jinns—into the technologies that they already used. Their preexisting frameworks were compatible with their new sources: makers of amulets could make Qur'anic amulets. Becoming a Muslim shaman or *pir* did not have to contradict the shaman's prior work. This is where the modern notion of "Abrahamic religion" fails us in its assumption that Judaism, Christianity, and Islam exist primarily as branches of a shared tree. The Abrahamic model isn't entirely unreasonable—of course, Muhammad did apparently self-identify as the fulfillment of biblical prophetic traditions and a biological descendant of Abraham—but to reduce these traditions to a single Abrahamic genealogy erases all of the other roots. Thinking of Judaism, Christianity, and Islam as Abrahamic cousins might seem applicable at a place like the Dome of the Rock or during an interfaith dialogue event on an American college campus; elsewhere, however, these traditions develop in other relationships, joined to other trees.

The conflict over where "authentic" Islam begins and ends

is an old one that has repeated itself in many forms throughout Muslim history. Nonetheless, the imperative felt by many Muslims to revive "true Islam" by purging it of deviations from local traditions, regulating the tradition through a strictly guarded roster of seminal thinkers, is a significantly modern one. Today, more Muslims than ever read figures such as al-Ghazali, treating elite theologians and philosophers as self-evident centers of classical Islam. This new brand of traditionalism comes at a cost. If we consider the classical tradition as represented only by the mighty scholars and thinkers of past centuries, we get a limited sample that fails to adequately represent historical Islam as lived in the world (unless, perhaps, we're reading someone like Ibn Taymiyya when he complains about the inauthenticity and deviance of popular practices).[182]

American Muslims have increasingly leaned toward textualist, scholar-centered endeavors that promise to "revive" Islam and more clearly enforce a division between "religious" (i.e., universal, global, and authentic) and "cultural" (unique, local, and often illegitimate) practices. This in part is a result of the unique demographics of American Muslim communities after the 1965 immigration reform in the United States, which brought highly educated, scientifically oriented professionals to the country. As a worldwide trend, Islam's intensified textualism and the popular imagination of scripturally sound "religion" as separate from ignorant "culture" mirror modern developments in other traditions. In the same era that Muslim reformers sought to purge Islam of local "shamanisms" and folk practices, Hindu reformers likewise sought to reconstruct Hinduism as a coherent "world religion," and Japanese Buddhist intellectuals insisted that a return to the textually authenticated teachings of the Buddha would rescue true, original Buddhism from the distortions of folk practices and solve the "problem" of Buddhist cultural diversity. Conventional scholarly narratives on Daoism, Louis Komjathy explains, have similarly divided Daoist tradition into "philosophical"/"original"/"pure" Daoism (the Daoism of scholarly elites) and "religious"/"degenerate"/"superstitious" Daoism, "undeserving of serious attention."[183] The effort to reconstruct "real Islam" strictly from textual canon looks a lot like projects to locate and restore the "real" versions of other traditions.

Heightened emphasis on rationalist scholarly textualism, resistance to "superstition," and this imagined religion-culture binary have left out the shamans, or even our chances to think about Muhammad's experience in shamanic terms. The irony that we find in this hadith of a black puppy devil, however, is that Muhammad-as-shaman lurks *within* the textual canon, even as many Muslims would avoid him. Celebrated in the tradition as an unlettered prophet, Muhammad did not become the Messenger by spending years in the seminary to master a textual canon, and the Qur'an did not first appear in a peer-reviewed academic journal. Muhammad's education came first through angels cutting open his body and pouring wisdom into his chest. As far as "shaman" can do anything for us as a category, Muhammad was a shaman. The canonical corpus provides enough material for multiple forty-hadith collections that reimagine him in the shaman's vocation—with no less historical credibility than constructions of Muhammad as philosopher, jurist, statesman, or theorist of economics.

33

DREAMING MUHAMMAD

Ibn 'Abbas narrated:
    The Prophet (God bless him and give him peace) said, "Whoever sees me in a dream has seen me, because the Devil cannot impersonate me."[184]

Early in Islam, hadith scholars claimed ownership over Muhammad's legacy by virtue of their methods and self-authorizing networks: they were the masters of oral traditions, trained in sciences of criticism, and mutually vetted to preserve and transmit prophetic knowledge. By the rules of their own system, however, they endorsed a hadith that could seemingly blow apart their custodianship of the tradition. Muhammad is not bound to the chains of scholarly transmission, but can continue to speak even millennia after his death by appearing in dreams. Hadith scholarship opened a window to certain nonscholarly modes of knowledge—what we might call mysticism—that could wield a living Muhammad against their chains of dead transmitters.

The dream of Muhammad potentially acts as what Deleuze termed a "line of flight," the route by which a structure grants escape from itself.[185] The classical hadith scholars did not seem to view it as such, however, as they also relied on the evidence provided in dreams to enforce their system. The tradition offers narratives in which hadith scholars report seeing Muhammad in a dream and asking him about the reliability of certain transmitters, with Muhammad offering his endorsement or disapproval. Adherents to competing legal schools also reported Muhammad visiting them in dreams to endorse one school over another.[186] In turn, hadith masters and representatives of schools (such as the traditionist Ibn Hanbal, epnonym of the Hanbali legal school) themselves could appear in dreams long after their deaths, granting or denying authority to scholars of later generations.[187] The Sunni traditionist widely regarded as the greatest hadith master in history, Imam al-Bukhari, was reportedly inspired to compile his supremely canonical collection after witnessing Muhammad in a dream, surrounded by flies. Al-Bukhari began swatting away the flies from Muhammad's face, which he later interpreted to mean that he would rescue the hadith corpus from forgeries that had been falsely attributed to the Prophet. Centuries after his own death, al-Bukhari would in turn make appearances in hadith scholars' dreams, answering their questions about the reliability of specific transmitters.[188]

The line of flight activated by dreams and visions can both destabilize and restabilize the structure. These encounters authorize the power of the textual corpus, its methodologies, and legendary experts, who graduate from mere human scholars into transcendent guides who speak from beyond this world— but the portal remains open. In 1229 in Damascus, the Anda- lusian Sufi master Ibn al-ʿArabi received not only a visionary encounter with the Prophet, but also a gift from him. "In his hand," Ibn al-ʿArabi recalls, "he was holding a book, and he said to me, 'This is the book of the *Fusus al-Hikam*. Take it and give it to humanity so that they may obtain benefit from it.'" The *Fusus* contains stories of prophets with wild interpre- tive leaps, most famously in its treatment of Noah. Departing from what Muslims would usually read as the plain-sense un- derstanding of the Qurʾanic narrative—in which Noah warns his idolatrous and sinful people, they reject him, and he sur- vives while they are destroyed—the *Fusus* seems to side with the idolaters against their divinely appointed warner. Noah fails in his mission because he cannot recognize the "idolaters" as true gnostics possessing advanced knowledge of God; their "idols" are only God's attributes, and their punishments of alle- gorically drowning in flood and burning in hellfire express the perplexity that comes with their advanced knowledge. While profoundly challenging to many Muslims' sensibilities—and even, for the shaykh's more severe opponents, taking him out of Islam altogether—the entire book of the *Fusus* counts to be- lievers in Ibn al-ʿArabi's station as a kind of hadith, a delivery from Muhammad himself to the world.

For all of his theological and prophetological provoca- tions, Ibn al-ʿArabi remained legally conservative. He main- tained a friendly relationship to the jurists of Damascus and did not fall prey to accusations of lawlessness or political sub- version that had led to the executions of other visionaries, such as Mansur al-Hallaj and Suhrawardi. Dreams and visions of the Prophet were not in themselves threatening to the establishment, so long as they did not lead the dreamer or visionary to disrupt earthly authorities. The definitive value of a dream encounter therefore becomes its relation to power. But while Muslim intellectual traditions sought to regulate the possibilities for what someone could gain from a Muhammad dream, denying dreams as a basis for legal opinions, should a dreamer listen to the scholars or the Prophet? Muhammad's ability to appear in dreams provides sites at which claims to power are made and contested. While some Muslims perform specific prayers and recite formulas in order to increase the chance of seeing Muhammad, sages have warned that only advanced knowers see the Prophet in his truest form; others see him in symbolic forms that reflect their own conditions.[189]

Depending how Muslim dreamers understand their dreams—I have personally dreamed of the Prophet, but do not hold a stable position on what that means—Muhammad becomes more than a historical person located in a tomb in Saudi Arabia; he becomes a force that still exists in the world and continues to interact with his community.

34

KNOWLEDGE IN CHINA

Anas narrated:
The Messenger of God (God bless him and give him peace) said, "Seek knowledge even in China, since the search for knowledge is a duty for every Muslim."[190]

If I were to compile a "Top 40" collection of the most popular hadiths among American Muslims, the "knowledge in China" hadith would easily make the top ten. It was quite likely the first hadith that I ever learned, with the possible exception of Muhammad's statement that paradise rested under the feet of mothers. Both hadiths appeared frequently in my early readings on Islam and made for useful talking points when I explained my conversion to others, arguing that Islam was neither hostile to the intellect nor misogynistic.

Often presented with the supplementary context that in Muhammad's era, China would have signified the absolute end of the earth, this narration circulates well in Friday sermons aimed at students. The hadith instantly resonates with numerous other prophetic traditions from canonical collections in which Muhammad commands the pursuit of knowledge as a religious obligation and praises scholars as heirs to the prophets. Calling attention to legacies of Muslim philosophers and scientists, the hadith establishes intellectual curiosity and dedicated study as Islamic virtues. For somewhat different reasons, it also finds frequent citation in media directed toward non-Muslims: the hadith counters negative preconceptions about Islam, Muslims, and organized religion, offering a Muhammad who does not demand "fundamentalist" tunnel vision but instead praises the worldly seeker of knowledge.

In terms of historical reliability, the "knowledge in China" tradition, like the "paradise under the mother's feet" tradition, does not fare well against the classical methods of hadith evaluation. Based on analysis of the transmitters, hadith scholars give these traditions low ratings. Neither enjoys much canonical support. The hadith about mothers appears in only one of the Six Books, and one of the least prestigious of the Six, an-Nasa'i's *Sunan*. The "knowledge in China" hadith is not only absent from the canon, but actually shows up in anticanonical collections of fabricated narrations. But their troubled evidence has apparently done little to slow down their circulation.

In the later twentieth century, these poorly evidenced hadiths enjoyed widespread dissemination via popular booklets that were often sold at street markets outside masjids in cities such as Cairo and Damascus. As Nerina Rustomji explains, these booklets offered "popular theology . . . easy and inspirational reads for Muslims."[191] Even if these hadiths failed to meet scholars' highest standards of authenticity, they became ubiquitous ingredients in Muslim public conversation and no less "mainline" than narrations with stronger canonical gravitas. It could be difficult today to find a Muslim, Sunni or Shi'i, who has not heard both of these hadiths.

If one of the most popular and widely recognizable hadiths in the world is not in the canon, what exactly does it mean to be canon? What are the limits of texts with "canonical" and "mainstream" privilege in presenting a tradition?

35

HADITHS FOR LOSERS

Abu Hurayra narrated:
It was said, "O Messenger of God, from what is our Lord?"
He said, "From water not of earth, nor of the heavens. He created a horse and made it run. It sweated, and then he created himself from that sweat."[192]

"There is something powerful in being wrong, in losing, in failing," writes J. Halberstam in *The Queer Art of Failure*, "and all our failures combined might just be enough, if we practice them well, to bring down the winner."[193] In *The Queer God*, theologian Marcella Althaus-Reid describes the relocation of God in marginalized and transgressive identities (such as "God the Whore" and "Sodomite God") as "a project doomed to failure," but goes on to say that "we should feel ourselves free to fail."[194] In *Queer Phenomenology*, Sara Ahmed asks, "So what does it mean to say that an object fails to do the work for which it was intended? . . . A hammer might be broken and not enable me to do one thing, but it could still let me do something else."[195] So I wonder about hadiths that have failed, and the chance that some of these seemingly broken or dysfunctional tools can be picked up for a different kind of task.

The story of Allah's self-creation with horse sweat does not bear the endorsement of any hadith master; you're not going to find it in the collections of Bukhari or Muslim, nor the rest of the broader Six Books canon, or even respected collections by lesser luminaries. It certainly did not show up in the Intro to Islam pamphlets and books that I encountered as a young convert. By all accounts, the narration is not to be treated as a source for any recognizably Islamic conception of God. The horse-sweat tradition represents an undesirable extreme, for which it has been rejected, reviled, and offered up as an example of dangerous content beyond the limits of acceptable, appropriate Islam. It stands forever outside. The hadith's transmitters have been marked as heretics, poor scholars, liars, and self-serving charlatans. The weight of "orthodox" Muslim intellectual tradition, an immeasurable mountain of books, has fallen upon this narration of divine horse sweat with all of its weight, its force of truth, to crush the hadith and its claims.

With its advocates long gone, the horse-sweat hadith appears as the kind of failed tradition that we learn about only from its opponents, but the hadith's condemnation is also where it gets interesting. The horse-sweat hadith and its implications about God might strike us as a radically unthinkable image of Islamic tradition, but it could not have been unthinkable (or undesirable) for *every Muslim ever*. Otherwise, the hadith would not have existed, let alone circulated enough to become known and merit refutation. To achieve the dissemination that could threaten responsible scholars, this hadith of God's self-creation had to make sense to someone. While it's not likely that *the* Muhammad ever said these words, there were nonetheless Muslims who regarded the hadith as compatible with Muhammad's message. Though their voices are lost to us—we have only the condemnations of the individuals named as the hadith's original reporters, and the master critics' suspicions of their motives—some people apparently believed this hadith to be true, or that it could be true, and these people apparently understood themselves to be Muslims. What was Islam at a time when this idea of God could flow between teachers and students? Where were Islam's limits in a world in which such hadiths posed a potential threat? What possibilities existed then that we can't have today? Finally, how did unacceptable hadiths lose? Was it simply by being "wrong"? I am interested in the Muslims who first spread this hadith, the Muslims who believed in its content, and the space that they occupied.

Sunni Islam has been called a "cult of authenticity" for the rigorous methodologies through which premodern scholars evaluated alleged statements of Muhammad, vetting transmissions and their transmitters in vast archives of commentary and critique.[196] It has even been argued that these methodologies led to the creation of Sunni Islam as a thinkable concept.[197] The hadith traditions emerged as a process of power, in which a sectarian movement, popularly called the Hadith Folk, circled the wagons around its master scholars and made claims for its methodological supremacy. The Hadith Folk produced compilations of Muhammad's reported words and deeds as proof of their exclusive authority over his legacy. This coterie of elite proto-Sunni scholars, which preexisted Sunnism, eventually won its fight and secured authorization to brand itself as the center of Sunni tradition, succeeding to such a degree that its texts are now regarded as simply Sunni texts.

Yet the cult of authenticity, defined by its obsessive redrawing of borders between truth and forgery—borders over which it claims exclusive domain to construct and police by its own rules—also becomes a cult of inauthenticity. The makers of "mainstream" Islam spent a great deal of time thinking about Islam's edges and fringes, and where that line of demarcation existed, just as an obsession with personal hygiene feeds an obsession with whatever undermines it: the dirt under your fingernails, flakes of dead skin, traces of sweat, snot, blood, pus, piss, and shit. A clean canon could be achieved only by identifying and eliminating pollutants. This restless vigilance against the inauthentic produced its own anticanon; just as the Hadith Folk scholars produced collections of Muhammad's reported sayings and actions that were supported by the strongest evidence, they also gave attention to the accounts that they condemned as weakly evidenced or outright forgeries. The scholars' massive biographical dictionaries, cataloging thousands of traditionists whom they privileged as trustworthy reporters of Muhammad's words, were mirrored by compendiums of transmitters whom they deemed unreliable: reporters blacklisted as forgetful and lazy scholars, greedy scholars for hire, sectarian ideologues, unacceptable heretics, immoral and impious people, and simple poseurs looking for attention. The traditionists' efforts at purifying the canon by exposing unreliable reports and reporters ironically meant that they also immortalized the dirt, producing and preserving a whole archive of the material that they sought to erase. Thanks to their work, my bookshelves are now lined with excluded voices and rejected possibilities, defeated visions of Islam.

Hadith scholars regarded the horse-sweat tradition as *mustahil*, a textual artifact so bizarre and absurd that one could reject its content even without going through the usual process of vetting its transmitters. Nonetheless, they discussed the reporters out of loyalty to method and form. Ibn al-Jawzi (1126–1200) traces the narration to Muhammad ibn Shuja' al-Balkhi, an alleged anthropomorphist and "zealot" who falsely attributed his forged hadiths to trustworthy sources; al-Balkhi in turn reported that he had heard from Hibban ibn Hilal Abu Habib al-Bahili, a Basran scholar who had given up hadith studies out of frustration at the sloppiness of other Basran scholars; al-Bahili's reported source was Hammad ibn Salama, a controversial Basran transmitter who was included in Muslim's Sahih but avoided by Bukhari.[198] The hadith is finally traced to a traditionist named Abu al-Muhazzim, who claimed to have reported it on the authority of Abu Hurayra, a Companion of the Prophet. Experts in the classical method of transmitter-based hadith criticism—*'ilm al-rijal*, literally the "science of men"—universally reviled Abu al-Muhazzim with their professional terms of exclusion and marginalization, marking him as *da'if* (weak), *da'if jiddan* (extremely weak), *matruk* (abandoned), and *la shay'in* (nothing). In Ibn Sa'd's *Tabaqat*, Abu al-Muhazzim's disqualification comes at the hands of his own student, Shu'bah bin al-Hajjaj. Shu'bah pronounced Abu al-Muhazzim a weak transmitter and charged that he saw him in the mosque of Thabit al-Banani, "lying

on the ground" (*mutruhan*, which brings the additional con-
notations of being thrown down or dumped) and offering
to report seventy hadiths for a *fals*, a copper coin valued at
one thousandth of a dinar.[199] Modern Orientalist scholars also
wrote him off: Ignatz Goldziher called Abu al-Muhazzim a
"hadith beggar," repeating Shu'bah's charge that he peddled
prophetic reports from the mosque floor.[200] If you're willing
to commodify and sell hadiths, it's in your interest to offer
rare hadiths that no one had heard elsewhere, which in turn
means that it's best for business to simply invent them.

By all scholarly assessments, Abu al-Muhazzim was a
loser. J. Halberstam writes, "All losers are the heirs of those
who have lost before them."[201] In many Muslim contexts, I am
also a loser; I tend to associate with the wrong groups and cite
the wrong sources. For quite a few Muslims, my name is dirt.
Some of the most significant lineages that I have constructed
for myself end up performing the opposite function that we
usually ask from lineages; they serve only to disqualify me
and delegitimize my opinions. This might lead me to a weird
sense of kinship with Abu al-Muhazzim, the hadith hustler
selling forgeries.

If we focus on its transmission by problematic losers, the
horse-sweat tradition also exposes vulnerable points in the
hadith edifice that could shock its whole system. Despite
Abu al-Muhazzim's poor reputation, he does show up in a
few chains within the Six Books canon. Abu al-Muhazzim
taught students who went on to become scholars of higher
rank than himself. In these teacher-student relationships,
Abu al-Muhazzim represents a crack in the structure, a point
of leakage between the inside and outside. Bukhari does not

use Abu al-Muhazzim's transmissions, but Tirmidhi, Abu Dawud, and Ibn Maja cite him in hadiths on topics such as the sale of dogs and permissibility of eating locusts. In the Qur'an commentary of Ibn Kathir, a medieval scholar favored in modern Sunni revivalist circles, Abu al-Muhazzim contributes to our understanding of the 113th sura's third verse. Citing Abu al-Muhazzim, who in turn cites Abu Hurayra, Ibn Kathir tells us that the Qur'an's mention of "the evil of night when it comes" refers to a star. Abu al-Muhazzim might have been a loser, but the walls and barriers that keep losers out of the tradition remain significantly porous.

Sunnis were not the only Muslims with an intellectual tradition that could be called a cult of authenticity: other Muslim communities shared this investment in finding authenticity and properly documenting the unacceptable. Mention of the horse-sweat hadith appears in the *Bab al-Shaytan* ("Gate of the Devil"), a tenth-century Isma'ili heresiography dedicated to cataloguing various groups that the compiler condemns as standing beyond the pale of Islam. The text offers an entry on a group known as the Minhaliyya, so named for their leader, al-Minhal ibn Maymun al-'Ijli, who apparently taught that God possessed attributes of length, breadth, and width, as well as the ability to change his form. The Minhaliyya reportedly articulated their position from a certain understanding of God's absolute power. Nothing is more powerful than God; therefore, no being can possess a power that God lacks; this means that if the tradition portrays angels and devils as capable of changing their forms, God must also have this ability. The Minhaliyya then employ this theological point to argue that God can (and does) materialize with the forms of humans, animals, plants, jinns, angels, and essentially any being or solid object.[202]

The critical problem with cases such as Abu al-Muhazzim and the Minhaliyya remains that they do not get to speak for themselves; we learn about them from "orthodox" scholars for whom they exist only as objects of suspicion and scorn. Relying on these polemical sources would be comparable to learning about Muslims today exclusively from Fox News. We should thus exercise caution when presuming knowledge of the Minhaliyya's theology or the intentions of hadith scholars who transmitted the horse-sweat tradition. We can't presume, as Ibn al-Jawzi had, that reporters fabricated bizarre hadiths and forged their sources as part of a sectarian conspiracy to discredit hadith science.[203]

In the archives of forgotten and failed masters, we also find Muhammad al-Zawawi, a fifteenth-century North African visionary who kept an extensive diary of more than one hundred dream encounters with the Prophet. He did not win the status that his dream records claimed for him, but the diary survives. In one dream, Muhammad carries al-Zawawi like an infant, first holding al-Zawawi over his shoulder as though the Prophet would burp him. Then the Prophet cradles al-Zawawi and places his nipple in al-Zawawi's mouth, nursing him. This was the nipple that felt the cold of God's own hand; it's notably the left nipple, closer to the prophetic heart that received knowledge through divine touch. The narrative echoes milk imagery found elsewhere, such as the hadiths found in Shi'i sources of Muhammad's uncle Abu Talib breastfeeding Muhammad when he was a toddler and of Husayn receiving milk through his grandfather's thumb.[204] The flow of milk from Muhammad's body into his grandson and al-Zawawi, beyond its loaded symbolism for al-Zawawi as a mystic heir to the Prophet's knowledge, gives us an imaginary of the Prophet that perhaps we had not expected: Muhammad as wet nurse or even mother.[205] I also want Muhammad's milk. If this dream from six centuries ago becomes a resource for me, and Muhammad becomes my mother, does something change in my Islam? What I really mean to ask: With a new way to think about the Prophet, does something change in me? Maybe, or maybe not. The rejected library is a space for experiments.

As an introduction to Muhammad, what potential value can we find in a hadith that Muslim intellectual tradition and its mighty scholars, Sunni and Shi'i alike, uniformly rejected as a flagrant forgery and betrayal of all comprehensibly Islamic ideas about God? Not all hadiths rejected by scholars as inauthentic will offer the tools to liberation: we should be thankful that premodern scholars denounced false hadiths such as "A Black man lives only for his stomach and his genitals"[206] and "The intellect of women is in their vaginas."[207] Power isn't always on the wrong side, and sometimes we'll find useful resources in the "official" Muhammad of canonical texts and establishment scholars. But perhaps it's worth remembering that beyond the limits of mainline scholarship, another Muhammad waits. The horse-sweat hadith reminds us that the Muhammad whom we pursue remains a contested terrain, a battlefield, and a burial ground where we encounter the winners of intellectual power struggles. We should remember that the losers are there too, their graves often unmarked but their bodies still fertilizing the soil.

36

QUEERING MUHAMMAD

> *Al-Sha'bi narrated:*
> A delegation from the tribe of 'Abd al-
> Qays came to the Messenger of God (God
> bless him and give him peace) and with
> them was a beardless boy of radiant beauty.
> The Prophet (God bless him and give him
> peace) seated him behind him. And he said,
> "The mistake of David was the gaze."[208]

According to this narration, Muhammad made an effort to avoid looking at a handsome young man, apparently to avoid temptation. What happens if we imagine the Prophet—the same one who reportedly said that he feared no sin for his community more than the sin of Lot's people—as a gay man?

First, we should exercise critical caution when discussing sexuality in another historical setting. People in seventh-century Hijaz who experienced physical or romantic attraction to people of their own gender would not have defined that attraction with the same categories that we use today. While various phenomena that we might reasonably mark with the label of "homosexuality" certainly existed in early Islam, our present category of homosexuality did not operate in that world. This also means that there was no heterosexuality either. Khaled el-Rouayheb's work on how Muslims historically thought of same-sex attraction, *Before Homosexuality in the Arab-Islamic World, 1500–1800*, could have just as accurately been titled *Before Heterosexuality*.

Beardless youths were the premier sex symbols of the broader Mediterranean world, and it seemed to have been a given that any man could experience temptation in their seductive power—even the Prophet himself. In *The Distinct Necklace on Love of Beardless Youth*, seventeenth-century Palestinian scholar Muhammad Abu al-Fath al-Dajjani says of this hadith: "And if God's messenger, unerring and free of all deformation, guilt or indeceny," feared his own gaze at the beardless boy, "what about all those who are not thus immune?"[209]

The Prophet apparently feared the acts of Lot's nation as a universal threat to which all men were susceptible. The Prophet's cousin and son-in-law 'Ali, when asked why sex between males had been forbidden, reportedly explained that if men could penetrate these youths, they would abandon women and the human species would become extinct.[210] This is not the objection to homosexuality that would become common in modern religious conversations, condemning same-sex love with the claim that it's unnatural, a betrayal of one's biological wiring. Just the opposite: according to no less an authority than 'Ali, sex with beardless youths is more naturally compelling for most men than their desire to biologically reproduce. The attraction is so natural that it requires regulation by artificial means: interventions of culture and law, and threats of punishment in this world and the next.

The great hadith masters and jurists of early Islam confess to the power and danger of beautiful boys. El-Rouayheb provides accounts of Sufyan al-Thawri (d. 778) stating that he feared a lone devil with every woman but no less than seventeen devils with every beardless youth, and Abu Hanifa (d. 767), eponym of the Hanafi legal tradition, making an attractive male student sit behind him to avoid "betrayal by the eye," thereby following the Prophet's own reported practice.[211] Medieval Hanbali scholar Ibn al-Jawzi (1126–1200), who refers to the story of the Abu Qays delegation in his *Dhamm al-Hawa* (Censure of Passion), took it as a fact of nature that boys were more tempting than girls.[212]

While scholars agreed upon the danger of beautiful young men, some appeared to be less vigilant than others. The great hadith transmitter and historian Khatib al-Baghdadi, author of the immense *Tarikh al-Baghdad*, kept the company of a handsome boy in Damascus, who had allegedly traveled with him from Baghdad. The chief of police, investigating accusations concerning al-Baghdadi and the boy, reportedly went to al-Baghdadi's house and found them alone together. Al-Baghdadi's critics used the story of his affair with the boy to discredit him, while more sympathetic writers admitted, "His story with the youth whom he loved is well known," but were willing to more or less look the other way, due to al-Baghdadi's importance as a scholar of hadith.[213] In her work on the significance of sexuality in the mystical thought of Andalusian Sufi master Ibn al-'Arabi, Sa'diyya Shaikh acknowledges the "heterosexist underpinnings" of Ibn al-'Arabi's ideas, but points out the master's reference to a "slave girl [*jariyya*] or slave boy [*ghulam*]" as the lover's potential beloved. "Unless Ibn 'Arabi is suddenly introducing a female subjectivity when speaking about the slave boy," Shaikh observes, "this extract creates an opening to investigate the implications for alternative sexualities in Ibn 'Arabi's framework. Is this a glimmer of acknowledgment that other types of sexuality might not be readily dismissed as fundamentally deviant and utterly problematic?"[214]

Modern discussions of tawhid generally take it for granted that God exists beyond gender. We often point to the ways that God's Ninety-nine Names can open us to contemplate God in both masculine and feminine terms and insist that the divine "he" shows up in the Qur'an due only to Arabic's gendered grammar. Yet God also appears in hadith traditions as a gorgeous and intensely embodied young man; reports call attention to God's lush hair, golden sandals, and green cloaks, and sometimes depict him reclining on a bed. Hadiths of God's gendered appearance often describe him in sensuous terms: in one controversial hadith tradition, God-as-boy transmits knowledge to Muhammad through physical encounter, placing his hand between Muhammad's shoulders. Narrating the episode to his Companions, Muhammad recalls that he felt the coolness of God's palm in his nipples. The Prophet's report of his physical sensation highlights the encounter as real and presents God's touch as penetrative, achieving a transmission into Muhammad's flesh—specifically at his heart, which was regarded in the premodern world of this hadith as the organ of intellect. As with other provocative or potentially troublesome hadith traditions, this story appears in a variety of versions. Shi'i hadith scholars recognized the hadith as authentic in its transmission history, but read it strictly as a dream. Only a single report of the safest version—the encounter happening in a dream and including the cold hand, but lacking the detailed description of God's "best form"—achieved a spot within the Six Books canon.

If God exists beyond gender, these hadiths amount to God performing a kind of drag, undermining masculinity through mimicry of its costumes and gestures. Could we also read the story as an erotic encounter? Is it an accident that God appears in the embodied form that countless men across the ancient Mediterranean praised as the ultimate object of sensual desire—or, for that matter, the illicit temptation that Muslim jurists most feared? The tradition reads as simultaneously homophobic and homoerotic. Muhammad, fearful that anal intercourse will destroy the men of his community, warns of the dangers in gazing at beautiful, beardless boys. In one hadith, Muhammad explains, "Looking at what is forbidden is an arrow from the Devil; therefore you should warn the righteous not to sit with beardless youths, nor to speak to them, nor to walk with them, for fear of mischief (*fitna*)."[215] But the Qur'an also invites contemplation of "eternal boys" as sensual rewards for the believers in paradise. Two of the Qur'an's three mentions of these boys appear within short sequences that also describe the *hur*, the paradisical maidens of large eyes, firm breasts, and eternally renewing virginity (52:20–24, 56:17–23). Though the boys' role in paradise is ostensibly to serve drinks to the believers, the Qur'an describes these boys and the hur with the exact same term, "well-protected pearls" (52:24, 26:23). Muhammad sees God in this very form, even calling it the "best form"; this is the

God who puts his own hand to Muhammad's skin, turning Muhammad's nipples cold. God prohibits men from gazing with desire at other male bodies but redirects that energy toward himself. Omid Ghaemmaghani observes a parallel tradition in Shi'i sources surrounding the twelfth Imam, the awaited Mahdi, who disappeared as a child centuries ago and will return to this world in the form of an exceptionally gorgeous youth (*shabb*, "youth," potentially signifying a man anywhere from his teens to his thirties) with deep black eyes, radiant complexion, lush hair (and often a beard), and a face that shines like the moon.[216] Muslims have also imagined the Prophet himself as a beautiful youth, as seen in the popular Iranian portrait. When I showed my Muhammad poster in class, one student's initial reaction was surprise that the artist had depicted Muhammad "as a woman," and others perceived the poster as eroticizing young Muhammad. In his reflection on Christ's masculine body and the challenges and opportunities that it poses to queer theology, Mark D. Jordan asks, "Is it surprising that an officially homophobic doctrine would take as its central image an *almost* naked man being tortured?"[217] What does it mean that in an "officially homophobic" vision of Islam, Muhammad's encounter with God can embrace a sensuality that both of them had allegedly condemned?

For a particular corner of Sufi tradition, men's contemplations of the sensuous male body were not in conflict or contradiction with the pursuit of God. Some Sufis, including notable thinkers such as Awhad al-Din Kirmani (d. 1237), Ahmad al-Ghazali (poet, mystic, and less famous brother of *the* al-Ghazali), and al-Ghazali's martyred disciple 'Ayn al-Qudat al-Hamadhani engaged in *shahid bazi* ("witness play"), the controversial practice of gazing at beautiful boys as a mode of contemplating God's attributes. Shahid bazi often accompanied practices that jurists and many sober-minded Sufis would disdain, such as musical concerts, dancing, ecstatic states, and spontaneous outbursts of poetry with possibly heretical or scandalous content. Critics condemned shahid bazi as idolatry and suspected that gazing and dancing inevitably led to touching; Kirmani was accused of ripping the shirts of young men so that their bare chests touched his as they danced together.[218] Opponents of shahid bazi linked theological and sexual subversion, accusing Sufi dervishes of exploiting boys with claims that they could transmit blessings and advanced knowledge through anal intercourse.[219] In his *Sufis & Saints' Bodies*, Scott Kugle calls attention to the love between Punjabi Sufi poet Shah Husayn (1539–1599) and his Hindu boyfriend, Madho Lal, that later poets celebrated as simultaneously a physical relationship and spiritual initiation.[220] The two remain entombed together in a shared shrine in Lahore, which regularly receives visits, respectful maintenance, and donations of flower petals, cash, and prayers; the site also includes alleged footprints of the Prophet.

Advocates of shahid bazi such as 'Ayn al-Qudat authorized their practice using the precedent of the Prophet, who witnessed God during his ascension in the precise form through which they contemplated God in the world.[221] Even as 'Ayn al-Qudat refers to the boy who receives his attention as an "idol," playfully accepting the outrage of his critics, he finds support in the divinely revealed Sunna: to encounter God's beauty in this embodied form imitates Muhammad's own experience as recorded in authoritative sources. Within the same hadith sources, we could also find subtle opposition to the practice. In his *Love Theory in Later Hanbalite Islam*, Joseph Norment Bell notes a compelling overlap: while the hadith masters present a number of traditions in which Muhammad repeatedly warns 'Ali about the danger of allowing oneself a second glance ("a poisoned arrow which stirs up desire in the heart"), the majority of Sufi orders (regardless of their Sunni or Shi'i orientation) happen to trace their chains of authority back to 'Ali. The hadith masters depict Muhammad warning 'Ali of the very practice that would become associated with groups that claim 'Ali as their spiritual template. With awareness that scholars forged hadiths to make interventions in contemporary issues, Bell speculates that this overlap might not be an accident or coincidence.[222]

If the act of "queering" a text or tradition, as Ellen T. Armour explains, means "to complicate, to disrupt, to disturb all kinds of orthodoxies," the immense and multivocal hadith corpus invites a queering of Muhammad in part through its unmanageable mass, the many thousands of scholars who contributed to its making, and the diversity of ways that Muslims decide which hadiths are most useful to them both within and beyond "canon." The very shape of the hadith corpus resists absolute coherence and stability, even when it acts as the supreme orthodoxy-making machine. The Prophet undergoes queering in the multiplicities that become possible for him and those who love him.

Queerness does not merely refer to sexual orientation, but rather points out the ways that gender and sexuality become devices to marginalize communities and portray them as monstrous. In this sense, Islam has already been queered by modern Islamophobia networks, which weaponize Muhammad's sexuality against him. Muhammad's marriage to young A'isha marks him as a "queer" monster, as Islamophobic media highlights their marriage to disparage the Prophet—and by implication, modern Muslims. In the nineteenth century, when child brides were still a relatively common part of American life, anti-Muslim critics ignored the A'isha question and instead focused on Muhammad's practice of plural marriage, resonant with anti-Mormon polemics. For Christians working with the model of a celibate Christ, a voraciously sexual Muhammad—portrayed in classical sources as having the libido of dozens of men—represented the antithesis of what it meant to be genuinely spiritual. Even if all of his sex partners were female, Muhammad became "queer" in Euro-Christian imaginations for his incompatibility with both the asexual Jesus and privileged monogamy.

During the holy month of Ramadan in the summer of 2016, following the mass shooting at Orlando's Pulse nightclub, members of the Muslim and LGBTQ communities at Duke and UNC came together to express their mutual support and alliance. Duke's Center for Sexual and Gender Diversity hosted an *iftar*, the evening breaking of the Ramadan fast, announcing the event as an open and safe space that welcomed everyone. The performance of the evening prayer reflected a careful and respectful negotiation between various Muslim commitments. The call to prayer was performed by a woman, signaling an investment in gender-egalitarian ritual reform that most Muslims would consider radical; nonetheless, the organizers negotiated with participants who believed that only men can lead a mixed-gender congregation, inviting me to lead the prayer. After the prayer and dinner, the organizers facilitated a conversation in which anyone who wanted to address the gathering had a chance to speak. Rather than target homophobia in Muslim communities or Islamophobia in LGBTQ communities, speakers called for solidarity against a shared oppressor, highlighting the forces of white patriarchy that target both communities. It was crucial to avoid the homonationalist traps of Republicans who suddenly claimed to care about LGBTQ safety now that the issue involved a Muslim enemy. Meanwhile, Muslims also took the conversation beyond the Orlando Statement, an unsatisfying attempt by Muslim community leaders and scholarly authorities to condemn the Pulse murders while also emphasizing an absolute distinction between Muslims' "Abrahamic morality" and LGBTQ communities (which they presented as entirely unrelated to Muslim communities). More than one speaker emphasized that as we pursue collaborations between Muslim and LGBTQ communities, we must recognize and center LGBTQ Muslims, who stood at the intersection of these identities and yet were frequently erased in both.

The post-Pulse iftar, as well as a "queer iftar" held by Muslim students at Duke and UNC the previous year, created new spaces and expanded possibilities for what it could mean to have Muslim community. Within the narrow constraints of my early Muslim experience, I could not have imagined these spaces existing, let alone claiming a foundation in the Prophet's legacy. For Muslims who find their community in a queer iftar, however, there remain visions of Muhammad that might nourish us, a Muhammad who stands with the excluded and endangered.

37

KNOWLEDGE OF SELF

'Ali narrated:
> The Messenger of God (God bless him
> and give him peace) said, "He who knows
> himself knows his Lord."[223]

This hadith resonates powerfully with Greek philosophical tradition, echoing the famed maxim of the Delphic oracle, "Know yourself and know your god." The great Muslim philosopher Ibn Sina (Avicenna) attributed it to Aristotle and, as L. E. Goodman explains, found in its command "an invitation to profound self-scrutiny."[224] The Delphic maxim had appeared in circulation as a prophetic hadith by Ibn Sina's time, having been popularized in Sufi circles, and had also circulated in Hellenized Jewish and Christian versions, enabling Platonic and biblical conceptions of selfhood to find homes in the same words.[225] This linkage of self-knowledge with knowledge of the divine could show the artifact that we're calling Muhammad to be a product of cultural intersection and exchange, rather than a singular individual from seventh-century Arabia who either said things or did not say things.

In the *maghazi* works of early Islam, chroniclers portrayed Muhammad as an epic hero of the battlefield as per the folkoric traditions that they inherited; in Central Asia, nomadic tribes embraced Muhammad as an ideal teacher in their model of the shaman; biblically oriented believers prioritized Muhammad's link to the prophetic tradition associated with Abraham, Moses, and Jesus; early Chinese Muslims rewrote Muhammad in Confucian and Buddhist terms, with some referring to God as "Buddha" rather than "Allah";[226] there were even communities in South Asia that understood Muhammad as an avatar of Vishnu. For Muslim readers of the Greek intellectual corpus, Muhammad naturally appeared in the mold of a supreme philosopher. Promoting this image of the Prophet, Muslim rationalists also circulated hadiths, some of dubious origin, in which Muhammad praised the authority of reason. Muslim philosophers came to imagine philosophy and prophethood as expressions of the same knowledge, each speaking in the language of its audience. In other words, prophets provided the truths of philosophy to common folk who lacked training as intellectuals and thus depended on allegorical expressions (such as the Qur'an's mention of God sitting on a throne), while philosophers pursued in their rigorous training the knowledge that unlettered prophets obtained by intuition. To study the thought of Aristotle, therefore, was not antithetical to studying the Qur'an, but rather offered a privileged key for unlocking the Qur'an's meanings.

A considerable body of literature in Muslim traditions

would either directly quote, creatively appropriate, or otherwise engage Muhammad's link of self-knowledge with the
quest for God. In his posthumous classic *What Is Islam?*, Shahab Ahmed cites this hadith in his argument for alternative
ways of conceptualizing the classical tradition. While some
would imagine the concern with self-knowledge to have been
trademarked as exclusively a value of post-Enlightenment
Western Europe, accessible to the rest of the world only as
a late modern import, Ahmed asserts that we should think
of the quest for self-knowledge as "centrally constitutive of
Islam" throughout Muslim history.[227] For Ahmed, the "Whoever knows himself" hadith was central to a popular conception of human selfhood at which we can observe resonances
between Muslim mystics, philosophers, and poets; the hadith
thus highlights an element of Muslim life no less significant
than the law-centered traditions that often get privileged as
properly "Islamic."[228] Again, this Muslim echo of the Delphic
maxim reflects many Muslims' senses of Muhammad: they
understand the statement as something that Muhammad
would or *did* say because they already have an idea of what
"Muhammad-ness" means. The hadith represents a Muhammad that speaks to and through their knowledge of the world,
which of course includes all of the other sayings and practices attributed to the Prophet, but also their resources beyond
what gets typically marked as "Islamic." For our purposes
here, Ahmed's observation that "human and historical Islam
is arguably as Neo-Platonic as it is Muhammadan"[229] could
also be read to say, "*Muhammad* is arguably as Neo-Platonic
as he is Muhammadan." If we acknowledge Muhammad as
being continually rewritten and reproduced by these makers

of "human and historical Islam" and consider the full range of their resources, it's not so absurd to comprehend visions of Muhammad as a Hellenic philosopher or even as Vishnu.

The enormously important Andalusian theosopher Ibn al-'Arabi regarded the hadith as authentic (*sahih*), but not by the hadith scholars' methods of assessing reporters and the chain of transmission. Rather, from his position as a sage who had achieved supreme spiritual advancement, Ibn al-'Arabi accepted the hadith as authentic through his intuition and mystical unveiling (*kashf*). In premodern modes of knowledge, this would have been an acceptable method; even the great hadith masters, despite being reimagined today as purely scientific collectors of data, often engaged dreams and visions as real sources of truth. The authority of mystical knowledge did undergo regulation—jurists denied mysticism the power to rewrite law, and any individual mystic could be discredited as a fraud or heretic, subject to book-burning or even execution—but mystical knowledge itself enjoyed popular acceptance as a measurement of truth. This hadith introduces Muhammad as a malleable and fluid entity. His words can be found beyond the corpus of stringently vetted hadith collections by jurists who sought to recover and restore the historical man; Muhammad's sayings and actions can also undergo vetting in the gut (at least the elite gut that has been qualified by sufficient training and cultivation).

For his often bewildering systematizations of theology, cosmology, and mystical pursuits, and the celebrations of paradox and contradiction that run throughout his work, Ibn al-'Arabi becomes vulnerable to misreadings. When one considers the ways in which Ibn al-'Arabi himself treated perplexity and the ambiguity of language, however, the question of what might constitute a "misreading" in his case becomes somewhat complicated; it is by no means a random accident that we now have scholarly monographs placing Ibn al-ʿArabi's thought in conversation with the *shaykh al-akbar* of French postmodernism, Jacques Derrida.[230] In his commentary on the "Whoever knows himself" hadith, Ibn al-ʿArabi emphasizes the fleeting impermanence of human existence, the ways in which humans are definitively not divine; one comes to know God by knowing the true smallness of being human, the absolute poverty of our existence in comparison to God. Sunni theologian (and Ibn al-ʿArabi's contemporary) Fakhr al-Din al-Razi gave a similar reading to the hadith: to know that you are temporary leads to appreciating your lord as eternal.[231] When humans recognize the limits of their own cognitive powers as utterly unequipped to comprehend God, knowledge of self leads to a sort of knowledge of the divine.[232] Another contemporary of Ibn al-ʿArabi, the poet-saint Rumi, interpreted the hadith as rendering each human being a potential "astrolabe of God." From the astrolabe of one's own existence, a human can attain knowledge of God, comparable to an astrolabe of mere copper mirroring the majestic heavens.[233]

Ibn al-ʿArabi remains a polarizing figure; opponents particularly take offense at his complex theology of *wahdat al-wujud* ("the unity of existence"), accusing him of pantheism, atheism, and belief in God's incarnation within material bodies.[234] Opponents and supporters alike read Ibn al-ʿArabi's kashf-based advocacy for this hadith alongside his wujudi system, his project of human development expressed as the "anthropocosmic/cosmoanthropic concept of the Perfect or Complete Human" (*al-insan al-kamil*),[235] and also the dangerous statements attributed to earlier Sufis such as al-Hallaj, who was accused of claiming to be one with the divine. Medieval critics of Ibn al-'Arabi indeed charged that a circle of his readers in Yemen had taken to calling each other God.[236]

*

The hadith became meaningful for me in my travels between "classical" Islam and American Muslim traditions. The Nation of Islam (NOI), a movement that originated among African American converts in 1930s Detroit, and whose most famous iteration is led today by Louis Farrakhan, taught that Black people were gods, and that becoming the highest god (Allah) involved a project of rigorous self-perfection. The NOI holds that Allah came in the person of its founder, Master Fard Muhammad. This does not mean that Allah otherwise exists as a transcendent, abstract spirit and then incarnated himself into Fard Muhammad's body, but rather that Fard Muhammad trained under elevated masters in Mecca to become Allah, the best knower and complete human, and then traveled to America to create an entire nation of gods. In conversation with Farrakhan's followers, I have encountered repeated references to the "whoever knows himself" hadith. In their reading, knowledge of self means comprehension of one's limitless potential for discipline, self-improvement, and achievement: to know one's power is the first step toward activating one's power as inherently divine, realizing one's personal godhood and in turn awakening the same knowledge of self in others. Whether or not Ibn al-'Arabi—or for that matter, the historical Muhammad—would have authorized this interpretation, the NOI's project of divine Black excellence processes itself in part as an expression of Muhammad's own words and the construction of Muhammad found in Sufi interpretive tradition.

I began to seriously explore NOI tradition by engaging the Five Percenters, a community that originated in the 1960s when a former NOI member renamed himself Allah and taught his interpretation of NOI Lessons to young Black and Latino men across Harlem and Brooklyn. This Allah shared the rights to his name with his disciples, recognizing them as gods and supreme knowers in their own right. In the Five Percenter context, knowledge of self means that one no longer worships an abstract, transcendent god that exists outside the self, but instead recognizes divine power within. For this reason, many Five Percenters told me that they should not be called Muslims, as they do not perform "surrender"/ "submission" (*islam*) to a power of the unseen. And yet, Muslim or not, performing islam or not, Five Percenters maintain a claim on Islam. Five Percenters sometimes justified their teachings to me using the Qur'an, and a number of Five Percenters engage Sufism to locate themselves in Islamic tradition. When I visited the Five Percenters, we shared in the greeting of "Peace, god," and many told me that what they called "knowledge of self" amounted to nothing less than the ultimate truth (*haqq*) of Islam: as custodians of this secret, they counted Ibn al-'Arabi and even the Prophet within Five Percenter tradition. They would read the widely disseminated prophetic hadith "Create yourself with God's traits"[237] through a lens informed by the Nation of Islam. While some Five Percenters shrugged off interest in Muhammad or Sufism, others located their godhood squarely in the hadith that Ibn al-'Arabi had promoted: more than one Five Percenter, engaging me as a stand-in for "orthodox Islam," insisted that Muhammad had said, "Whoever knows himself knows his Lord." Ibn al-'Arabi's critics had charged that his ideas had dangerously undermined the distinction between divinity and humanity, but this accusation did not trouble Five Percenters, who regarded such a distinction as purely imaginary.

One elder of the Five Percenters, First Born Prince Allah, self-identified as both a Muslim and Five Percenter, alienating many of his peers in both communities. Though Five Percenters generally reject prayer in the sense of appealing to a transcendent "Other" outside the self (if you're God, who do you pray to?), First Born Prince Allah regularly attended congregational Friday prayers at Sunni masjids. Despite critics' objections, he did not perceive his Sunni prayers to be in conflict with his Five Percenter godhood. In fact, he regarded one as a route to the other; it was during a Sunni ritual practice that First Born Prince Allah attained the truth of the Five Percenters. While washing in preparation for prayer, First Born Prince Allah glanced at the bathroom mirror, stared into his own reflection, and realized that he only prayed to himself. First Born Prince Allah's recognition of his godhood while engaged in Sunni practice becomes a lodestone for Five Percenters invested in Muslim tradition: in the Five Percenter community, the category-defying First Born Prince Allah even became paradoxically known as the "Sunni god." For Five Percenters who studied Sufi tradition, First Born Prince

Allah represented the knowledge of self that they understood as the pinnacle of Sufi advancement.

While a student of the Five Percenters, I also accepted initiation in the Nimatullahi Order, a Sufi community that had originated in fourteenth-century Iran and could be called a wujudi order for its investment in Ibn al-'Arabi's teachings. When I visited Nimatullahi lodges in Boston, New York, and San Francisco, fellow dervishes met me with the greeting "Ya al-Haqq" ("O Reality"). Calling each other by al-Haqq, a Name of God, we affirmed the secret of Mansur al-Hallaj, who had reportedly earned his martyrdom for proclaiming himself al-Haqq while in a fit of mystical ecstasy. To my ears, the Nimatullahi greeting naturally linked this experience to my Five Percenter experience. It also happened to be in a Nimatullahi lodge's library that I came across a short book of commentary on the "Whoever knows himself" hadith (unreliably) attributed to Ibn al-'Arabi.

Like the Five Percenters, the Nimatullahi Order—which began as a Sunni Sufi order at the end of the fourteenth century, became a Shi'i Sufi order as the rest of Iran became Shi'i, and sought some degree of distance from formal Muslim identity after Iran's Islamic Revolution in 1979—discouraged overemphasis on overtly Muslim-ish elements of their heritage. "We don't advocate reading the Qur'an," a Nimatullahi shaykh told me at my first visit, adding that Nimatullahis did not prioritize the five daily prayers. Echoing the "Whoever knows his lord" hadith, Nimatullahi literature informed me that seeking knowledge of self was more valuable than interpreting sacred scripture. Even the greeting of "Ya al-Haqq" related to the group's rebranding: dervishes in the 1970s had greeted each other with "Ya 'Ali." Though I certainly wouldn't suggest that a name of God was less "Islamic" than the name of 'Ali, these names would undergo a new coding in the post-'79 context. The switch to "Ya al-Haqq" celebrated an executed heretic over the first Shi'i Imam and emphasized the Nimatullahis' Hallajian/wujudi orientation over Khomeini's state-Shi'ism project.

Regardless of how "Muslim" or "non-Muslim" it might have appeared, the Nimatullahi Order still boasted a teaching lineage (*silsila*) that connected its current master back through the centuries to its founder, Shah Nimatullah Wali, whose chain of teachers extended in turn to the ascetic luminary Hasan al-Basri and through him achieved a connection to 'Ali, himself the spiritual heir to the Prophet. Whether concerned with the label of "Muslim" or not, the order regarded itself as an authoritative heir to that knowledge. In a move that would strike many as paradoxical, the Nimatullahis maintained a claim on their sense of Islam without feeling much pressure to properly perform as a Muslim community, and deauthorized Muslim religious practice while remaining authorized by its link to Muhammad—even publishing collections of hadiths, drawn from a considerable range of Muslim sources, that anchored the order in commitment to its prophetic lineage. But paradoxes were not a problem for me. Traveling between the Nimatullahi lodge in downtown Manhattan and the Five Percenters' Allah School in Harlem, and also a number of Sunni and Shi'i masjids throughout New York, I became a happy pastiche of seemingly random references that didn't feel random. Even in my doctrinal instability, I felt personally coherent. And while all of this was happening, I also enrolled in Shahab Ahmed's seminar on Ibn al-'Arabi at Harvard.

In *What Is Islam?*, Shahab Ahmed introduces the problem guiding his book's title by asking a series of questions, one of which concerns Sufi masters who claimed, by virtue of having attained "experiential oneness with the Real Truth, *al-haqiqah*," to transcend the legal and ritual bounds of shari'a. Asking whether this could amount to an "Islamic" claim, he proceeds to examine the Sufi project of human development—accepted in popular, "mainstream," and even politically advantaged expressions as indeed "Islamic"—for more than a thousand years.[238] For Ahmed, these provocative claims were not only Islamic, but definitively so, as they engage the divine revelation to Muhammad.[239] What mattered was the process of making meaning through the revelation, rather than the specific methods and sources that one chose for the work, or, for that matter, the conclusions that one reached. It became thinkable that even a self-identified apostate, leaving what s/he considers to be the boundaries of Islam, remains "Islamic" when s/he exits through an Islamic escape route. If Muhammad appears to you in a vision and tells you to no longer be a Muslim, and you obey him because you accept his authority over you as the Prophet of God, and you also believe that the Prophet of God can communicate with you in visions and dreams, does your obedience really take you out of Islam?

I had once mentioned the Five Percenters during a discussion of wujudi Sufi poets in Ahmed's seminar, specifically the ways in which Five Percenter hip-hop artists such as the RZA could satisfy multiple registers with their lyrics.

When the RZA says "Allah," for example, this word means radically different things to "orthodox" Muslims and to Five Percenters, but both can read the verse on their own terms and thus accept it as true on their own terms. Like a classical Sufi poem, the lyrics invite a variety of interpretations, some more publicly acceptable than others. Five Percenter MCs, at least to my ears, spoke as the ambiguous Sufi poet-sages of their world. Ahmed gave me a look as though I had jumped out of my seat and stabbed the student next to me, and I remained silent for the rest of the semester; the Five Percenters and Louis Farrakhan certainly did not register to him as heirs of what he called the "Sufi-philosophical amalgam" of the classical "Balkans-to-Bengal complex." But taking Ahmed's brilliant seminar in Boston while bouncing between readers of the "Whoever knows himself" hadith, I found a place for myself within multiple orientations—including not only the Five Percenters and Nimatullahis, but also the "regular," "normative," "mainstream," and "orthodox" mosques—that claimed Islam in different ways while drawing from a shared set of references. Though agreeing that the border between Creator and creation might be flimsy and even an illusion, Nimatullahis and Five Percenters could find themselves theologically beyond reconciliation if pushed on the finer points of their ideas: in Nimatullahi contexts, we encounter the suggestion that only God really exists, and human existence is nothing; Five Percenters tend to argue the opposite, asserting that humans represent God because no mystery god outside humanity exists. But even if people found antithetical truths in its words, the "knowledge of self" hadith enables the construction of a bridge. It facilitates travel between wildly divergent ideas about the relationship between God and humanity. The Sufi lodge and Five Percenter school (and even the Sunni masjid) all possessed their own truths that they could anchor in the same statement of Muhammad. There was a sense of Islam to be experienced in both Muhammad's potential for multiplicity and my own doctrinal incoherence.

Like every introduction to Muhammad, this hadith showcases some versions of Muhammad and excludes others. The "Whoever knows himself" tradition provides an important glimpse into historical Islam, regardless of how one judges its connection to the historical Muhammad. For luminaries such as Rumi, the hadith conveys a meaningful element of the Muhammadi project, indeed the project of being human. A wealth of Muslim intellectual, spiritual, and artistic traditions engaged the hadith as foundational to Islam and a true statement of Muhammad, reflecting an image of Muhammad as supreme gnostic, esoteric philosopher, and still-present guide on the mystical path (and also contributing to further renditions of that image). As I heard echoes of the hadith among my Nimatullahi teachers, the core of Muhammad's message materialized as follows: each human being has been endowed with a particular capacity for knowing God, his/her cup; our purpose in this world is to fill our cups with knowledge of the divine to their fullest capacity, and perhaps expand our cups in order to hold more.

This image of Muhammad gets less play in the modern world than articulations of the Prophet as supreme lawgiver, social engineer, and statesman; but looking at Islam through the ages, our wujudi gnostic Muhammad appears to have been at least as historically mainline as the Muhammad of law and governance. There were contexts in which wujudi Sufism, including orders such as the Nimatullahis, enjoyed access to imperial power and patronage, even a place in the making of Islamic "orthodoxy." The modern narratives that popularly envision Sufis as beyond the pale of established Muslim authority, thereby pitting "political," "law-obsessed," and "ritualistic" (thus supposedly spiritless) Islamic "orthodoxy" against "spiritual" (thus supposedly uninterested in politics, law, or ritual) or even "heretical" Sufism, would not have made sense in all other times and places. Today, this hadith carries us to the margins, but at another time would have brought us to the center, or at least *a* center among multiple centers, and a center that would surprise many non-Muslims and Muslims alike.

38

HAIR AND SKIN

'Abu Humayd and Abu Asayd narrated:
The Messenger of God (God bless him and give him peace) said, "When you hear a hadith from me and your hearts recognize it, and your hair and skin become soothed with it, and you feel that it is near to you, I am the nearest of you to it. And when you hear a hadith from me that your hearts deny, and your hair and skin shy from it, and you feel that it is far from you, I am the most distant of you from it."[240]

I owe this hadith to Muslim scholar and activist Laury Silvers, who shared it with me when I confessed my own struggles with aspects of Muhammad's life. There is a Muhammad of textual record, Muhammad as delivered by the sources. Or rather, lots of Muhammads. Due not only to the radically different world that we inhabit in our modern condition, but also the incoherent vastness of the classical hadith corpus—

assembled over multiple generations by thousands of scholars who represented numerous and often clashing networks and ideologies—the sources give us a multiplicity of Muhammads, some more approachable than others. Some hadiths soften my heart and bring me to tears; I cling to the image of Muhammad as a gentle grandfather who lets his daughter's sons Hasan and Husayn climb onto his back as he prays. Other hadiths, even after we have agonized over them for years, seem to offer only confusion and angst. While accepting that Muhammad lived nearly fifteen centuries ago, and recognizing that this vast historical gulf creates some obvious challenges in understanding the Prophet and his world—it's hard enough for me to appreciate the historical contexts that shaped my own grandparents and their values—Muslims can also wrestle at times with the Prophet's potential limits as a transcendent figure, a mercy to *all* of the worlds, whose truth-making power is supposed to stand outside of time.

The producers of the hadith corpus were not a monolithic block, even after the emergence of the Hadith Folk movement; when we search through the chains of transmission even in canonical sources, we find adherents to doctrinal positions and sectarian groups that the Hadith Folk found unacceptable. While the Hadith Folk's project might have been to stabilize and concretize Muslim authority with their own sources and methods as the center, they inherited massive heterogeneous and fragmented networks across the lands of Islam. As Muslims today are even more immeasurably diverse than the premodern hadith masters, we do not all find treasures and troubles in the same hadiths. An elderly uncle in my community, informed by the particular notions of rationality that characterized many Muslim intellectuals in the early twentieth century, confidently asserted to me that any hadiths that depicted Muhammad as having supernatural powers or properties—healing the sick with his saliva, for example, or splitting the moon—must have been later fabrications. The real Muhammad, he insisted, preached a simple and clear message, entirely compatible with modern ideals, that appealed to reason and required no miracles, fantastic tales, or resorts to what he called superstition. While this uncle took issue with hadiths that threatened to place Islam in contrast with his own ideas of civilization, reason, and progress, however, he was mostly unfazed by hadiths that many of us would read as misogynistic or homophobic. Other Muslims would struggle with the seemingly unquestioned heterosexism of the sources, but take less interest in erasing the miracle stories. Still other Muslims would prioritize the sectarian implications of certain hadiths as they appear in Sunni or Shi'i collections to privilege one position over another.

Whatever hadiths become central to our engagements of the tradition and Muhammad himself, as Aisha Y. Musa notes, Muslims navigate the hadiths with concerns of authenticity and authority.[241] In the question of authenticity, Muslims ask whether Muhammad really said or did what has been reported in his name; in the matter of authority, Muslims decide the significance of a particular hadith (or the hadith corpus at large) for answering questions of Muslim belief and practice. Through their judgments of authenticity and authority, Muslims give different weight to the hadith corpus. Some would argue that the canonical hadith sources are both reliable and binding: Muhammad's Sunna itself amounts to a divine revelation that has been faithfully protected and transmitted by master scholars across the generations. Others suggest that Muhammad's teachings and precedents are binding in principle, but that the canonical sources have not reliably preserved them, leaving us to evaluate specific hadiths on a case-by-case basis. There are also Muslims who dismiss the hadiths altogether as unreliable, asserting that even if hadiths could be trusted as historical sources, they should have little or no power to regulate our lives, because the Qur'an alone reflects the speech of God. Some Muslims envision a Muhammad-centered din in which Islam becomes inconceivable without the hadith corpus, while others construct Islam as founded upon the Qur'an to such a degree that it becomes virtually Muhammad-less. For the Qur'an-only position, in which Muhammad is compared to a postal worker who only delivers the Qur'an to humanity and then disappears, any problems with the tradition remain external to the perfect Qur'an, and thus troublesome hadiths offer no trouble at all.

I remember the moment of disconnect that I felt when, as a young Muslim, I first encountered the famous Hadith of the Fly. Fully endorsed within the most canonical Sunni sources, this narration depicts Muhammad as advising that if a fly lands in your drink, you should submerge it completely, because one of its wings contains the cure to whatever disease its other wing might bring. Because I had been so invested in Islam as not only compatible with modern science, but even miraculously providing us with scientific truths that the modern world was only starting to discover—as well as the literal, empirically verifiable truth of every hadith supported by Bukhari—the Hadith of the Fly punched me in the gut. Sharing my anxiety, modern Muslims have produced a number of responses to this tradition, including claims of scientific evidence, allegorical interpretation, and critical re-evaluation of the hadith's transmission history. Today I find myself less challenged by hadiths that speak within the logics of science and nature from another age (which would include every hadith that discusses the tiered structure of the heavens and earth, informed as they are by classical Mediterranean cosmologies). I have relocated my priorities. Whether or not Muhammad believed that we should dip flies in our drinks or that paradise and hellfire were locatable sites within physical reality is not where I personally feel the stakes to be highest. I want to know Muhammad's way of being human.

The hadith corpus provides us with cases in which events from Muhammad's multiple vocations—statesman, judge, husband, and so on—can challenge our own ideas of how to properly move in those fields. In one example frequently cited by anti-Muslim media to portray Islam as inescapably vio-lent, hadith literature portrays Muhammad slaughtering all the men of a Jewish community, Banu Qurayza, and taking its women and children as prisoners, as punishment for vio-lating an agreement. We can question the narrative's historic-ity on numerous grounds, such as the lack of archaeological evidence that we'd expect to find at a site of mass genocide, differences in ways that the event is portrayed across liter-ary genres and their respective producers (comparing hadith scholars against historians and biographers, for example), and the unresolved question of whether we should trust our earli-est sources, being that they're nowhere near as "early" as his-torians would prefer. Some would argue for the importance of historical context and ask how policies that are unthinkable in today's world might have been understood in the seventh century (or rather our ninth-century sources).

On a case-by-case basis, we can attempt to sift through the reported events of Muhammad's life and search the evidence to retrieve a verifiably "real" Muhammad, hoping that he satisfies us. Each approach to a question such as Banu Qurayza, however, comes with a price that we might not be willing to pay. If historical relativism solves the problem— Muhammad lived in his world, we live in ours—some Muslims would charge that we have undermined his transcendent moral authority across time and space, depriving ourselves of a Muhammad whose life and teachings can critique and correct our present. On the other hand, if we're willing to throw out the Banu Qurayza episode as fiction, we risk wounding the integrity of our sources, and therefore face the question of just how much we can claim about the historical Muhammad with any confidence. Is the Sunna knowable but irrelevant, or still authoritative but hopelessly inaccessible?

There's another mode of relating to the Prophet, one in which we trust our hearts to preserve him. Scholar Vernon Schubel shared an anecdote with me from his travels in South Asia, in which he heard a Muslim dismiss the narratives of Banu Qurayza with the firm insistence, "*My* Prophet would never have done that." Schubel's conversation partner was simply not interested in the chains of trustworthy reporters that produced the Banu Qurayza stories, nor the verdicts that these accounts had received from classical hadith masters. For this particular Muslim, no Bukhari could overrule his intuitive sense of Muhammad as the greatest of creation and God's mercy to all of the worlds. In my own experience as a Muslim and member of Muslim communities, I have heard similar responses to the question of A'isha's age at the time of her marriage. These Muslims do not necessarily possess the Arabic proficiency to engage hadiths without reliance on translators, let alone the skills in classical hadith evaluation to assess a tradition's chains of narrators; but with or without scholarly approval, they know that *their* Prophet did not marry a child. The heart holds an authority of its own. When Muhammad lives in the hearts of those who love him and wish to travel in his Sunna, textually transmitted knowledge does not always have the last word—at least not without allowing some space for movement and negotiation.

A comparable approach to the problems of texts and reliability appears in Buddhist traditions. According to classical narratives, the First Council codified the Buddha's teachings immediately after he left this world. As with Muslims, Buddhists have found the authority of these sources challenged by modern scholarship. The problem of uncertainty over whether a saying of the Buddha really came from the Buddha, however, could be solved from within the tradition: "Whatever is well spoken is the word of the Buddha." John S. Strong explains, "whatever accords with the Dharma and is conducive to nirvana is canonical."[242] Such an approach can help keep the door open both for troublesome hadiths to find their way out, or, as seen with the intuitive hadith evaluation by Sufi masters such as Ibn al-'Arabi, hadiths of weaker evidence to find their way in.

This suggestion that we can rely on our visceral reactions to hadiths would strike many as enabling an unstable, irrational, and incoherent Islam, in which everyone simply follows what feels right and abandons anything that becomes personally difficult. I would counter that this is often how Muslim life already works on the ground; trained experts in classical hadith-vetting have never been the only producers of Islam, and they have never achieved the absolutely centralized power to regulate Muslim behavior that they might claim for themselves. Much of what we know about popular religion in premodern Islam, after all, comes from elite scholars condemning the practices of the masses and complaining that no one listens to them. Yes, we negotiate with scholarly authorities in our social lives as members of Muslim communities, but much of the time, we're trusting our guts.

The first time I came home from a trip to Pakistan more than two decades ago, I carried a nine-volume set of Bukhari's *Sahih* through airports on my shoulders, a performance of my commitment to the textual tradition. After visiting Lahore this year, I brought home a magical artifact, perhaps a sign of my shifting priorities. The piece, a chart of special names and prayers designed to enlist God's help against one's enemies, provoked a conversation with friends and family as to whether Islam permitted us to curse people. An elder auntie stated confidently that Muslims never curse anyone. I attempted to provide the nuance that I had heard from clerical scholars: that it is permissible to curse broad categories of people, such as oppressors or tyrants, but not specific individuals or communities by name. The auntie cut me off and insisted, "No, we don't do that. It is not the right thing. We leave people alone." She was not a religious anarchist who lived outside the law, nor a Qur'an-only Muslim who rejected the hadith corpus and intellectual tradition wholesale; this auntie would regularly consult the local imam on matters of practice and etiquette, and kept books of prophetic traditions in her house. But without asking any scholar or consulting a hadith collection, she already knew that *her* Prophet never cursed anyone. Remembering the words of al-Ghazali's teacher al-Juwayni— "You may cling to the din of old women"—I trusted her answer.

Whenever the textual tradition risks undermining its own authority and gives us a potential opening, we'll find a scholar standing in the way, blocking our line of flight. Though Muhammad can speak to us in dreams, clerical jurists would attempt to regulate that experience and limit its possible consequences. If this hadith of hair and skin looks like an escape hatch out of the structure, the structure's scholarly guards can turn it into a tunnel that only leads us in a circle, taking us right back inside. The Prophet tells us that we can reject hadiths based on our visceral reactions to them, but the custodians of textual tradition warn us that not all intuitions are equal; only the mixture of rigorous scholarly training and advanced piety prepares elite intuitions to detect forgeries by a hunch.[243] I am not a hadith scholar in anything close to the classical sense of someone who sits at elder shaykhs' feet to memorize narrations and their transmitters, nor am I particularly developed in my piety, but as I wander through the corpus, I might still have a decent sense for what wounds me, what heals my wounds, and the Prophet who calms my hair and skin.

39

THE MERCY OF DIFFERENCE

Ibn 'Abbas narrated:
The Messenger of God (God bless him
and give him peace) said, "The disagreement
of my community is a mercy for you."[244]

If there's one big takeaway that I hope my students retain
after exploring hadith traditions, it's that Muhammad does
not always agree with himself. The hadith corpus, even in its
most narrowly canonical scope, contains a sufficient diversity of content that Muslims can compile entire forty-hadith
collections to argue for opposing perspectives. Skimming the
reports in any particular collection from Sunni Muslims' Six
Books canon, for one limited example, will reveal competing
networks and differing views of the Prophet, now blended
into one another by their shared home in a set of bound volumes. The myth of unity offered by the material artifact of
the volumes, and the name of a single master compiler across
the spines, belies considerable tension inside.

The multivocality inside any hadith collection is matched outside its volumes by the diversity of its readers. Muslims enter the books in search of answers, explore a variety of well-lit chambers and dark hidden rooms, and come back to the world with the jewels that they consider valuable. This also means that they leave things behind. For every hadith on the excruciating punishments of hell, we can find hadiths of divine mercy and compassion that more or less extinguish the fire.

Looking out our windows, we can also agree that the so-called Muslim world contains enormous diversity, and recognize that different communities, favoring their own sources, methods, and authorities, say lots of different things about what it means to be a Muslim. But is Muslim diversity a blessing or a problem? In my travels as a Muslim, I have encountered two hadiths on Muslim diversity with increasing frequency, each offering a counter to the other's implications. First, in a number of varying narrations, Muhammad predicts that his community will divide into seventy-three distinct groups or sects, but that seventy-two are in tragic error and only one can be correct. We don't need to treat seventy-three as a precise number here; in late antiquity, seventy-two was a generic way of saying "a lot." Muhammad explains that the singular legitimate community is al-Jama'a, "the Assembly" or "the Congregation," apparently suggesting an original and mainline body of Muslims from whom the other seventy-two groups break away as sectarian offshoots.[245] In other versions, Muhammad specifies that the only correct group is the one that follows him and his Companions. In modern Muslim discourses, this variegated tradition has become a calling card of the Sunni revivalist phenomenon known as Salafism (and the particular Saudi-networked brand of Salafism, popularly termed Wahhabism), which enjoys broad appeal for its promise to cut through centuries of accumulated tradition and restore true, original Islam. This hadith resonates with the Qur'an's own warnings against the community falling into division and factionalism after receiving clear signs (3:105).

Navigating a vast sea of Salafi print and digital media, you will often encounter identification of Salafi Muslims as the only true *Ahl al-Sunna wa-l-Jama'a,* "People of the Sunna and Assembly," and the one "Saved Sect." Among those Muslim traditions disqualified by Salafi revivalism, we find first and foremost Shi'i and Sufi Muslims, but also Sunni Muslims whom the Salafis deem insufficiently Sunni, such as the pilgrims to shrines and tombs, or those who adhere to unacceptable theological methods and positions. The potential irony of Salafism is that in denouncing the vast majority of Muslims as unacceptable in their ideas and behaviors, Salafis cast themselves out of the "mainstream Islam" (al-Jama'a) they claim to represent; as they condemn divisive sectarianism but mark themselves as a separate and distinct community, they could be engaging in the very thing that the Prophet warned us against doing. The Salafi response—that they're not breaking away to form something new, but only preserving the original and pure—would be the same response offered by false sects.

Whether or not the Salafiyya represent the one Saved Sect, their discourse of Sunni revival has proven enormously successful, mirroring the rise of textualist revival/reform trends in Christian, Hindu, and Buddhist media. Salafism became a globalizing and "mainstream" force with the twentieth-century formation of a Salafi (or "Wahhabi") state in Saudi Arabia, and the popularity of Salafi themes transcends the bounds of communities that would explicitly self-identify as Salafi.

There's another way of thinking about Muslim difference. This position finds support in another hadith that appears with some variation in its wording, the gist of which holds that the Prophet said, "Disagreement in my community is a mercy."[246]

For many Muslims, this hadith itself is a mercy. More than once, I've heard or read this hadith cited in response to a heated argument between Muslims over matters such as correctly identifying the start and end of the holy month of Ramadan (should we sight the moon or follow calculations?), the degree to which genders must be segregated in a masjid (barrier or no barrier?), or the permissibility of celebrating the Prophet's birthday. Someone can lighten the debate or even add humor by reminding us that the Prophet saw difference as a good thing.

As with any hadith, Muslims apply this narration to different ends. Though it opens space for Muslim pluralism, communities will name the precise limits of that pluralism at different points. For some, the scope of "disagreement-as-mercy" remains limited to the multiple opinions found within and between the Sunni legal schools now recognized as legitimate: Hanbali, Hanafi, Maliki, and Shafi'i. Others would expand this scope to include Sufism—perhaps with limits and qualifications—and Shi'i tradition (at least Ithna Ash'ari or Twelver Shi'ism, while still excluding Isma'ilis) within the bounds of acceptable difference. For Islam to remain coherent, many Muslims would still preserve some sense that the mercy of disagreement can't allow room for everything.

Salafi scholars, for their part, often dismiss the hadith using Salafi methods; that is, they denounce the hadith as an inauthentic fabrication due to problems with its transmitters. Gibril Fouad Haddad writes that the hadith had originated as a legal maxim among traditionists from the early generations of Islam, only to later find false attribution to the Prophet.[247] Within a certain narrow context, from this point of view, the saying did have some application; but because it was not a genuine statement from Muhammad, it does not break down the gates to let all possible perspectives count.

While the hadith has not found its way into "official" canon, it nonetheless travels as an authentic representation of lived Muslim pluralism and diversity. Even if Muhammad had never said the words, Muslims still receive the hadith as a genuine reflection of his love for their communities.

40

THANK ALLAH FOR AMINA WADUD

Anas narrated:
The Messenger of God (God bless him and give him peace) said, "One of you does not believe until s/he loves for another what is loved for self."[248]

This hadith, which might read to Christian eyes as Islam's parallel to the Golden Rule, remains one of the most well-circulated hadiths throughout Muslim history and easily one of the more famous hadiths in modern Islam. It also boasts impeccable prestige of canon. With numerous chains tracing it back to the Prophet's Companion Anas, this hadith can be found in five of the Six Books, as well as other important collections such as Ibn Hanbal's *Musnad* and the compilations of Darimi, Ibn Hibban, Tayalisi, and Tabarani. Perhaps most important, the hadith appears in al-Nawawi's popular arba'in collection that floods our world in countless reprints, translations, online archives, and commentaries.

Claimants upon a religious tradition have numerous modes by which they can disqualify each other as illegitimate. You pray wrong; you dress wrong. You read the wrong books, or perhaps read the right books wrong. Your understanding of God's attributes is wrong. Your prophetology is wrong. Your preferred scholarly authorities are wrong. Your opinions about permissible and forbidden acts are wrong. This hadith reminds us that we can get everything right, have all of the mainline scholars affirming our beliefs and rituals and rules as correct, and still fail as Muslims on the grounds that we're selfish pricks. As Muhammad came to perfect the noble traits, just being a good person can mark a high demand of his Sunna.

It's easy for academics to smirk and roll their eyes at the suggestion that "just being a good person" is the heart of the matter. Scholars of early Christianity might laugh at the popular modern reduction of Christ's teachings to "just being a good person," and scholars of Islamic studies would push back against such a construction of Muhammad. Within both academic and confessional contexts, such dismissal often comes with an assumption that the sentiment reveals a lazy, shallow, loosey-goosey, "spiritual but not religious" condition, and represents the least demanding part of the master teacher's lesson. In the tradition of the "greater jihad" as the jihad against the ego, however, Muhammad reminds us that becoming less of a selfish prick would confront many of us as an epic struggle. Being a good person isn't the easy part.

This hadith and the specific form in which it manifests here came to me from Qur'an scholar and theologian amina wadud. Through her books, *The Qur'an and Woman* and *Inside the Gender Jihad*, dr. wadud has opened the gates for a diverse field of scholars that engage the Qur'an with gender as a guiding concern; through the power and love with which she walks her Islam and embodies her scholarship, and the ways in which community grows around her, she has become our sun. (I am reminded here that in Arabic, the sun is a feminine noun, and in the Qur'an, the masculine moon follows her [91:1–2]).

Mentioning my forty-hadith project to dr. wadud, I asked if there was any one hadith that she would choose as her preferred representation of the Prophet. Another of al-Nawawi's forty hadiths, after all, quotes the Prophet as telling us, "The religion is sincere advice." wadud's immediate answer was this famous hadith of wanting for others as you would for yourself, but with her own translation. The hadith almost always appears in English as "One of you does not believe until he loves for his brother what he loves for himself." Reading the hadith in Arabic, we indeed find *akhihi*, "his brother"; in some versions, it's *jarihi*, "his (male) neighbor." wadud instead offered a gender-inclusive translation that expands its scope. Because we're no longer talking only about brothers, the hadith highlights the fullness of its challenge: if men do not want for women what they have always claimed as their own privileged domain—full membership in the community, meaning full agency to participate as authorities in the making of tradition and textual meaning—men are not complete in their faith.

This reading of the hadith reflects wadud's Tawhidic Paradigm, in which humanity's role as God's representative

on earth means that we must pursue a nonhierarchical human unity that mirrors the perfect unity of Allah. When we
violate our shared humanity with ideologies of patriarchy,
homophobia, transphobia, racial and ethnic supremacy, pa-
triotism, religious bigotry, or ableism, we perform a kind of
idolatry. Growing as a believer and one who surrenders, in
wadud's reading of tawhid, means resisting these culturally
learned impulses to deify ourselves at the expense of others.
Divine unity thus becomes a social ethic. Recognizing Allah's tawhid means recognizing shared humanity, which in
turn means affirming others as equally deserving of human
dignity. wadud's prioritization of this hadith hasn't led her to
any "loosey-goosey" spirituality or withdrawal from ongoing
struggles for justice. She has fought and suffered for her theology and its real-life ethical consequences.

The way that this hadith found its way into my project
calls me to acknowledge that what I call "Islam" and "Muhammad" are both conglomerations of my experiences, the
traditions and literatures that I can access, my particular
scholarly training, and the numerous teachers—both formal
and informal—who have contributed to various points of my
journey as a Muslim. My collection of forty hadiths could
never amount to simply a conversation between the textual
tradition and myself: between every hadith and every reader
stands a process that makes their encounter possible, and the
details of this process unavoidably transform both sides of the
encounter. Beyond the original chain of transmitters that escorted this hadith into the textual canon, I must also consider
the multiple chains of books and teachers and masjid conversations through which these words find routes into me today.

In each body that has been changed by him, Muhammad is not a singular man with his own life but a montage of images, an arrangement of moving parts. In my own Muhammad, some of those parts would have been the various books and pamphlets that I read around the time of my conversion (during which I would have first learned this hadith), or the countless Friday sermons in which an imam could have quoted this tradition to the congregation. Every teacher, book, academic journal article, and hadith opens a portal to a specific image of Muhammad that in turn starts a path to a specific vision of self. But assemblage also means fragmentation: the ingredients of my Muhammad often come to me as shattered pieces that have been chipped away from something else. As I build this house for myself, each stone that I choose is actually a broken piece of a bigger stone, appropriated and repurposed. If someone objects to me with the clichéd charge that I treat Islam "like a buffet," I answer that I treat it like a dozen buffets. But this means that in my selection of pieces, I also perform breaks and refusals, and I am responsible for my choices.

Recently a reader reached out to me via social media after having finished one of my books. She generously thanked me for helping her to feel comfortable in her own skin as a Muslim. Looking at her profile, I noticed that she had also posted a quote from Yasir Qadhi, a Muslim scholar whose engagement of Islam stands in sharp contrast to my own. In terms of our personal priorities and the various materials and linkages and network flows that make us, you might reasonably position us as irreconcilable antitheses to each other; but here we both were, sharing space in a third Muslim's bag of ingredients. I have to wonder about the image of the Prophet that this reader assembles for herself.

The process by which Muhammad becomes a concept that can do things in my head has been nourished by the scholarship and friendship of dr. wadud. If I am left to build the Prophet for myself from what resources I have, I'll look to amina wadud's Muhammad, and it is a joy to give her the last word. Peace and gratitude to my teachers—Sunnis and Shi'is, Sufi shaykhs, feminists, Five Percenters, DMT, all of them.

ACKNOWLEDGMENTS

First, always: Sadaf and Mom.

So much of this book reflects my PhD experience at the University of North Carolina at Chapel Hill, and I remain in immense debt to my mentors and friends at UNC, first and foremost Juliane Hammer. I am thankful not only for Juliane's guidance at UNC but especially for our continued friendship. I hope that my work positively reflects the impact of Dr. Hammer's training; please recognize her at the better parts. Gratitude to Carl Ernst, Omid Safi, Jessica Boon, Cemil Aydin, the UNC and Duke Muslim Students Associations, and all of my North Carolina colleagues and friends. Beyond the Carolinas, my doctoral research concerning the Prophet benefited from Scott C. Lucas's work as well as his participation on my dissertation committee.

This book allowed me to go exploring in a number of directions, but was initially inspired by the Muhammad seminar that I taught at Kenyon College, and remained profoundly informed by my teaching experiences. I am grateful for my students at Kenyon, UNC Chapel Hill, and my new home at the University of Central Florida.

Laury Silvers is the one who brought me into this ring.

Kecia Ali has been a consistent voice of guidance and

encouragement, and I have benefited not only from her published work but also her personal advice. Of particular salience for my writing, Kecia opened my eyes to the consequences of our citational practices. If my own work demonstrates any observable mindfulness in that regard, give credit to Dr. Ali.

Thank you to everyone at Soft Skull who made this happen. First, gratitude to Yuka Igarashi for courageously and patiently sharing in the journey of this project, and deep appreciation for Wah-Ming Chang. My deep thanks to Kathleen Boland, Lena Moses-Schmitt, Megan Fishmann, Dory Athey, and Jennifer Kovitz for their efforts to support this work.

This book happened because of the most supportive agent in all of the worlds, Allison Cohen.

For everyone who thought that my words might deserve a look, and especially those who are here after reading my other things: I get that I cut a weird profile, so I thank you for your generosity with your time.

NOTES

I: INTRODUCING THE INTRODUCTIONS

1. Al-Nasawi, *al-Arba'in lil-Nasawi*, #43. IslamWeb.

2. Suleiman Mourad and James Lindsay, *Islamic History and Civilization: The Intensification and Reorientation of Sunni Jihad Ideology in the Crusader Period: Ibn 'Asakir of Damascus (1105–1176) and His Age, with an Edition and Translation of Ibn 'Asakir's* The Forty Hadiths for Inciting Jihad (Leiden: Brill, 2012).

3. Shah Wali Allah ad-Dihlawi, *Al-Arbain*, trans. Safaruk Zaman Chowdhury (London: Turath Publishing, 2015).

4. Scott C. Lucas, "Forty Traditions," in *Encyclopedia of Islam*, 3rd ed., Kate Fleet, Gudrun Kramer, Denis Matringe, John Nawas, and Everett Rowson, eds. (Leiden: Brill, 2015).

5. Kecia Ali, *The Lives of Muhammad* (Cambridge: Harvard University Press, 2015), 241.

6. Nurhafihz Noor, *40 Hadith Reflections on Marketing and Business* (Nurhafihz Noor, 2014).

7. Omar Usman, "40 Hadiths on Social Media," Fiqh of Social Media. Accessed May 2017.

8. Thomas R. R. Cobb, *An Inquiry into the Law of Negro Slavery in the United States of America* (Philadelphia: T. & J. W. Johnson; Savannah: W. Thorne Williams, 1858), 118–19.

9. Imam Jalal Ad-Din as-Suyuti, *Al-Arba'in*, trans. Aisha Bewley (London: Turath Publishing, 2015), 29.

10. Harald Motzki, "The Musannaf of 'Abd al-Razzaq al-San'ani as a Source of Authentic Ahadith of the First Century A.H.," *Journal of Near Eastern Studies* 50, no. 1 (Jan. 1991), 1–21.

11. Wael B. Hallaq, "The Authenticity of Prophetic Hadith: A Pseudo-Problem," *Studia Islamica*, no. 89 (1999), 75–90.

12. Denise Spellberg, *Politics, Gender, and the Islamic Past: The Legacy of 'A'isha bint Abi Bakr* (New York: Columbia University Press, 1994). Asma Sayeed, *Women and the Transmission of Religious Knowledge in Islam* (Cambridge: Cambridge University Press, 2013).

2: PUNK ROCK AND BEDOUIN PISS

13. Ibn Hanbal, *Musnad*, #13117. Islamweb.
14. Ahmet T. Karamustafa, *God's Unruly Friends* (Oxford: Oneworld, 2007), 70–78.

3: THE PROPHET IN HIS WORLD

15. Bukhari, *Sahih*, kitab al-a'tasam bi-l-kitab wa-l-sunna, #6888. Islamweb.
16. Greg Fisher, *Between Empires: Arabs, Romans, and Sasanians in Late Antiquity* (Oxford: Oxford University Press, 2011), 71.
17. Ibid., 36–38.
18. Peter Brown, *The World of Late Antiquity: AD 150–750* (London: W. W. Norton, 1989), 148.
19. Ibid., 109.
20. Almut Hintze, "Monotheism the Zoroastrian Way," *JRAS*, Series 3, 24:1 (2014), 225–49.
21. Touraj Daryaee, *Sasanian Persia: The Rise and Fall of an Empire* (London: I. B. Tauris, 2009), 71.
22. Christopher Haas, "Mountain Constantines: The Christianization of Askum and Iberia," *Journal of Late Antiquity* 1.1 (Spring 2008), 101–26.
23. Norbert Nebes, "Martyrs of Najran and the End of the Himyar," in *The Qur'an in Context: Historical and Literary Investigations into the Qur'anic Milieu*, Angelika Neuwirth, Nicolai Sinai, and Michael Marx, eds. (Leiden: Brill, 2010), 35–40.
24. Ibid.
25. Ibid.
26. Christian Julien Robin, "Arabia and Ethiopia," in *The Oxford Handbook of Late Antiquity*, Scott Fitzgerald Johnson, ed. (Oxford: Oxford University Press, 2012).
27. Fred Donner, *Muhammad and the Believers: At the Origins of Islam* (Cambridge: The Belknap Press of Harvard University Press, 2010), 7–13.

28. Touraj Daryaee, *Sasanian Persia: The Rise and Fall of an Empire* (London: I. B. Tauris, 2009), 36.

29. François de Blois, "Islam in Its Arabian Context," in *The Qur'an in Context: Historical and Literary Investigations into the Qur'anic Milieu*, Angelika Neuwirth, Nicolai Sinai, and Michael Marx, eds. (Leiden: Brill, 2010), 615–24.

30. G. R. Hawting, *The Idea of Idolatry and the Emergence of Islam* (Cambridge: Cambridge University Press, 2009), 6.

31. Ibid.

32. Ibid., 2.

4: THE HADITH OF GABRIEL

33. Al-Nawawi, *Riyad al-Salihin* (Beirut: Sharikat Dar al-Arkam ibn Abi al-Arqam), 40.

34. Sachiko Murata and William C. Chittick, *Vision of Islam: The Foundations of Muslim Faith and Practice* (London and New York: I. B. Tauris, 1996), xxv–xxvii.

35. Ibid.

36. Jamillah Karim, *American Muslim Women: Negotiating Race, Class, and Gender Within the Ummah* (New York: New York University Press, 2009), 242.

37. Tirmidhi, *Jam'a*, kitab al-diyan, #1325. Islamweb.

38. N. Hanif, *Biographical Encyclopedia of Sufis: Central Asia and Middle East* (New Delhi: Sarup Book Publishers, 2002), 312–14.

39. Fred Donner, *Muhammad and the Believers: At the Origins of Islam*, op. cit.

40. Patricia Crone, *The Nativist Prophets of Early Islamic Iran: Rural Revolt and Local Zoroastrianism* (Cambridge: Cambridge University Press, 2012), 8–11.

5: THE END OF PROPHETHOOD

41. Ibn Hanbal, *Musnad*, #12128. Islamweb.

42. Al-Kulayni, *al-Kafi*, vol. 1, Muhammad Sarwar trans. (New York: Islamic Seminary, 2015), 218.

43. Ingrid Mattson, *The Story of the Qur'an: Its History and Place in Muslim Life* (Oxford: Blackwell Publishing, 2008), 218. Barbara Freyer Stowasser, *Women in the Qur'an, Traditions, and Interpretation* (New York and Oxford: Oxford University Press, 1994), 77.

44. Hartmut Bobzin, "The Seal of the Prophets: Towards an Un-

derstanding of Muhammad's Prophethood," in *The Qur'an in Context: Historical and Literary Investigations into the Qur'anic Milieu*, Angelika Neuwirth, Nicolai Sinai, and Michael Marx, eds. (Leiden: Brill, 2009), 565–84.

6: WHO CREATED GOD?

45. Muslim, *Sahih*, kitab al-iman, #199. Islamweb.
46. Abu Dawud, *Sunan*, kitab al-iman wa al-tudhur, #2859. Islamweb.
47. Harald Motzki, *Reconstruction of a Source of Ibn Ishaq's Life of the Prophet and Early Qur'an Exegesis* (Piscataway: Gorgias Press, 2017), 65–66.

7: MUHAMMAD THE "PURE GREEK"

48. Ibn Sa'd, *Tabaqat al-Kubra*, vol. 1. Muhammed Abd al-Qader 'Ata, ed. (Beirut: Dar Al-Kutub Al-Ilmiyah, 2012), 320.
49. Robert Hoyland, "Physiognomy in Islam," *Jerusalem Studies in Arabic and Islam* 30 (2005), 361–402.
50. Majid Fakhry, *A History of Islamic Philosophy, 3rd Edition.* (New York: Columbia University Press, 2004).
51. Robert Hoyland, "A New Edition and Translation of the Leiden Polemon," in *Seeing the Face, Seeing the Soul: Polemon's Physiognomy from Classical Antiquity to Medieval Islam*, Simon Swain, ed. (Oxford: Oxford University Press, 2007), 330–463.

8: PORTRAIT OF THE PROPHET AS A YOUNG MAN

52. Christiane Gruber, "Images of the Prophet Muhammad In and Out of Modernity: The Curious Case of a 2008 Mural in Tehran," in *Visual Culture in the Modern Middle East: Rhetoric of the Image*, Gruber and Sune Haugbolle, eds. (Bloomington: Indiana University Press, 2013), 25–45.
53. Oleg Grabar, "The Story of Portraits of the Prophet Muhammad," *Studia Islamica* 96 (2003), 19–38.
54. Christiane Gruber, "Images of the Prophet Muhammad In and Out of Modernity," op. cit.
55. Amina Inloes, "Racial 'Othering' in Shi'i Sacred History: Jawn ibn Huwayy the 'African Slave,' and the Ethnicities of the Twelve Imams," *Journal of Shi'a Islamic Studies* VII, no. 4 (Autumn 2014), 411–39.

56. As Sayyid Isa Al Haadi Al Mahdi, *The Book of Laam: The Message of the Messenger Is Right and Exact* (Brooklyn: Tents of Kedar, 1989), 301.

9: MUHAMMAD THE ORPHAN

57. Bukhari, *Sahih*, kitaab al-talaq, #4918. Islamweb.
58. Ibn Hisham, *The Life of Muhammad*, A. Guillaume, trans. (Oxford: Oxford University Press, 2012), 68–69.
59. Ibid., 70–71.
60. Ibid., 73, 79–82.
61. Ibid., 81.
62. Ibid., 72.
63. Uri Rubin, *Eye of the Beholder: The Life of Muhammad as Viewed by the Early Muslims: A Textual Analysis* (Princeton: Darwin Press, 1995).
64. Tayalisi, *Musnad*, #1643. Islamweb.
65. Ibn Hanbal, *Musnad*, #17798. Islamweb.
66. Ron Buckley, "The Buraq: Views from the East and West," *Arabic* 60 (2013), 569–601.
67. Kecia Ali, *The Lives of Muhammad*, op. cit.

10: THE MOUNTAIN OF LIGHT

68. Bukhari, *Sahih*, Kitab al-tafsir, #4672. Islamweb.
69. Tayalisi, *Musnad*, #1632. Islamweb.
70. Shahab Ahmed, *Before Orthodoxy: The Satanic Verses in Early Islam* (Cambridge: Harvard University Press, 2017), 32–33.

11: THE ASCENSION

71. Al-Kulayni, *al-Kafi*, vol. 1, 446.
72. Ibn Sa'd, *Tabaqat al-Kubra*, vol. 1, Muhammed Abd al-Qader 'Ata, ed. (Beirut: Dar Al-Kutub Al-Ilmiyah, 2012), 320.

12: "HIS CHARACTER WAS THE QUR'AN"

73. Ibid., 273.
74. William C. Chittick, *The Sufi Path of Knowledge* (Albany: SUNY Press, 1989), 21–26, 283–86.
75. Marion Holmes Katz, *Body of Text: The Emergence of the Sunni Law of Ritual Purity* (Albany: SUNY Press, 2002), 176.

76. Laury Silvers, "'In the Book We Have Left Out Nothing': The Ethical Problem of the Existence of Verse 4:34 in the Qur'an," *Comparative Islamic Studies* (2008), 171–80.

13: THE PEOPLE OF WUDU'

77. Ibn Maja, *Sunan*, Kitab al-zuhd, #4280. Islamweb.

14: THE SEVEN OFT-REPEATED

78. Bukhari, *Sahih*, Kitab tafsir al-qur'an, #4426. Islamweb.

15: FORGIVE HIS HANDS TOO

79. Muslim, *Sahih*, Kitab al-iman, #171. Islamweb.

16: HADITHS OF INTENTION

80. Ibn Maja, *Sunan*, Kitab al-fitan, #4063. Islamweb.

17: THE GREATER JIHAD

81. Bayhaqi, *al-Zuhd al-Kabir*, #383. Islamweb. Ibn al-Jawzi, *Dhamm al-Hawwa*, #72. Islamweb.
82. Joseph Norment Bell, *Love Theory in Later Hanbalite Islam* (Albany: SUNY Press, 1979), 17.

18: DEATH OF THE PROPHET

83. Bukhari, *Sahih*, Kitab fard al-khums, #2885. Islamweb.
84. Ma'mar ibn Rashid, *The Expeditions*, Sean W. Anthony, trans. (New York and London: New York University Press, 2014), 185.
85. Ibn Sa'd, *Tabaqat al-Kubra*, Vol. 2, Muhammed Abd al-Qader 'Ata, ed. (Beirut: Dar Al-Kutub Al-Ilmiyah, 2012), 210.

19: MUHAMMAD AS LIGHT

86. Al-Kulayni, *al-Kafi*, vol. 1, 444.
87. Uri Rubin, "Pre-Existence and Light—Aspects of the Concept of Nur Muhammad," *Israel Oriental Studies* 5 (1975), 62–119.
88. Ibn Hanbal, *Musnad*, #16740, #23599. Ibn Sa'd, *Tabaqat*, vol. 1, 118.
89. Uri Rubin, "Pre-Existence and Light," op. cit.

20: THE CITY AND THE GATE

90. Tirmidhi, *Jami'*, Kitab al-da'awat, #3686. Islamweb.
91. Scott C. Lucas, *Constructive Critics, Hadith Literature, and the Articulation of Sunni Islam: The Legacy of the Generation of Ibn Sa'd, Ibn Ma'in, and Ibn Hanbal* (Leiden: Brill, 2004).
92. Denise Spellberg, *Politics, Gender, and the Islamic Past*, 118–19.
93. Scott C. Lucas, *Constructive Critics, Hadith Literature, and the Articulation of Sunni Islam*, op. cit.

21: THE PEOPLE OF THE HOUSE

94. Imam Muhammad ibn Jafar al-Kattani, *Al-Arba'in: Forty Hadiths on the Duty of Loving the Noble Family of the Prophet Muhammad* (May Allah Bless Him and Give Him Peace), Safaruk Zaman Chowdhury, trans. (London: Turath Publishing, 2009), 43.
95. Ibid., 67.
96. Ibid., 39.
97. Ibid., 47.
98. Ibid., 60–61.
99. Ibid., 62–66.
100. Ibid., 11–12.
101. Ibid., 54–55.
102. Ibid., 15–18.
103. Ibid., 16.
104. Ibid., 32–33.
105. Ibid., 18–25.

22: THE LADY OF LIGHT

106. Al-Kulayni, *al-Kafi*, vol. 1, 469.
107. Ibn Hanbal, Ahmad bin Muhammad, *Musnad al-Imam Ahmad ibn Hanbal*, Vol. 8 (Beirut: 'Alam al-Kutub, 1998).
108. Mahmoud M. Ayoub, *Redemptive Suffering in Islam* (The Hague: Mouton Publishers, 1978), 214.
109. Verena Klemm, "Formation of an Islamic Legend: Faṭima, the Daughter of the Prophet Muhammad," in *Ideas, Images, and Methods of Portrayal: Insights into Arabic Literature and Islam*, Sebastian Gunther, ed. (Leiden: Brill, 2005), 181–207.
110. Al-Kulayni, *al-Kafi*, vol. 1, 218.
111. Ibid., 464–65.

112. Verena Klemm, "Formation of an Islamic Legend: Faṭima, the Daughter of the Prophet Muhammad," op. cit.

113. Karen G. Ruffle, "May Fatimah Gather Our Tears: The Mystical and Intercessory Powers of Fatimah al-Zahra in Indo-Persian, Shi'i Devotional Literature and Performance," *Comparative Studies of South Asia, Africa and the Middle East* 30, no. 3 (2010), 386–97.

114. Ibid.

23: MUHAMMAD THE GRANDFATHER

115. Bayhaqi, *Dala'il al-Nubuwwa*, #2812. Islamweb.

24: LIKE THE STARS

116. Ibn 'Abd al-Barr, *Jami' Bayan al-'Ilm wa Fadlahi*, #1061. Islamweb.

117. Aisha Geissinger, "'A'isha bint Abi Bakr and Her Contributions to the Formation of Islamic Tradition," *Religion Compass* 5/1 (2011), 37–49.

118. Wilferd Madelung, *The Succession to Muhammad: A Study of the Early Caliphate* (Cambridge: Cambridge University Press, 1997), 84.

119. Sarah Bowen Savant, *The New Muslims of Post-Conquest Iran: Tradition, Memory, and Conversion* (Cambridge: Cambridge University Press, 2013), 61–90.

120. Kecia Ali, *The Lives of Muhammad*, 119.

25: MOTHER OF THE BELIEVERS

121. Ibn Abi Shayba, *Musannaf*, #34724.

122. Ibid., #34736.

123. Nadia El Cheikh, *Women, Islam, and Abbasid Identity* (Cambridge: Harvard University Press, 2015), 108–109.

124. Denise Spellberg, *Politics, Gender, and the Islamic Past*, 86.

125. Aisha Geissinger, "Mary in the Qur'an: Rereading Subversive Births," in *Sacred Tropes: Tanakh, New Testament, and Qur'an as Literature and Culture*, Roberta Sterman Sabbath, ed. (Leiden: Brill, 2009), 379–92.

126. Eve Kosofsky Sedgwick, *Between Men: English Literature and Male Homosocial Desire* (New York: Columbia University Press, 1985).

127. Denise Spellberg, *Politics, Gender, and the Islamic Past*, 154–55.

128. Ze'ev Maghen, *Virtues of the Flesh: Passion and Purity in Early Islamic Jurisprudence* (Leiden: Brill, 2005), 121.

129. Jane I. Smith and Yvonne Haddad, "Women in the Afterlife: The Islamic View as Seen from Qur'an and Tradition," *Journal of the American Academy of Religion* 43.1 (1975), 39–50.

130. Denise Spellberg, *Politics, Gender, and the Islamic Past*, 64.

131. Ibid., 129.

132. Marion Holmes Katz, *Women in the Mosque: A History of Legal Thought and Social Practice* (New York: Columbia University Press, 2014).

26: PROPHETIC SEXUALITY

133. 'Abd al-Razzaq, *Musannaf*, kitab al-Talaq, #13649.

134. Ze'ev Maghen, *Virtues of the Flesh*, 106–107.

135. Ibn Sa'd, *Tabaqat*, #866. Islamweb.

136. Abu Nu'aym, Akhbar Isbahan, #2250. Islamweb.

137. Ze'ev Maghen, *Virtues of the Flesh*, 75–110.

138. Ibid., 107.

27: THE A'ISHA QUESTION

139. Muslim, *Sahih*, kitab al-nikah, #2557. Islamweb.

140. Kecia Ali, *Sexual Ethics & Islam* (Oxford: Oneworld, 2006), 143.

141. Pernilla Myrne, *Narrative, Gender and Authority in 'Abbasid Literature on Women* (Gothenburg: University of Gothenburg, 2010), 185.

142. Kecia Ali, *The Lives of Muhammad*, 159–60.

143. Nicholas L. Syrett, *American Child Bride: A History of Minors and Marriage in the United States* (Chapel Hill: University of North Carolina Press, 2016).

144. Ibid., 49.

145. Ibid., 208–209.

28: MUHAMMAD THE LAWGIVER

146. Ibn Maja, *Sunan*, Kitab al-Hudud, #2537.

147. Sarah Eltantawi, *Shari'ah on Trial: Northern Nigeria's Islamic Revolution* (Berkeley: University of California Press, 2017), 62.

148. Scott C. Lucas, "'Perhaps You Only Kissed Her?' A Contrapuntal Reading of the Penalties for Illicit Sex in the Sunni Hadith Literature," *Journal of Religious Ethics* 39.3 (2011), 399–415.

149. Najam Haider, "Contesting Intoxication: Early Juristic Debates

over the Lawfulness of Alcoholic Beverages," *Islamic Law and Society* 20-1-2 (2013), 48–89.

150. Khaled El-Rouayheb, *Before Homosexuality in the Arab-Islamic World, 1500–1800* (Chicago: University of Chicago Press, 2005), 118–22.

151. Jorgen S. Nielsen, "Sultan al-Zahir Baybars and the Appointment of Four Chief Qadis, 663/1265," *Studia Islamica* 60 (1984).

152. Henri Lauziere, *The Making of Salafism: Islamic Reform in the Twentieth Century* (Oxford: Oxford University Press, 2015), 158.

153. Hina Azam, *Sexual Violation in Islamic Law: Substance, Evidence, and Procedure* (Cambridge: Cambridge University Press, 2015), 246–47.

29: DELEUZIAN FINGERNAILS

154. Ibn Sa'd, *Tabaqat al-Kubra*, #10612. Islamweb.

155. Ibn Sa'd, *Tabaqat al-Kubra*, vol. 6, 'Ali Muhammad 'Umar, ed. (Cairo: Maktaba al-Khanji, 2001), 30.

156. Daniel Colucciello Barber, *Deleuze and the Naming of God: Post-Secularism and the Future of Immanence* (Edinburgh: Edinburgh University Press, 2014), 4–9.

157. Shahab Ahmed, *What Is Islam? The Importance of Being Islamic* (Princeton: Princeton University Press, 2016), 92.

158. Ibid., 93.

159. Gilles Deleuze and Felix Guattari, *A Thousand Plateaus: Capitalism and Schizophrenia*, Brian Massumi, trans. (Minneapolis: University of Minnesota Press, 1987), 206.

160. Jiangping Wang, *Glossary of Chinese Islamic Terms* (London: Routledge, 2016), 12.

161. Ibid.

162. Harry Munt, *The Holy City of Medina: Sacred Space in Early Islamic Arabia* (Cambridge: Cambridge University Press, 2014), 109.

163. Gilles Deleuze and Felix Guattari, *A Thousand Plateaus*, 503.

30: MUHAMMAD AND THE ANIMAL

164. Ibn Hanbal, *Musnad*, #1681. Islamweb.

165. Ibid., #1752.

166. Beyondhalal.org.

167. Richard Folz, *Animals in Islamic Tradition and Muslim Cultures* (Oxford: Oneworld, 2006).

168. Mahnaz Moazami, "The Dog in Zoroastrian Religion: 'Videvdad' Chapter XIII," *Indo-Iranian Journal* 49, no. ½ (Spring 2006), 127–49.

169. Wendy Doniger, *On Hinduism* (Oxford: Oxford University Press, 2014), 504.

170. Giorgio Agamben, *The Open: Man and Animal* (Berkeley: Stanford University Press, 2003).

171. Sarra Tlili, *Animals in the Qur'an* (Cambridge: Cambridge University Press, 2012), 116–23.

172. Christopher Melchert, "God Created Adam in His Image," *Journal of Qur'anic Studies* 13.1 (2011), 113–24.

173. Lloyd Ridgeon, "The Controversy of Shaykh Awhad al-Din Kirmani and Handsome, Moon-Faced Youths: A Case Study of Shahid-Bazi in Medieval Sufism," *Journal of Sufi Studies* (2012), 1–28.

174. Javad Nurbakhsh, *Dogs from a Sufi Point of View* (London and New York: Khaniqahi-Nimatullahi Publications, 1989).

31: THE BAG OF MEAT

175. M. J. Kister, "'A Bag of Meat': A Study of an Early 'Hadith,'" *Bulletin of the School of Oriental and African Studies, University of London*, vol. 33, no. 2 (1970), 267–75.

176. Shahab Ahmed, *Before Orthodoxy*, op. cit.

177. M. J. Kister, "'A Bag of Meat,'" op. cit.

32: MUHAMMAD THE SHAMAN

178. Abu Muhammad Abd 'Allah al-Darimi, *Sunan al-Darimi*, Mustafa Dib al-Bugha, ed. (Beirut: Dar al-Mustafa, 2011), 19.

179. Jeroen W. Boekhoven, *Genealogies of Shamanism* (Barkhuis, 2011).

180. J. R. Porter, "Muhammad's Journey to Heaven," *Numen* 21 (1974), 64–80.

181. Anwarul Karim, "Shamanism in Bangladesh," *Asian Folklore Studies* 47, no. 2 (1988), 277–309.

182. Muhammad Umar Memon, *Ibn Taimiya's Struggle Against Popular Religion* (Paris: Mouton & Co., 1976).

183. Louis Komjathy, *The Daoist Tradition* (London: Bloomsbury, 2013), 4–5.

33: DREAMING MUHAMMAD

184. Tirmidhi, *Jami'*, kitab al-ru'ya, #2207. Islamweb.
185. Gilles Deleuze and Felix Guattari, *Anti-Oedipus*, Robert Hurley, Mark Seem, and Helen R. Lane, trans. (London and New York: Continuum, 2004). *A Thousand Plateaus*, Brian Massumi, trans. (London and New York: Continuum, 2004).
186. Leah Kinberg, "The Legitimization of the Madhahib Through Dreams," *Arabica* 32 (1985).
187. Ibid.
188. Joel Blecher, *Said the Prophet of God: Hadith Commentary Across a Millennium* (Berkeley: University of California Press, 2017), 23.
189. Hadrat 'Abd al-Qadir al-Jilani, *The Secret of Secrets*, Shaykh Tosun Bayrak al-Jerrahi al-Halveti, trans. (Cambridge: Islamic Texts Society, 1992), 112–13.

34: KNOWLEDGE IN CHINA

190. Mulla 'Ali al-Qari, *Encyclopedia of Hadith Forgeries*, Gibril Fouad Haddad, trans. (London: Beacon Books, 2014), 134.
191. Nerina Rustomji, *The Garden and the Fire: Heaven and Hell in Islamic Culture* (New York: Columbia University Press, 2013), 159.

35: HADITHS FOR LOSERS

192. Al-Marisi, *Naqd*, #118. Islamweb.
193. Judith Halberstam, *The Queer Art of Failure* (Durham: Duke University Press, 2011).
194. Marcella Althaus-Reid, *Queer God* (London: Routledge, 2003), 98.
195. Sarah Ahmed, *Queer Phenomenology* (Durham: Duke University Press, 2006), 48–49.
196. Jonathan A. C. Brown, *Hadith* (Oxford: Oneworld, 2009), 78.
197. Scott C. Lucas, *Constructive Critics, Hadith Literature, and the Articulation of Sunni Islam*, op. cit.
198. Merlin L. Swartz, *A Medieval Critique of Anthropomorphism: Ibn al-Jawzi's Kitab Akhbar as-Sifat* (Leiden: Brill, 2002), 87–89.

199. Ibn Sa'd, *Tabaqat al-Kubra*, vol. 7, Muhammed Abd al-Qader 'Ata, ed. (Beirut: Dar Al-Kutub Al-Ilmiyah, 2012), 177.

200. Ignaz Goldziher, *Muslim Studies*, vol. 1, S. M. Stern, ed. (London: Routledge, 2005), 170.

201. J. Halberstam, *The Queer Art of Failure* (Durham: Duke University Press, 2011).

202. Wilferd Madelung, *An Ismaili Heresiography: The "Bab al-Shaytan" from Abu Tammam's Kitab Al-Shajara* (Leiden: Brill, 1998).

203. Merlin L. Swartz, *A Medieval Critique of Anthropomorphism*, 87–89.

204. Al-Kulayni, *al-Kafi*, vol. 1, 452–53, 469–70.

205. Jonathan G. Katz, *Dreams, Sufism and Sainthood: The Visionary Career of Muhammad al-Zawawi* (Leiden: Brill, 1996), 170.

206. Mulla 'Ali al-Qari, *Encyclopedia of Hadith Forgeries*, Gibril Fouad Haddad, trans. (London: Beacon Books, 2014), 563.

207. Ibid., 429.

36: QUEERING MOHAMMAD

208. Ibn al-Jawzi, *Dhamm al-Hawwa*, #232. Islamweb.

209. Dror Ze'evi, *Producing Desire: Changing Sexual Desire in the Ottoman Middle East, 1500–1900* (Berkeley: University of California Press, 2006), 91.

210. Khaled El-Rouayheb, *Before Homosexuality in the Arab-Islamic World, 1500–1800*, 16.

211. Ibid., 113.

212. Joseph Norment Bell, *Love Theory in Later Hanbalite Islam*, 23.

213. Fedwa Malti Douglas, "Controversy and Its Effects in the Biographical Tradition of Al-Khatib al-Baghdadi," *Studia Islamica* no. 46 (1977), 115–31.

214. Sa'diyya Shaikh, *Sufi Narratives of Intimacy: Ibn 'Arabi, Gender, and Sexuality* (Chapel Hill: University of North Carolina Press, 2012), 191–92.

215. Dror Ze'evi, *Producing Desire*, 91.

216. Omid Ghaemmaghani, "Numinous Vision, Messianic Encounters: Typological Representations in a Version of the Prophet's *hadith al-ru'ya* and in Visions and Dreams of the Hidden Imam," in *Dreams and Visions in Islamic Societies*. Özgen Felek and Alexander D. Knysh, eds. (Albany: SUNY Press, 2012), 51–76.

217. Mark D. Jordan, "God's Body," in *Queer Theology: Rethink-*

ing the Western Body, Gerard Loughlin, ed. (London: Wiley-Blackwell, 2007).

218. Lloyd Ridgeon, "The Controversy of Shaykh Awhad al-Din Kirmani and Handsome, Moon-Faced Youths: A Case Study of Shahid-Bazi in Medieval Sufism," *Journal of Sufi Studies* (2012), 1–28.

219. Khaled El-Rouayheb, *Before Homosexuality in the Arab-Islamic World, 1500–1800*, 37–38.

220. Scott Kugle, *Sufis & Saints' Bodies: Mysticism, Corporeality, & Sacred Power in Islam* (Chapel Hill: University of North Carolina Press, 2007), 181–220.

221. Lloyd Ridgeon, "The Controversy of Shaykh Awhad al-Din Kirmani and Handsome, Moon-Faced Youths," op. cit.

222. Joseph Norment Bell, *Love Theory in Later Hanbalite Islam*, 19–20.

37: KNOWLEDGE OF SELF

223. Suyuṭi, *Tadrib al-Rawi* (Beirut: Maktabat al-Kawthar, 1995), 626.

224. L. E. Goodman, *Avicenna* (London and New York: Routledge, 1992), 164.

225. Alexander Altmann, *Studies in Religious Philosophy and Mysticism* (Ithaca: Cornell University Press, 1969), 1–40. Soren Giversen, Tage Petersen, and Jorgen Podemann Sorensen, *The Nag Hammadi Texts in the History of Religions* (Copenhagen: Kongelige Danske Videnskabernes Selskab, 2002), 85–86.

226. Sachiko Murata, *Chinese Gleams of Sufi Light* (Albany: SUNY Press, 2000).

227. Shahab Ahmed, *What Is Islam?*, 329–43.

228. Ibid., 333.

229. Ibid., 174.

230. Ian Almond, *Sufism and Deconstruction* (London: Routledge, 2004).

231. Mahmoud M. Ayoub, *Qur'an and Its Interpreters* (Albany: SUNY Press, 1984), 406.

232. William C. Chittick, *The Sufi Path of Knowledge* (Albany: SUNY Press, 1989), 345.

233. William C. Chittick, *The Sufi Path of Love* (Albany: SUNY Press, 1984), 65.

234. Alexander Knysh, *Ibn 'Arabi in the Later Islamic Tradition: The*

Making of a Polemical Image in Medieval Islam (Albany: SUNY Press, 1998).

235. Shahab Ahmed, *What Is Islam?*, 79.
236. Alexander Knysh, *Ibn 'Arabi in the Later Islamic Tradition*, op. cit.
237. Shahab Ahmed, *What Is Islam?*, 475.
238. Ibid., 19.
239. Ibid., 449–75.

38: HAIR AND SKIN

240. Ibn Hanbal, *Musnad*, #15725. Islamweb. Jonathan A. C. Brown, "The Rules of Matn Criticism: There Are No Rules," *Islamic Law and Society* 19 (2012), 356–96.
241. Aisha Y. Musa, *Hadith as Scripture: Discussions on the Authority of Prophetic Traditions in Islam* (New York: Palgrave Macmillan, 2008), 4.
242. John S. Strong, *Buddhisms* (Oxford: Oneworld, 2015), 92.
243. Jonathan A. C. Brown, "The Rules of Matn Criticism: There Are No Rules," *Islamic Law and Society* 19 (2012), 356–96.

39: THE MERCY OF DIFFERENCE

244. Mulla 'Ali al-Qari, *Encyclopedia of Hadith Forgeries*, 309.
245. Ibn Maja, *Sunan*. Kitab al-Fitan, #3990. Islamweb.
246. Mulla 'Ali al-Qari, *Encyclopedia of Hadith Forgeries*, 308–309.
247. Ibid.

40: THANK ALLAH FOR AMINA WADUD

248. Author's correspondence with amina wadud.

MICHAEL MUHAMMAD KNIGHT is a novelist, essayist, journalist, and scholar. He converted to Islam at sixteen and traveled to Islamabad at seventeen to study at a madrasa. His books include *The Taqwacores, Blue-Eyed Devil, Tripping with Allah: Islam, Drugs, and Writing*, and *Why I Am a Salafi*. He is Assistant Professor of Religion and Cultural Studies at the University of Central Florida in Orlando.